DATE DUE

COLD WAR RHETORIC

Recent Titles in
Contributions to the Study of Mass Media and Communications

COLD WAR RHETORIC

Strategy, Metaphor, and Ideology

Martin J. Medhurst,
Robert L. Ivie,
Philip Wander,
and Robert L. Scott

Contributions to the Study of Mass Media and Communications,
Number 19
Bernard K. Johnpoll, Series Editor

Greenwood Press
New York • Westport, Connecticut • London

Library of Congress Cataloging-in-Publication Data

Cold war rhetoric : strategy, metaphor, and ideology / Martin J.
  Medhurst . . . [et al.].
      p.   cm.—(Contributions to the study of mass media and
  communications, ISSN 0732-4456 ; no. 19)
    Includes bibliographical references
    ISBN 0-313-26766-9 (lib. bdg. : alk. paper)
    1. United States—Foreign relations—Soviet Union. 2. Soviet
  Union—Foreign relations—United States. 3. United States—Foreign
  relations—1945- 4. Cold war. 5. Rhetoric—Political aspects—
  United States. I. Medhurst, Martin J. II. Series.
  E183.8.S65C644   1990
  327.73047—dc20   89-25906

British Library Cataloguing in Publication Data is available.

Library of Congress Catalog Card Number: 89-25906
ISBN: 0-313-26766-9
ISSN: 0732-4456

First published in 1990

Greenwood Press, 88 Post Road West, Westport, CT 06881
An imprint of Greenwood Publishing Group, Inc.

Printed in the United States of America

The paper used in this book complies with the
Permanent Paper Standard issued by the National
Information Standards Organization (Z39.48-1984).

10 9 8 7 6 5 4 3 2 1

In
Memory of
Wayne Brockriede,
Scholar,
Teacher,
Friend

Contents

x Contents

Acknowledgments

No book comes into existence without the able assistance and encouragement of many hands. The present work is no exception.

Texas A&M University provided funding for a research assistant, computer facilities, and office space.

Colleagues at Texas A&M, San Jose State University, and the University of Minnesota read portions of the manuscript and provided valuable feedback.

Our editorial assistant, Linda Benefield, provided crucial support without which the volume would not have come into being.

Bernard K. Duffy provided encouragement and guidance, as did Mildred Vasan, Maureen Melino, and Patricia Meyers at Greenwood Press.

To all of the people involved in this project, we express sincere thanks.

Introduction

In 1970, two books appeared that have special significance for the present study. One was *The Origins of the Cold War* by Lloyd C. Gardner, Arthur Schlesinger, Jr., and Hans J. Morgenthau. The other was *Moments in the Rhetoric of the Cold War* by Wayne Brockriede and Robert L. Scott.[1] The significance of the first work is structural in nature. Three scholars, each representing a different philosophical perspective on the origins of the Cold War, joined together to present their divergent views within the covers of a single volume. In so doing, these authors provided a broad overview of the dominant theories concerning Cold War origins, theories identified with the revisionist, traditionalist, and realist schools of thought. The significance of the second book—*Moments in the Rhetoric of the Cold War*—is not so much structural as methodological and substantive. Brockriede and Scott selected several crucial moments in Cold War rhetoric and examined those moments through the method of rhetorical criticism and the critical lens of such dimensions as liking, power, distance, attitude, format, channels, people, functions, methods, and contexts.[2]

Cold War Rhetoric: Strategy, Metaphor, and Ideology draws its inspiration from both of these earlier volumes. Like *The Origins of the Cold War*, the present work is the product of multiple authors each of whom is charged with presenting a distinct approach to the analysis of Cold War discourse. Martin J. Medhurst describes the assumptions and working hypotheses of strategic analysis and then illustrates those assumptions and hypotheses with two critical case studies, one focusing on Eisenhower's "Atoms for Peace" speech, and the other on Kennedy's March 2, 1962, address on the resumption of atmospheric testing of nuclear weapons. Robert L. Ivie, following the same pattern, first introduces the intricacies and presuppositions of metaphorical analysis, which he then follows with two critical illustrations, one on the Murrow-

McCarthy confrontation on the CBS program "See It Now," and another on the rhetoric of prominent Cold War critics. Philip Wander rounds out the tripartite approach by first describing the parameters of an ideological approach to Cold War discourse then providing two applications of an ideological critique. In the concluding chapter, Ivie suggests how all three approaches might contribute to a broadened view of how Cold War discourse functions for both its practitioners and its consumers. While the approaches are distinct, Ivie argues that there are areas of overlap that allow practitioners of one approach to engage in dialogue with practitioners of different approaches. Indeed, there is a sense in which all three emphases are necessary correlates of one another—necessary if rhetoric is to be understood in its fullest dimension as a linguistic sign of who we are as a people. And it is this sense of rhetoric as central to being human and constitutive of culture and society that points to Brockriede and Scott's earlier work.

Moments in the Rhetoric of the Cold War located the art of rhetoric as a generative principle of Cold War politics. Rhetoric was not something added on or peripheral to or substituting for the "real" issues. No, rhetoric was *the* issue; it constituted the central substance that required serious attention if the Cold War was to remain cold and rhetoric was to continue to be used in place of instruments of death. A Cold War is, by definition, a rhetorical war, a war fought with words, speeches, pamphlets, public information (or disinformation) campaigns, slogans, gestures, symbolic actions, and the like. By taking seriously this point of view, Brockriede and Scott were able to illuminate in new and creative ways such events as Khrushchev's 1959 American tour and Truman's famous speech on aid to Greece and Turkey.

Like Brockriede and Scott, we wish to place rhetoric at the center of debate and analysis. Unlike their earlier work, we offer not one but three distinct approaches that we bring to bear on different moments in the discourse of Cold War. While the methodological approaches are different and the particular moments distinct, we see *Cold War Rhetoric: Strategy, Metaphor, and Ideology* following the intellectual lead of Brockriede and Scott inasmuch as rhetoric is seen as a central defining characteristic of Cold War. Further, like those authors, we believe that scholars of speech, rhetoric, and communication studies have much of significance to contribute to Cold War scholarship. From the early studies by William Underhill, Robert P. Newman, and Robert T. Oliver to the current studies listed in the concluding bibliography of this volume, rhetorical scholars have made important contributions to a deeper understanding of the discourse that is Cold War. If the present volume does nothing more than call attention to this body of rhetorical scholarship, it will have fulfilled an important goal. If it should go beyond this limited goal to instruct in rhetorical methodology and criticism, the authors' purposes will be realized.

Robert L. Scott has graciously provided an opening essay for this volume. In his essay, Scott seeks to outline some of the tasks remaining for students of Cold War discourse. That the very term "Cold War" has a vaguely oxymoronic quality to it suggests that further exploration into the purely linguistic dimensions of the Cold War might prove fruitful. Yet no sooner has one stepped into the house of language than one becomes imprisoned, for while a given terminology is a way of seeing the world it is also, as Kenneth Burke taught us long ago, a way of not seeing as well. Language, Scott argues, does not so much describe reality as constitute that reality. When we study Cold War, be it in speech, letters, or other symbolic actions, we are studying a linguistically mediated act that cannot be separated easily from the discourses that call it into being, sustain, structure, and ultimately define it. Scott provides a way of thinking about Cold War discourse—indeed, all discourses—that makes rhetoric a central component of what it means to know or have knowledge about a topic.

Scott's quest to know more about Cold War rhetoric began over twenty years ago when, with the late Wayne Brockriede, he wrote *Moments in the Rhetoric of the Cold War*. That book, the first significant volume on the Cold War produced by communication scholars, began a trend that is now entering its third decade—the sustained analysis and close reading of seminal Cold War texts. We are pleased that Professor Scott has written the opening chapter for this book, and even more pleased to be able to dedicate the work in its entirety to the memory of our friend, Wayne Brockriede, a man whose work lives on as testimony to the insights that rhetorical analysis can offer, and who was a leader in the current renaissance of rhetorical studies.

Martin J. Medhurst

NOTES

1. Lloyd C. Gardner, Arthur Schlesinger, Jr., and Hans J. Morgenthau, *The Origins of the Cold War* (Waltham, Mass.: Ginn and Co., 1970); Wayne Brockriede and Robert L. Scott, *Moments in the Rhetoric of the Cold War* (New York: Random House, 1970).

2. For the theoretical basis of Brockriede and Scott's analysis, see Wayne E. Brockriede, "Dimensions of the Concept of Rhetoric," *Quarterly Journal of Speech* 54 (1968): 1-12.

COLD WAR RHETORIC

1

Cold War and Rhetoric: Conceptually and Critically

Robert L. Scott

On February 1, 1980, President Jimmy Carter addressed the National Conference on Physical Fitness and Sports for All. After a brief introduction in which he quipped about his well-known penchant for jogging being no threat to marathon runners Bill Rogers and Frank Shorter, the president said:

This is a time of determination, a time of sober assessment, a time of challenge. I changed my prepared remarks at the last minute to say a few things that I think are important to the American people and particularly to you. I'd like to begin by paying a special tribute to a group that deserves the praise and support of all Americans, the United States Olympic Committee. Recently, I declared on behalf of the American people that unless the Soviet forces are withdrawn from Afghanistan, that the 1980 Olympic games should be moved from Moscow, canceled, or postponed. Both Houses of Congress, I think speaking accurately for the American people, have concurred strongly in that judgment. And last weekend, the United States Olympic Committee voted, I believe unanimously, to support the strong national sentiment on this issue. It was not an easy decision for me, nor for the Congress, nor for the U.S. Olympic Committee. Their decision was difficult, and it was a courageous action which deserves our praise and our support.[1]

Of course we know now that the Olympics were neither moved from Moscow nor canceled or postponed, and that few other nations joined the United States in boycotting the summer games. Further, the boycott raised some controversy in this country. Soviet troops remained in Afghanistan.What did Jimmy Carter hope to achieve? That question is difficult to answer in detail, but it is not risky to say that he hoped to achieve more than he did.

In almost any human situation, response is important. Carter indicates as much in his speech in citing the action of Congress as "speaking accurately for the American people" and the action of the U.S. Olympic Committee. The national executive worked hard to assure those responses. That the president of the United States will respond in some fashion to any important action of the Soviet Union in today's world can be taken for granted and, to some degree, the nature of that response can also be taken for granted, for the United States and the USSR have been locked for decades in a Cold War.

The Cold War is not entirely a war of words; in the instance at hand, the presence or nonpresence of athletes representing the United States in Moscow in the summer of 1980 was an important moment in that war, just as was the embargo of grain shipments from this country to the Communist world.

Standing up to the USSR has been a mainstay in the conduct of U.S. foreign affairs since the end of World War II. Just what that phrase means, however, is constantly being interpreted by various parties within this country and abroad. Actions are justified by that phrase, and alleged lack of action, condemned.

We constantly interpret what others do. Carter could scarcely help doing so: "Some have said, many have said, that we should not allow politics to interfere with Olympic competition. I agree completely."[2] Here the word "politics" is key in assigning meaning to the situation. "Some" or "many" had responded to Carter—for indeed the possibility of the Carter administration's involving the Olympics in its reactions to the Soviet's entering Afghanistan had hit the news in early January and had been avidly discussed since—and Carter responded: "But the issue now before our country and the world is not politics by any reasonable definition of that word."[3] But what is a reasonable definition?

It is not politics when one nation sends 100,000 of its heavily armed troops across a border and subjugates its peace loving, deeply religious neighbor. It is not politics when one nation invades this nation's capital, installs a puppet regime, and participates in the assassination or death of the leaders which it does not like, including the families of those leaders. It's not politics when an army of invaders sweeps the countryside, as is presently taking place, killing those who dare to stand in its way. It's aggression, pure and simple. And I'm determined that the United States will make it clear to the Soviet Union, just as other countries are doing, that no country can trample life and liberty of another and expect to conduct business or sports as usual.[4]

Do Carter's statements constitute a definition? In the context in which he is operating, they surely do. It is a definition that he expects will win assent, for the context calls for winning. The repetition and word choice mark someone who is trying to be hard-hitting, not willing to conduct "business . . . as usual." The latter phrase echoes through Cold War controversies. Confronted with situations demanding response, leaders frequently declare that they refuse to conduct "business as usual," while others are criticized for allegedly doing so.

Interestingly enough, as the Carter administration was coming to its decision to make U.S. participation in the summer games contingent on what the USSR did in Afghanistan, a decision that unfolded in a variety of statements and reports during January 1980, the United States was preparing to host the winter games. What did the situation and principles that Carter alludes to dictate to the executive in regard to these? "I also want to make it clear," he continued in his speech February 1, "that I welcome athletes from all over the world who are now coming to Lake Placid, including those from the Soviet Union, to participate in the winter Olympic games."

THE CONCEPT OF THE COLD WAR

If we ever look back on the Cold War as something past, then the series of actions that eventuated in the U.S. boycott of the 1980 summer Olympics will be a minor skirmish at most. It is very difficult to say at this juncture how all our actions regarding the guerrilla war in Afghanistan may be regarded. Can the support that the United States has given the guerrillas and the diplomatic, and perhaps undiplomatic, efforts of a highly diverse sort at a myriad of times be well described as a victory? We are inclined to see some "victories" in the Cold War, for example, the USSR's "backing down" under the pressure of the Kennedy administration's "quarantine" (the threatened interception of Soviet ships) during what we call "the Cuban Missile Crisis." On the other hand, we took a good many Cold War losses quite aside from the military actions during the hot conflicts in Korea and Vietnam.

If the alleged placing of missiles in Cuba and the subsequent dismantling of the sites is a part of a Cold War, and if a hot war was carried on by the United States against armies supplied by the Soviet Union while the Cold War proceeded, the question of discerning something that is a "Cold War" becomes difficult.

Some dictionaries contain the entry "cold war." For example, *The American Heritage Dictionary* defines it as "1. a state of political tension and military rivalry between nations, stopping short of actual full-scale war. 2. *Capital C, capital W* The state of such rivalry existing between the Soviet and American blocs of nations following World War II."

During World War II, the Soviet Union was often pictured very romantically as an ally in the popular press, but quickly after the end of the war disenchantment with its actions and intentions set in. Tensions increased until "The Cold War" became the common description for the relationship between the United States and the USSR, or the United States and its allies and the USSR and its satellites. America sees itself as having "allies" while the Soviet Union has "satellites." Further, we often express ourselves as opposing the Soviets in such a way as to make the nations of Western Europe feel as if, in our eyes, their interests and influence are of little consequence. The terms expressing the dominance of the Soviet Union tend to suggest, and often quite blatantly, a counter, dominant power: the United States.

Whatever the causes, the tensions, the actions and reactions both verbal and nonverbal, the constant maneuvering, shifts, and assessments make up what we sense to be a state of being—a state we choose to call the Cold War.

Of course, once in our reflective consciousness, the term seems strange, even inappropriate. Can a war be cold? If so, it is an oxymoron expressing some degree of ambivalence. Even the most vigorous of cold warriors, those completely convinced of the diabolical nature and intentions of their nation's adversaries, are ambivalent; that is, their words and actions have thus far stopped short, and stopping short is essential to the meaning of cold war. Ambivalence is built into the concept.

If the Cold War gets hotter, and it often has, how hot does it have to get before it is no longer a cold war? Questions of this sort ridicule the concept. There are always relations among nations that at any moment can be seen as some sort of a situation. Most obviously, whatever the "situation" is at any moment is made up of a myriad of instances—forces resulting in a sort of state, a stasis, but the forces shift and so do those states. Wars among nations, too, involve shifting states, and, looking back, we can see preliminary states that lead to the wars. What is gained by talking about a Cold War as if it is a stable condition?

The answer to the question is, in part, that we have to talk some way. Concepts generally are not perfect reflections of the reality around us. Even words that appear at first glance to be object words refer to a shifting reality. For example, one can refer to something very concrete, such as the Black Forest. You can go there and point at it. Or can you? You can point at this tree and that, but the whole thing, which is more than the trees—in fact, more than the physical objects within the boundaries of the forest (and we shall bypass the problem of saying with precision where the boundaries are)—is rather difficult to take in at a moment, and in the next moment it has changed. "The Black Forest" includes all the songs and poems in which these words have been repeated, that is, there has grown up around that place something that is more than the place.

We could continue this exercise with some small object that can seemingly be taken in at a glance, but that too, symbolized by a word, is a shifting reality.

But shifting as the phenomena about us may be, there are better and worse ways to talk about them. One might grant that assertion and, in doing so, one must confront the evaluative implications of the better and worse ways. In regard to the Cold War, one might object that it lacks precision; but, on the other hand, it engages attention. One might object that it encourages us to think of the Soviet Union as adversaries to be beaten; on the other hand, it may encourage us to keep our confrontations cold. I am not trying to suggest that all arguments are equally balanced so that they make no difference; I would say rather that they make great differences and we should be evaluating them.

Whatever we say about it, the concept of Cold War is well established. For better and worse, it is a way of grappling with the complex and perplexing situation that is both a fascinating puzzle and a terrifying prospect.

RHETORIC AND REALITY

The expression "the Cold War" may be well established, but one might say that it is rhetoric rather than reality. Ironically, one of the greatest burdens that rhetoric must bear is itself rhetorical—the attraction of alliteration and antithesis that brings the phrase "rhetoric or reality" so readily into many discussions.

What do we mean by "reality?" Things as they really are, of course. Notice how easily the word "really" creeps into the statement. Since "really" repeats "reality," the redundancy is to gain emphasis. If we omit that word, then the burden falls on "things." What is a thing? Or better, perhaps, what is *not* a thing? So whatever is, in whatever condition that it is, is reality. But such statements get us nowhere in particular, unless we admit rhetoric into the picture. If we do, then we see these statements as quite rhetorical. The redundancy of "really" adds force to a statement; the statement does not simply exist, but is stated by someone for a purpose. Moreover, it is probably stated to someone; it is addressed. The character and relationship of speaker and audience is markedly important in considering these statements.

But can we not make a more satisfactory description of "reality" than these statements? One that is perhaps less informal, more careful? Putting aside the distinctly rhetorical characteristics of these questions, let us answer simply "yes." As the *Random House Dictionary* suggests, reality is "[the belief in] the existence of things independent of words about them." If one inserts the words I have bracketed, rhetoric may again appear, since traditionally rhetoric has meant appeals designed to inculcate belief. One need not insert the bracketed words, of course, but a statement not believed in is empty. If one says that it makes no difference whether anyone believes the statement or not, the statement is *true*—then truth is empty. It is difficult to believe that anyone who says belief makes no difference understands what he or she is saying, since the trouble of saying so, not to mention the vigor that enlivens the saying, seems enough to warrant that belief does make a difference.

Accepting the belief that reality exists independently of words about it (independently of thought about it, too), one will probably not leave reality long without words.   Talk about reality is often a powerful sorting instrument—"in reality," "that's rhetoric, not reality," "reality shows us" and similar statements serve to mark the good, to curb the bad, to encourage accepting, or to scourge nonaccepting.   In short, reality is a most useful rhetorical concept.

If we take reality to be the stuff of the world that affects our lives moment to moment (as in "reality is a hard teacher"), then rhetoric is bound up with what reality is for us.   The writer of the Rubáiyát gave us this verse:

> Ah, Love! could you and I with Him conspire
> To grasp this sorry Scheme of Things Entire,
>   Would we not smash it to bits—and then
> Re-mould it nearer to the Heart's desire!

(Fitzgerald translation)

We might like to grasp things in their entirety, but we probably won't. We shall rather deal with bits and pieces of reality.   In doing so, we are inevitably emphasizing and, whether explicitly or not, personalizing—that we choose to talk about something indicates a degree of value in doing so, and the value is often quite intense, especially when we appeal to the reality of our operations in doing what we do.

Jimmy Carter was singling out and personalizing when he called on the Soviets, the International Olympic Committee, the U.S. Olympic Committee, Congress, and the American people: this is important (not business as usual); I am acting in our interest, support me.   But was his description realistic?   Questions like that are ambiguous in this sense: people who ask others to be realistic may be asking that they report accurately, but they are even more apt to be instructing others to be pragmatic.   Of course those two aspects of the common question may well harmonize.

In this case, one could certainly argue that Carter was not accurate. Part of the difficulty would be in agreeing on meaning for the key descriptive term.   Is "aggression" an accurate description of what the Soviets did?   Did they install a "puppet" or were they invited by a legitimate government to aid in quelling insurrection?   Those questions would appear to make accuracy focal.   Can we obtain the necessary cooperation in getting the site of the Olympics changed or the games postponed?   If not, will a boycott of the games do much to bend the will of the Soviets?   Those questions would appear to make the pragmatic focal.   (And we know the answers now.)

Acting effectively given accurate descriptions of events might be another way of defining reality. But in this statement, just as in the questions of accuracy and pragmatics, values are evident. One cannot act effectively unless one has some criteria, explicit or implicit, for judging effectiveness. If one will act in concert with others, the criteria must be in some measure agreed upon. In short, the question must be answered: by whose standards? Which is similar to saying, from whose point of view? These sorts of questions can often be answered conventionally, which means that they have been more or less settled in past practice. However well settled, past practice needs to become relevant to current concerns. In short, rhetoric was probably a part of the past that led to a consensus widely enough recognized to be thought of as convention, and rhetoric will be a part of guiding present conduct conventionally. Rhetoric will intensify especially if, as they often do, the conventions seem incommensurate with present concerns.

Put a little differently: What is reality for us, that is, our day-to-day experiences, is apt to be compounded with rhetoric. Even if we write in passive voice, assiduously avoiding personal pronouns and appealing constantly to procedures and standards that we have learned to label as objective, rhetoric will not be avoided. It may be less apparent and it may be more comfortable for some persons, but it will be present. It will be present because we cannot leave "reality per se," whatever that may be, voiceless. We approach it through language and interpret it constantly; further, we engage others in seeking their cooperation in understanding and action.

Of course rhetoric is an abstract concept, that is, it is one of the convenient labels we use to work with the stuff of our lives. Words are part of that stuff, and so are other people. We can dispense with rhetoric in the sense that we can find a vocabulary that avoids the term and other terms traditionally associated with it. Depending on the audiences we are involved with, such an avoidance may be wise. But the problems that arise from being engaged in the events of our lives, of having to communicate about those with others in circumstances that make our concerted actions vital, or at least seem vital to us, will assure us that rhetoric, by whatever label, will be present.

One cannot choose between rhetoric or reality, for rhetoric is reality, although not the whole of reality to be sure. To leave it out, for one need not discuss it at every turn, is to leave out a part of reality. "That's rhetoric, not reality" is rhetoric of a particularly vicious sort that exploits, wittingly or unwittingly, a misunderstanding. Persons making the claim often simultaneously disparage authority while tacitly laying claim to their own or to that of their party of interest. Calling a remark "vicious" is to assess it. Rhetoric should be assessed. How does one go about such a task? There is no short, simple answer to that question, since rhetoric is a multifaceted tradition rather than a single, agreed-upon method. Descriptions, advice, and examples sprawl over 2,500 years of Western culture.

In part, answering that question is the task of this book. The writers here have undertaken to assess the rhetoric of the Cold War or, more accurately, some of the rhetoric of the Cold War.

RHETORICAL HISTORY

What we are engaged in here—writing a rhetorical history of the Cold War—is a task that will need a great deal more work to complete. The term "rhetorical history" is ambiguous in the same way that terms for other sorts of history are ambiguous. "Economic history" may mean either a history of economics or a more general history taking an economic premise as explanatory. The ambiguity is not always reduced in a particular instance; the tension between a concept as subject matter and a concept as a perspective on subject matter may be productive. Ambiguity is not necessarily a fault.

Rhetorical history takes rhetoric as its subject matter and perspective. It is akin to intellectual history in that it helps to trace the ideas that motivate people in the shaping of those patterns we call history. It is akin to political history in that the task of rhetoric—inducing cooperation—and politics are closely interwoven. It is akin to social history in that the patterns of appeal and the temper of interaction are products of the matrix that the lives of people form; rhetoric cannot be well understood apart from these disciplines.

All that was is history in one sense. We often use the word "history" to refer to anything past. In another sense, however, nothing is history until someone makes it so, that is, the leavings of the past are raw material for a process from which history will issue. History in this second sense is the selection and combination of material accompanied by explanations that make meaning of the past; that is, the patterns that to some degree we find in and to some degree impose on the relevant materials. The purposes, processes, and products of history are all open to discussion, and such discussions seem never to cease. History, too, has its rhetoric.

Rhetoric, then, is simply one perspective among others to take in struggling to understand the past. Like any perspective it will have its frailties and advantages. What is important is not that we do definitive histories, although that word is often used in giving rhetorical force to our judgments about particular accomplishments, but rather that we do as well as possible in order to appreciate the richness of human life and put ourselves in better positions to take a perspective toward the future.

Writing rhetorical histories of the Cold War may be especially perilous. We both sense the shifting reality that we attempt to focus on with our key terms and recognize that we are very much involved in its events. Our well-being is immediately at stake. The tempers of writers of history, of any sort, and their audiences are as vital as the tempers of speakers and audiences in any circumstance. Clearly, those who create rhetorical analyses are themselves being rhetorical. Their houses are glass.

RHETORIC IN THE COLD WAR

Although rhetoric does not compose the whole Cold War experience, it is essential to our understanding of the phenomena that we interpret through the key term. But just as the Cold War is not one thing but a congeries of actions, including verbal actions, neither is the rhetoric. We might seek some overall pattern of talk that would typify the rhetoric. A tempting question is, What is the relationship of a cold war to a hot war? One answer is that the relation is metaphoric: the "new" sense of war draws from the older, more conventional sense to establish its efficacy.

However, the question remains in another form: Is the metaphor a substitute for armed conflict or a prelude to armed conflict? Put differently, is the rhetoric preparatory for war or preventative of war? The terms take on a decidedly causal character.

Let us take an example. The defeat of Nazi Germany was not an end to armed conflict in Greece. Greek Communists, who had fought the Germans, did not lay down their arms, but began guerrilla warfare to overthrow the government supported by Western European nations, most specifically by Great Britain. The aftermath of World War II had left Great Britain in a desperate economic condition. Particularly severe weather in the winter of 1946-47 worsened difficulties of every sort, bringing extreme suffering and even starvation throughout Europe. The British government decided that it was no longer in a position to render aid, economic or military, to the government of Greece, and communicated that decision to Washington. The result was what came to be called the Truman Doctrine. The speech that first stated publicly the position of this country regarding the situation in Greece (and in Turkey) was a "request" to Congress which met in joint session on March 12, 1947.

We can look back after more than forty years and say that the policy was a success; that is, the Soviet Union did not intervene on behalf of the guerrillas and the Western-supported government prevailed. But are we ready to argue that the rhetoric had the desired effect? Before we do, we should think a little further.

The Truman Doctrine, with its obvious overtones of the Monroe Doctrine, put the United States in a position of pursuing, or failing to pursue, a policy that became known as "the containment of communism." Once well enough established so that people could think through those terms, the terms themselves invited this response: containment is not enough; we should liberate those under the heel of communism. If one can justify keeping Greece "free," should we not "free" nations in captivity? Soon a great deal was being argued about mere containment versus liberation.

Perhaps encouraged by broadcasts from such sources as The Voice of America and Radio Free Europe, in 1956 some citizens of the "captive" nation of Hungary revolted against their Communist government apparently believing that the Western allies, and particularly the United States, would step in to support their struggle. No such support came and the insurrection was crushed decisively.

In 1947, Truman addressed Congress. Doing so was proper and pragmatic: he needed the cooperation of Congress in forming and carrying out a policy. But time was important from the standpoint of the American administration: events were occurring in Greece that needed to be influenced. Truman's speech was addressed to the Soviet Union. But parties other than the governments of the United States and the Soviet Union heard the speech and were meant to. The speech was broadcast throughout the world in eight languages; summaries of it were broadcast in twenty-five languages.[5] This one many-faceted speech joins with other communication, some of which was initiated by the American government, but much of which was not, to form what can be taken as an early, major episode in Cold War rhetoric.

Even if a conventional rhetorical event seems to exist rather sharply by itself, say something like the "Great Debate" between John F. Kennedy and Richard M. Nixon during the presidential campaign in 1960, these trace into a bewildering tangle of precursors and successors, until the arguments arising continuously on every side seem to form a sort of climate of thought and communication with many shifts in the weather.

A policy of "containment" and the rhetoric creating it opposed communism and immediately called up half-forgotten echoes of the virulent anticommunism that followed World War I and re-enacted to some degree the responses common to the international communism of the 1930s. The policy and its rhetoric pushed forward into the presidential campaign of 1952, with the controversy over President Harry Truman's firing of General Douglas MacArthur as commander in Korea fresh for citation and allusion. In those days, being "tough" or "soft" were understood immediately as serious claims or charges not needing the addition of the words "on communism" to be clear. The constant calculating of the military capacity of this country and the Soviet Union made the arms race a reality, that is, a lens through which we constantly assessed our status, one used heavily for more than forty years. In 1960, we worried about "a missile gap."   In 1988, the Reagan administration achieved an agreement with the USSR to reduce the number of medium-range missiles in Europe.   The patterns of persuasion surrounding the deployment of missiles and their Cold War use—yes, use, since clearly missiles have been used in many ways other than firing them—would reveal a great deal about the forces that form climates of opinion.   This sort of study, and a myriad of others, remains to be done.   The rhetoric of the Cold War is a relatively neglected topic.

Neglected though it may be, some conclusions may be risked.

1. The rhetoric of the Cold War has lead to armed conflict.   To the "insurrection" in Hungary, we may add the United Nations's "police action" in Korea and the long, costly conflict in Vietnam.   Some would add the rhetoric that, if it did not lead to has enabled to continue, the resistance to the Sandinista government in Nicaragua by forces former president Ronald Reagan preferred to call "freedom fighters."

2. The rhetoric of the Cold War has lessened the likelihood of armed conflict.   A premier example is the well-articulated campaign that threatened a "quarantine" of shipping during the Cuban Missile Crisis, a campaign that became a reality for most Americans with President John F. Kennedy's speech broadcast October 22, 1962.   Although the arguments would need to be made in some detail, the vigorous, even violent, exchanges of words in dozens of instances—from that surrounding the building of the Berlin Wall to that of the Soviet downing of Korean Airline flight 007—may well have helped defuse passions and substituted to some degree for other sorts of action.

The first two conclusions argue that the rhetoric of the Cold War has been both a substitute for and a prelude to armed conflict.

3. U.S. foreign policy generally has been monitored by the rhetoric of the Cold War.   Keeping a bulwark against communism often has been interpreted as necessitating cooperation with authoritarian governments on the grounds that these will be staunch opponents of anything seen as Communist intrusion.   This argument, especially important in Latin American policy, has been a mainstay around the world, as, for example, in support for the Shah Muhammad Riza Pahlavi in Iran and Chiang Kai-shek and his successors in Taiwan.

4. The rhetoric of the Cold War has often been a touchstone in domestic affairs that seem, at least at first glance, quite remote from the zones of tension between the superpowers.   The civil rights movement in this country, for example, was haunted by charges of "Communist influence" or "giving comfort to the Communists."

5. Cold War rhetoric that justifies large expenditures of money and confers great status on "defense" is in turn buttressed by persons with vested interests in the industrial and commercial defense superstructure.   Thus, proposed closings of military bases or the attempt to curtail expensive weapons systems draw dire warnings of America's vulnerability and often explicit charges of being soft toward or duped by our adversaries. Put differently: From some points of view, the Cold War is an economic asset.

6. The economics of the Cold War are pictured in some rhetoric as a detriment to peace and survival. Dwight D. Eisenhower worried about the survival of representative democracy in his farewell address as president on January 17, 1961, the speech that gave us the phrase "the military-industrial complex." Prior to the summit conferences at both Reykjavik, Iceland, in 1987 and in Moscow in 1988, Russian sources charged that the American arms industry, fearing a loss of markets, was a major obstacle to lowering tensions between the two powers.

However one listens to Cold War rhetoric, economic arguments are apt to be at hand, if not explicitly, then implicitly.

7. In the world of Cold War rhetoric, the more vigorous the denunciations, the more room for pacific overtures. That only a well-anointed Communist basher like President Richard Nixon could possibly approach the Chinese to ease the impossibly high tensions that had existed for more than twenty years is almost a truism today. Many nodded sagely when Reagan, after nearly seven years of the most virulent interpretations of Soviet motives and behaviors, sought, apparently successfully, very significant arms reductions and a great easing of tensions with Mikhail Gorbachev in 1988.

8. In the world of Cold War rhetoric, all foreign aid by the United States and the USSR is military aid. That is an overstatement, but aid that is not explicitly military—the supplying of arms and training, for example—is best justified as keeping our friends strong or denounced as propping up client states, if one takes an American point of view.

9. In the world of Cold War rhetoric, all science is military science and all art, propaganda. Again, this is an overstatement, but many examples tend toward hyperbole. The outbreak of anguished self-examination in this country after the Russians successfully flew their Sputnik I in 1957 and the succession of congressional acts and executive actions to control the travel of scientists and the general flow of scientific information would give many cases in point. The tours of musical organizations, plays, and collections of paintings to the Soviet Union from the United States or vice versa seem to rise and fall with the tide of Cold War rhetoric and are justified by arguing that these are the best ways to learn about the cultures of our opponents with the assumption, often articulated, that such learning will lead to understanding and respect, thus encouraging amity; a further assumption is that they will, of course, want to be more like us once they are exposed to our art or experience the freedom of our world.

10. So universal has Cold War rhetoric been that it has been a force in dividing the world. At first we thought of the political world as divided into two parts; in this country we were content for years to contrast what we called the free world with the Communist world, which we characterized with various negative descriptors. That divided world created a friction that was energy not long left unexploited. Many nations saw an advantage in being unaligned and letting the superpowers bid for their support—mainly verbal support in the United Nations and other international forums. Soon the unaligned nations began to think of themselves as a force, and the concept of the Third World was born.

If these conclusions point to anything, they point to work to be done. In view of that work, they can be taken as crude hypotheses, hypotheses that will be refined in dozens of studies of Cold War rhetoric. These conclusions also indicate that rhetoric is not something added to reality but a creative force in our grasping and modifying the situations we constantly find ourselves in as we sense the shape and meaning of the lives we live.

PLURALISTIC CRITICISM

The rhetorical criticism in this book will proceed from several points of view. One might expect as much simply because several different persons are involved in writing, but even if that obvious pressure toward diversity were not the case, pluralism makes sense.

The rhetoric of the Cold War being the subject at hand, the diversity of the subject matter is readily apparent. The parties to the rhetoric represent different points of view and even when speaking the same language give different voices to the various exchanges that make up a single debate. The singularity, however, is usually too broad to be grasped immediately. If it is to be grasped at all, it must be so by dint of a great deal of preliminary work necessarily taken in pieces.

Subject matter makes its own demands. Just as the grain in wood or in stone yields more readily to cuts from some angles than others, with some tools but not others, so will the verbal actions that make up the rhetoric in which we are interested. Given the diversity of this subject matter, then, a pluralism in the criticism of the rhetoric of the Cold War should not only be expected but welcomed. To begin to understand the Cold War will be to begin to understand the rhetoric in its diversity. That the diverse instances making up the rhetoric of the Cold War will be best understood by analysis and reanalysis from many points of view with multiple methods is hardly startling.

The claim I am making here, however, should not be understood as assuming that, given time, we shall be able to gather the bits and pieces of the criticism of Cold War rhetoric to fit neatly together rather in the style of a picture puzzle. Our task will not be so simple. Rather we shall be faced with pieces difficult to make fit and perhaps will be forced to put them to one side. More disquieting, regardless of the glimpses we may believe we see of some larger picture, we shall be constantly confronted with blank spaces and edges that shade away tantalizingly.

What we experience, and shall continue to experience, is change. Struggling with the changing reality of the Cold War and its rhetoric, we may hope to gain a clear sense of the whole and with that sense a greater confidence that we understand and will be able to account for the shifting patterns, especially if relations between the blocs of nations we call East and West shift until the concept of Cold War is no longer generally appropriate. That is, if we can take that reality as remote as we take the Hundred Years War, we may gain significant advantage in working toward more satisfying, overarching explanations.

Although our confidence may increase with time, the plural will remain with us. We shall continue to strive to grasp patterns, to reach understandings. Further, the parties to these understandings will be plural even though the ratio of agreement may rise. The likelihood is that they will rise and fall and shift. Any unitary sense of the *we* that works to grasp patterns and gain understanding will be momentary. The parties interested in any critical give-and-take concerning the Cold War, or any other complex topic, will be not only a plurality but one that shifts.

Inevitably the life of concepts, as well as biological life, will evolve. "Once and for all" is an illusion. Even if we gain a highly satisfactory state of being, we can count on that state being temporary. We may endeavor to maintain whatever equilibrium we gain—regardless of the sort of equilibrium on which we focus—but we should recognize that equilibrium is fundamentally a consistency of change.

Regarding the rhetoric of the Cold War, whoever examines it will examine it in a certain context—that is, the context in which she or he is indeed situated. Situations make relevancy a crucial question for particular human beings. Understandings, then, constantly need addressing and relating to the ongoing flow of events and to the concepts through which people grasp and create such reality as they are privileged to experience.

What I have said concerning the pluralism sensible in regard to the rhetoric of the Cold War applies equally to the instruments themselves. They are not only varied in answering the demands of the material but also in answering the demands of situated critics.

Part of what makes rhetorical criticism inevitably pluralistic is the nature of what we call rhetoric in the sense of means to various ends; the ends themselves, what is created by the means, may also be called rhetoric. But as instruments, if that metaphor is at all appropriate, what we have are sets of concepts and stated relationships among these concepts. Such conceptualizing has been a continuous—although scarcely smooth—endeavor for approximately 2,500 years of a spreading, changing Western culture.   Rhetoric, in its instrumental sense, is a tradition. Traditions generally are so because they persist over a length of time and involve the understandings, though not necessarily the high awareness, of a number of persons.   In short, diversity and evolution would seem to be necessary features of anything we might regard as a tradition.   Tradition, then, suggests a strong sense of pluralism.

Traditions appear at their liveliest when they engage the cross-currents of other traditions.   Rhetoric has continually crossed, drawn from, and been diverted from other conceptual, that is, intellectual, traditions.

The long and often messy relationships among rhetoric and poetics as well as philosophy reveal moments of strength and weakness, of borrowings and rejections, but they most of all reveal a constant reassessment of instruments, their relationships to one another, and their applications. Rhetoric as criticism has been diverse even though we may create a sort of unity in grasping the patterns of its history.

The terms that are key to the three critics included in this volume are traditional terms.   They not only represent the tradition, but also the particular styles that reflect the working habits of these persons and, to some degree, others of similar bents.   Each of them will comment on their own methods of seeking critical insight within the tradition of insight, so it would be superfluous for me to comment further.

The pluralism of this book reflects the greater pluralism of the events and any means of grasping those events.   Most emphatically, the pluralism of this book reflects the pluralism of the tradition we call rhetoric.

SUMMARY

The goal of this book is to contribute to what we hope will be an increasingly rich and varied rhetorical history.   The sprawling, often exasperating, often fearsome reality of the Cold War desperately needs a rhetorical history—one that interacts with its political, social, and economic histories.   In addition, we hope to contribute to a sense of rhetorical history generally and to help develop the instruments of its making.

NOTES

1.   Jimmy Carter, "National Conference on Physical Fitness and Sports for All," *Public Papers of the Presidents of the United States*, 1980 (Washington, D.C.: U.S. Government Printing Office, 1981), 259.

2. Ibid., 260.

3. Ibid., 260.

4. Ibid., 260.

5. "Speech Broadcast throughout the World," *New York Times*, Late City Edition, 13 March 1947, 10.

PART I
STRATEGY

2

Rhetoric and Cold War:
A Strategic Approach
Martin J. Medhurst

A strategic approach to Cold War rhetoric is predicated upon a realist view of the world; not the world as it ought to be or as we might wish it to be, but the world as it currently exists with its varying political systems, governmental philosophies, economic assumptions, power relationships, and dominant personalities. By adopting a realist position, one also embraces an accompanying axiom: that systems, philosophies, assumptions, relationships, and personalities change and that one's response to any given situation must change with them, reflecting reality as it currently exists or is perceived to exist rather than what existed last week, last month, or last year or what might exist tomorrow, next week, or next year. Decisions are made according to a reading of the current situational configuration. Such a reading involves the collection, analysis, and interpretation of numerous pieces of data and the weighing of that data in light of the strategic assumptions and goals held by those in decision-making positions.

Cold War, like its "hot" counterpart, is a contest. It is a contest between competing systems as represented, for example, by the Soviet Union and the United States. It is a contest involving such tangibles as geography, markets, spheres of influence, and military alliances, as well as such intangibles as public opinion, attitudes, images, expectations, and beliefs about whatever system is currently in ascendancy. The contest, in other words, is both material and psychological in nature.

The currency of Cold War combat—the tokens used in the contest—is rhetorical discourse: discourse intentionally designed to achieve a particular goal with one or more specific audience. While the weapons of a hot war are guns, bombs, missiles, and the like, Cold War weapons are words, images, symbolic actions, and, on occasion, physical actions undertaken by covert means. For the most part, however, Cold War is a matter of symbolic action, action intended to forward the accomplishment of strategic goals—social, political, economic, military, or diplomatic.

Cold War rhetoric, then, is by definition a strategic rhetoric. It comes into being for the purpose of realizing a goal or goals and is shaped and executed with these goals in mind. It seems clear, therefore, that any adequate evaluation of Cold War discourse must take as its beginning point the strategic nature of the enterprise and the specific goals that form its reason for being.

To analyze Cold War rhetoric the critic must first become a strategist, seeking to understand the goals being pursued, the historical, political, economic, diplomatic, and military constraints that exist, and the precise situational configuration—the situation as it currently exists or as it existed at the time a particular decision was made or symbolic action undertaken. By understanding the goals, the constraints, and the configuration of forces that interact to form the situational context—the chess board upon which the game of superpower politics is played—the critic is in a much stronger position to analyze, interpret, and judge any particular piece of Cold War discourse. It is only when one knows what possibilities for rhetorical modification exist that one can adequately judge whether those possibilities are being most fully exploited by the practitioners of Cold War rhetoric.

COLD WAR GOALS

It is impossible to evaluate Cold War discourse adequately without a thorough understanding of the goals policy makers hope to achieve by employing symbolic means. Such goals are often opaque, resisting easy identification, classification, or simple explanation. In almost all cases, for example, reliance upon testimony, political ideology, or explicit language usage alone is misleading. Foreign policy goals are generally greater than their architects admit, broader than the ideology of the era might suggest, and more complex than any literary interpretation—analogical, psychoanalytic, structuralist, or literal—can reveal. The goals are the ends for which the Cold War strategy and tactics are the means.

One overarching goal of the Cold War era has been, and continues to be, the avoidance of hot war between the superpowers; the prevention of World War III. Coexistent with this goal is the desire of both superpowers to maintain and, in some cases, to expand their respective spheres of influence without sacrificing the concomitant goal of avoiding world conflagration. It is these two poles—the avoidance of all-out war on the one hand and the maintenance or improvement of one's strategic position on the other—that define the broad parameters of the Cold War era. Within these parameters numerous strategies and tactics are employed in much the same manner as one makes moves on a chess board, trying always to maintain a potentially winning posture without making the fatal move that results in the capture of one's queen—or capital. Every move, then, is a strategic one, undertaken for specific purposes in the glare of transcendent, and seemingly eternal, goals of survival and ideological struggle.

To evaluate adequately any particular move—any specific campaign, movement, speech, diplomatic maneuver, or military exercise—one must consider not only the overarching goals but the specific goals of the moment as well. To learn about such goals in all of their rhetorical complexity is the critic's task. This task cannot be accomplished, however, apart from the historical, critical, archival, and field research that allows the critic to reconstruct the strategic motives that give birth to Cold War discourse. Specific goals can only be determined in light of an objective examination of the rhetorical constraints surrounding any particular discourse event. Historical, political, economic, diplomatic, and military constraints are almost always factors in the selection and pursuit of specific goals and must be considered by the critic if he or she hopes to fashion a fully rounded assessment of the Cold War rhetoric under study.

CONSTRAINTS IN THE RHETORICAL SITUATION

Cold warriors face numerous constraints, factors that have the potential either to accelerate or retard the realization of the strategic goals. Some of these factors can be influenced by discourse; some cannot. Those which can be influenced by symbolic means are rhetorical constraints. Lloyd F. Bitzer notes that rhetorical constraints are "made up of persons, events, objects, and relations which are parts of the situation because they have the power to constrain decision and action."[1] Sources of constraint might include "beliefs, attitudes, documents, facts, tradition, images, interests, motives and the like."[2] In Cold War discourse five constraining factors are always present: the history of superpower relations, domestic political concerns, the status of both the domestic and world economies, present diplomatic negotiations, and the ever-present possibility of military engagement.

These five factors are endemic to the very nature of post-World War II life in the Western democracies. Each impinges on the others in a constantly changing mosaic of relationships. The history of superpower interactions is an ever-present constraining force and source of arguments, evidence, and beliefs about motives, actions, and likely outcomes. History is often the rationale for undertaking or failing to undertake certain diplomatic initiatives. History "teaches" us how to negotiate with the Soviets. Past "lessons" constrain the form such negotiations may take. We have "learned" from history how to act "wisely" and how to "read" Soviet attitudes and actions.[3] By undertaking particular diplomatic initiatives, we often affect political, economic, or military relationships. A change in any one part of the mosaic alters the overall picture formed by the interaction of the parts. Talk that leads to an arms treaty, for example, likely affects not only the military, but the domestic political fortunes—for good or ill—of those who negotiate the treaty as well as the economic relationships that depend upon the old military needs and requirements.

These five factors—historical, political, economic, diplomatic, and military—are contextual constraints that inhere in any set of modern foreign relations, including the set called U.S.-USSR. While contextual factors may or may not be rhetorical in nature—may or may not be capable of modification through symbolic means—other constraining factors are inherently rhetorical without regard to context. Such factors include the medium employed, the timing, place, occasion, spokesperson, content, targeted audiences, and intended or actual outcomes. It is immediately clear that all of these inherently rhetorical constraints involve choices on the part of the decision makers—choices that are based on strategic thinking and analysis and that, therefore, reflect the mind's response to contingent reality. The choices made could have been other than what they were; they reflect the mind's studied and strategic response to the situation as read—to the situation as perceived, analyzed, and interpreted in light of transcendent geopolitical goals.

That such choice-making is, itself, often a product of historical images and beliefs is clearly evident in even the most cursory reading of the Cold War era. Alexander L. George puts the matter well when he notes: "Consistency striving plays a role also in enabling opponents in an acute conflict situation such as the Cold War to maintain basic images of each other as hostile and malevolent in the face of seemingly contradictory evidence. When one attributes 'inherent bad faith' to the opponent, such an image can easily become self-perpetuating, since the assumption of 'inherent bad faith' does not easily admit of evidence that could invalidate it. Thus, when the opponent behaves in a seemingly conciliatory fashion there is a strain toward rendering such discrepant information consistent with one's preexisting negative image of him, and this leads to various stratagems for discounting, ignoring, or discrediting the new information."[4] One's choice-making reflects not only a reading of the situation, but also the terms, languages, vocabularies, and images with which one is doing the reading. Such symbols are, themselves, rhetorical in the sense that they are weighted; they project an attitude toward the person, place, or thing being described.

But Cold War rhetoric is not a matter of words or images alone. Certain individuals carry within themselves a rhetorical dimension. They are symbols that stand for ideas, beliefs, and actions that transcend the individual. The person selected to deliver a particular speech, for example, is a rhetorical choice. Shall the speech be delivered by the president, the secretary of state, the secretary of defense, the national security advisor, the ambassador to the United Nations, or some other functionary? The very selection of a spokesperson is, itself, a sort of message, a message indicative of importance, intended audience, motive, and desired outcome. Likewise, the selection of a place or occasion for delivery of the speech is also a rhetorical choice. By careful selection of a speaking site, astute rhetors can add to the persuasive force of their messages by building in a nonverbal or psychological source of reinforcement. Every component of the speaking situation—speaker, message content, place, occasion, timing, immediate audience, medium of expression, intended outcomes—are rhetorical choices, choices that are, to a large degree, under the direct control of the message source: president, national security council, cabinet, or Cold War advisory board. The task of such rhetors is to examine both the contextual and rhetorical resources at their disposal and to select from among them the proper mix of factors to achieve the immediate and long-term goals. The task, in other words, is to think and act strategically.

THE RHETORICAL AND SITUATIONAL CONFIGURATION

To be successful, the critic of Cold War rhetoric cannot operate in a vacuum. Mere abstractions, though helpful for theory building or model construction, are not sufficient for the description, analysis, and interpretation of actual historical events. The critic's task, then, is to fit the abstract critical concepts to the concrete rhetorical behaviors manifested by cold warriors. The task is to examine the contextual and rhetorical forces as they exist in "configured interplay"[5] at any given moment. The critic must thoroughly understand the situational configuration before he or she can successfully turn to the acts of analysis and interpretation. Eisenhower's "Atoms for Peace" speech provides a clear example of these forces in configured interplay.

The contextual factors are crucial for a proper understanding of the speech: how it came about, why it was structured as it was, and what the goals were, both short-term and long-term. To understand the exigencies of superpower politics in 1953 is to understand the strategic nature of Eisenhower's "Atoms for Peace" speech; and understanding its nature is prerequisite to an appreciation of its rhetorical artistry and pragmatic effect. History, politics, economics, diplomacy, and military necessity all conspired to yield the "Atoms for Peace" speech and the follow-up campaign based upon the principles articulated in it.[6]

By 1953, U.S.-USSR historical relations were at an all-time low. Soviet troops remained in Eastern Europe. Six hundred million Chinese had been lost to Communism. The USSR had managed to acquire the secret of the atomic bomb and to develop its own nuclear arsenal. American troops continued to fight and die in Korea. Not only was peace far removed, but the very possibility of mutual coexistence was in doubt. Then something happened: Stalin died.

With the death of the Russian dictator American strategists perceived an opportunity to exploit the transfer of power in the Soviet Union and at the same time try to reposition the American public for what many policy makers believed would be an age of great peril, an age that could result in all-out nuclear war. This was the immediate historical context within which the genesis of the atoms-for-peace idea was born, a context made even more frightening by the detonation in August 1953 of the first Russian H-bomb. People were scared. Part of the motivation for Eisenhower's speech was the desire to channel American thoughts and actions toward more pragmatic responses to the nuclear age. But there was more.

Eisenhower had been swept into office on the pledge to reduce the influence of government over private enterprise and to turn away from deficit financing and public works projects in a move toward balancing the federal budget. Administration economists and strategists, including Eisenhower himself, were concerned that the ongoing conflict in Korea and the long-term ideological battle with the Soviet Union might so sap American productive power that wins on the battlefield would be matched by economic ruin at home. And this at a time when the Soviet economy was in a state of sustained growth.

The need to economize on the one hand and to stay ahead of the Soviets militarily on the other led to the adoption of what came to be called the New Look defense posture. In brief, the New Look called for heavy reliance on nuclear weapons as both strategic deterrence and tactical, battlefield options. "Massive retaliation" became the watchword and "more bang for the buck" the slogan. But America could not afford to acquire the public image of a nuclear bully, threatening the peace of the world by an all-out reliance on weapons viewed by many as immoral and unthinkable. Hence, another purpose of the "Atoms for Peace" speech was to position the United States as a benefactor of technological miracles, miracles such as radioactive isotopes, nuclear medicine, irradiated food, and atomic power—all of which could and would be shared with friendly nations throughout the world. By emphasizing the peaceful applications of nuclear science, Eisenhower hoped to divert attention and criticism from the ongoing build-up of nuclear weapons that was simultaneously being pursued under the banner of the New Look doctrine.

On the diplomatic front, Eisenhower's speech was the opening salvo in an intensive persuasive campaign to put the Soviets at a public relations disadvantage by challenging them, in public, to join with the United States in the development of an International Atomic Energy Agency. The president hoped either to embarrass the Soviets and thus reduce their appeal to poor Third World countries or to start the Russians down the road of cooperation with the United States and thereby reduce the international tensions that could, he feared, lead to World War III. In either case, the United States's strategic position would be enhanced.

The contextual factors of history, politics, economics, diplomacy, and military necessity structured the strategic nature of the response and invited the choice of particular rhetorical options: Eisenhower as speaker; the United Nations as place; the closing U.N. session as occasion; the last day of a three-power Bermuda summit as timing; a live public speech as medium, with simultaneous broadcast via shortwave radio in thirty-three languages; arrangement of the speech to achieve maximum rhetorical impact; and careful selection of the speech content to convey different messages to three distinct audiences. The contextual and rhetorical constraints were carefully coordinated to achieve a strategic response to a very complex situation.

To understand the rhetorical dynamics of "Atoms for Peace" or any other instance of Cold War rhetoric, the critic must achieve an insight into the strategic thinking that went into the invention of the discourse. Such insight is possible only when the contextual and rhetorical forces are identified and their "configured interplay" in a concrete historical situation is understood. Cold War rhetoric, by definition, is a strategic rhetoric, a strategic mode of discourse that requires an equally strategic view of language as symbolic action for its explanation, analysis, and interpretation.

One clear example of a strategic rhetoric is John F. Kennedy's address to the American people on the evening of March 2, 1962. Unlike Eisenhower's "Atoms for Peace" speech, a speech characterized by its implicit argumentative techniques, Kennedy's strategy emphasized the rhetorical resources inherent in the persona of the speaker. Though Kennedy had to take into account the contextual constraints of history, politics, economics, diplomacy, and the possibility of military gain or loss, it was the peculiar persuasive possibilities of his public persona that constituted the dominant strategic dimension of the speech.

The public Kennedy—the candidate who made public arguments, took public positions, voted for and against public policies—was the chief constraining factor he faced on the night of March 2, 1962. Kennedy's public persona as an opponent of the arms race and an advocate of arms control was at war with his dominant rhetorical purpose—to announce the resumption of atmospheric testing of nuclear weapons. The rhetorical artistry of the speech lay in the strategic choices made by the speaker in his effort to shape audience perceptions, both at home and abroad, of his intentions and motivations.

Kennedy used his public persona to great advantage as he addressed such constraining factors as world opinion, domestic political opposition, British reluctance to support renewed testing, and the greatest constraint of all—his own belief that renewed testing was not the final answer and that arms control was the only way ultimately to secure the peace. By using strategically selected rhetoric to form a portrait of himself as a particular kind of person, a person caught in a maelstrom of historical forces over which he had virtually no control, Kennedy was able both to maintain his persona and to achieve his purpose, the launching of a new series of atmospheric tests.

The studies that follow—one on Eisenhower's "Atoms for Peace" speech and one on Kennedy's March 2, 1962, address on the resumption of nuclear testing in the atmosphere—are examples of an explicitly strategic approach to rhetorical analysis. By examining goals, constraining factors in configured interplay, and audience invitations and responses, these studies reveal the essentially strategic nature of Cold War discourse. They also reveal the equally strategic means used to communicate that nature to or conceal that nature from the intended audiences. To be a critic of Cold War rhetoric is, therefore, to assume the mantle of teacher: to instruct about situations, motives, and choices as well as about techniques, arguments, and strategies. It is also to become a prophet of sorts: to look to the past as both warning and antidote for the future.

NOTES

1. Lloyd F. Bitzer, "The Rhetorical Situation," *Philosophy and Rhetoric* 1 (1968): 8.

2. Ibid., 8.

3. For one example of how reliance on such past "lessons" affected Cold War discourse, see Martin J. Medhurst, "Truman's Rhetorical Reticence, 1945-1947: An Interpretive Essay," *Quarterly Journal of Speech* 74 (1988): 52-70.

4. Alexander L. George, *Presidential Decisionmaking in Foreign Policy: The Effective Use of Information and Advice* (Boulder: Westview Press, 1980), 65.

5. The notion of rhetoric in configured interplay is developed at length in Eugene E. White, "Rhetoric as Historical Configuration," in *Rhetoric in Transition: Studies in the Nature and Uses of Rhetoric*, ed. Eugene E. White (University Park, Pa.: Pennsylvania State University Press, 1980), 7-20. Also in the same volume, see Lloyd F. Bitzer, "Functional Communication: A Situational Perspective," 21-38.

6. For more information on the follow-up campaign to "Atoms for Peace," see Martin J. Medhurst, "People and Power: Rhetorical Dimen-

sions in Eisenhower's 'Atoms for Peace' Campaign." Paper presented at the 1988 Western Speech Communication Association Convention in San Diego, California.

3

Eisenhower's "Atoms for Peace" Speech: A Case Study in the Strategic Use of Language

Martin J. Medhurst

Personally, I think this [speech] will be a "sleeper" as far as this country is concerned—but one of these days when the deserts do bloom, and atomic reactors are turning out electricity where there was no fuel before, and when millions of people are eating who never really ate before . . . the President's December 1953 speech and proposal will be remembered as the starting point of it all.[1]

C. D. Jackson, Special Assistant to the
President for Psychological Warfare
February 5, 1955

More than thirty years later the deserts have not bloomed, famine is still a reality, and the nuclear reactor, once the hopeful sign of a better tomorrow, stands as a technological indictment of humanity's inability to see beyond the visions of the moment.

Dwight Eisenhower was not the first president to speak of the peaceful uses of atomic energy, yet it was his "Atoms for Peace" speech, delivered in front of the United Nations's General Assembly on December 8, 1953, that marked the public commencement of a persuasive campaign the dimensions of which stagger the imagination. Planned at the highest levels of government, shrouded in secrecy, aided by the military-industrial complex, and executed over the course of two decades, the campaign to promote the peaceful use of the atom was conceived in pragmatism, dedicated in realism, and promoted in the spirit of idealism. At each stage of the campaign rhetorical purposes, some lofty, some base, motivated both words and deeds.

Space does not permit a complete explication of this persuasive effort nor even a perfunctory glance at each of its component parts. That must await some future forum. In this essay the pragmatic atmosphere that prompted Eisenhower to deliver a speech advertised as a step away from the nuclear precipice will be described. At the same time, the realist assumptions and motives that reveal Eisenhower's true purposes for delivering his "Atoms for Peace" speech on December 8, 1953, will be explicated.

The argument has three parts. First, despite American protestations to the contrary, Eisenhower's "Atoms for Peace" speech was, in fact, a carefully crafted piece of Cold War rhetoric specifically designed to gain a psychological victory over the Soviet Union. It was part of an American peace offensive launched, in part, as a response to an ongoing Soviet peace offensive.

Second, the speech creates one audience on the level of explicit argument, but a much different audience when the implicit arguments are examined. Explicitly, the speech is addressed to the world at large, particularly those nonaligned nations in the midst of industrialization. It is aimed at that amorphous animal called world opinion. Implicitly, it is addressed to the Soviet Union, partly as warning, partly as challenge.

Third, the speech is intentionally structured to invite the world at large to understand "Atoms for Peace" as a step toward nuclear disarmament. In addition to the internal structure, the persuasive campaign carried on immediately before and after the speech was designed explicitly to portray "Atoms for Peace" as part of the free world's (read America's) commitment to nuclear arms control. That the speech was not, in fact, related to disarmament talks but was, rather, an attempt to gain a psychological Cold War victory will be demonstrated.

CONCEIVED IN PRAGMATISM

To understand fully how "Atoms for Peace" evolved to the form in which it was delivered, one must return to the opening weeks of the Eisenhower administration, specifically the events of February, March, and April of 1953. Three events are particularly worthy of note.

In February, a top-secret report commissioned by President Truman was delivered to the new secretary of state, John Foster Dulles. Known internally as the Oppenheimer Report, the document "declared that a renewed search must be made for a way to avert the catastrophe of modern war." Essential to this goal, the report held, was "wider public discussion based upon wider understanding of the meaning of a nuclear holocaust."[2]

As discussion of the policy implications of the Oppenheimer Report ensued, a new factor changed the complexion of American foreign policy: Stalin died. Announced to the world on March 6, 1953, the death of Stalin was viewed as a unique opportunity for advancing the cause of freedom, both in the occupied countries of Europe and within the Soviet Union itself. As historian Louis Halle puts it, the hope was "widespread throughout the West, that the Soviet state, unable to resolve the problem of the succession, would fall into confusion and helplessness upon Stalin's removal from the scene."[3]   Nowhere was this hope more evident than within Eisenhower's inner circle.

C. D. Jackson, special assistant to the president for Cold War strategy (also known as psychological warfare) and the man who would later be primarily responsible for the drafting of "Atoms for Peace," viewed the death of Stalin with both elation and alarm.   On March 4, 1953, Jackson wrote to General Robert Cutler, head of the National Security Council:

This morning's developments, both in Moscow and in Washington point up both a great need and a great opportunity. As to the need, it is hardly an exaggeration to say that no agency of this government had in its files anything resembling a plan, or even a sense-making guidance, to cover the circumstances arising out of the fatal illness or death of Stalin. . . . It is both fair and safe to say that, left to itself, the existing machinery will be incapable of assuming the initiative and moving on the first really great opportunity that has been presented to us.

Conversely—and this is the opportunity—if we do not take the initiative and capitalize on the dismay, confusion, fear, and selfish hope brought about by this opportunity, we will be giving the enemy the time to pull himself togther, get his wind back, and present us with a new monolithic structure which we will spend years attempting to analyze. . . .

In other words, shouldn't we do everything possible to overload the enemy at the precise moment when he is least capable of bearing even his normal load. . . . During the present moment of confusion, the chances of the Soviets launching World War III are reduced virtually to zero, and will remain in the low numbers so long as the confusion continues to exist. Our task, therefore, is to perpetuate the confusion as long as possible, and to stave off as long as possible any new crystallization.

It is not inconceivable that out of such a program might come further opportunities which, skillfully exploited, might advance the real disintegration of the Soviet Empire.[4]

Thus was set in motion a systematic plan to exploit the weakness perceived to accompany a Soviet transfer of power.   Within the week plans were being laid, amidst much internal dissension, to take advantage of the historical moment.   Against the wishes of John Foster Dulles, Jackson convinced the president to launch an American peace offensive and, with the assistance of Walt Rostow and Emmet Hughes, began to draft a major foreign policy address designed, in Rostow's words, "to hold up a vision of the specific long-range objectives of American diplomacy but to make the negotiations designed to achieve that vision contingent upon a prior Korean settlement."[5]

After "some fourteen drafts"[6] the "Chance for Peace" speech was delivered before the American Society of Newspaper Editors on April 16, 1953.   It was the opening shot in the psychological warfare advocated by Jackson as a means "to preempt a possible Soviet peace offensive."[7] The speech laid out American objectives: settlement in Korea, peace in Indochina, unification of Germany, an Austrian peace treaty, and, in one line, the peaceful use of atomic energy. Atoms for peace, long sought after by scientists and visionaries, now joined the Cold War effort.

Having launched the offensive, Jackson, at Eisenhower's direction, continued to probe for opportunities to exploit the situation. In an effort to line up the American public behind the offensive and to prepare them for the twilight struggle that lay ahead, Jackson and Hughes were charged with producing drafts of what came to be known as Operation Candor—a straightforward report to the American people on the destructive capacity of nuclear weapons.

Both Eisenhower and Jackson agreed with the findings of the Oppenheimer Report: that the public must come to understand the full implications of nuclear war. Moreover, the Soviet peace offensive and public weariness with the Korean War made incorporation of the American audience behind the U.S. effort an absolute necessity lest Americans, in the words of Konrad Adenauer, be tempted "to succumb to the blandishments of a détente which for the time being was nothing but a pipedream."[8] It was time to be completely candid with the American public concerning the possibility of mutual destruction, a possibility that now defined the very nature of superpower politics.

Numerous drafts of the "Operation Candor" speech were produced from late April to early October of 1953. None proved adequate to the task at hand. Furthermore, in the intervening months the situation had changed radically once again. On July 26 a Korean truce had been signed; the war was over. Two weeks later, on August 12, 1953, the Soviet Union tested their first hydrogen bomb. Unbeknownst to the American public, the type of thermonuclear weapon tested by the Soviet Union indicated that they were much closer to the capacity for delivering a hydrogen bomb than anyone imagined.[9] The need for "Candor" was now greater than ever. The public must be prepared for the worst, but there were problems.

On September 2, Jackson wrote to Gordon Arneson at the State Department: "I am afraid that the Candor speech is slowly dying from a severe attack of Committee-itis."[10] Though Jackson tried to establish new guidelines for production of the speech, the difficulty of the concepts involved along with a well-publicized leak to *Washington Post* columnist Stewart Alsop, resulted in the death of Operation Candor.[11] On September 28, 1953, James Lambie distributed the following memo to the twenty people who were by then involved in the Candor question: "C. D. Jackson asks me to use this outworn method (rather than the more expeditious one of going directly to Stewart Alsop) to make sure you are apprised of the following: Subject Operation, *as a series* of connected and integrated weekly talks is canceled. The President may deliver a single speech of his own in the general area to have been covered by subject series. As of now, however, no final decision has been taken as to such a speech by the President—what, when or whether."[12]

Though no final decision had been made, Eisenhower wanted to continue the search for an appropriate speech, though with a different emphasis. Consulting with Jackson, Cutler, and Admiral Lewis L. Strauss, Chairman of the Atomic Energy Commission, Eisenhower proposed, in a very general sort of way, an international pool of fissionable material that could be used strictly for peaceful purposes. It was this idea, first shared with his three top advisors on September 10, that eventually matured into "Atoms for Peace."[13]

The story of the evolution of Project Wheaties, the code name given to the newly resurrected "Atoms for Peace" speech, is an essay unto itself and must not detain us here. Suffice it to note that starting with the first complete draft on November 3, 1953, "Atoms for Peace" went through eleven major revisions before its presentation on December 8. The last four drafts were completed at the Big Three conference in Bermuda from December 4-7, with the final draft being edited on the flight from Bermuda to New York City on the afternoon of December 8. There is much to be learned from examining the eleven drafts of the speech, but that, too, is a separate essay.[14] I turn now to the speech delivered by Eisenhower at 4:30 p.m., December 8, 1953, in front of 3,500 delegates, guests, and media representatives at the United Nations building in New York City.

DEDICATED IN REALISM

The address was a masterpiece of realpolitik long before the term became fashionable. Every line was included (or excluded) for a purpose, and that purpose was strategic advantage, whether defined in terms of placing the Soviet Union at a psychological disadvantage, or in terms of preparing the American audience for an age of peril, or in terms of ingratiating the foreign audience.

From the outset, the public posture of the U.S. was that this was *not* a propaganda speech, but a serious proposal that could, if accepted by the Soviets, lead to a climate more conducive to nuclear disarmament. As Eisenhower himself would later maintain in his memoirs, "if we were successful in making even a start, it was possible that gradually negotiation and cooperation might expand into something broader."[15] Possible, yes, but not probable. Indeed, given the relative strengths of each side's nuclear forces, the relative scarcity of mineable uranium within the USSR, and the diplomatic tradition which held that serious proposals were made through private, not public channels, it seems clear that any public offer would have had a propaganda *effect* by placing the Russians on the spot in front of a worldwide audience. Even if the American offer was sincere, it placed the USSR in a position of either accepting the offer (and thereby implicitly testifying to America's long-professed desire for peace) or rejecting the offer (and thereby appearing to the world at large as an aggressor unwilling to explore a plan that, as presented by Eisenhower, would benefit directly the underdeveloped nations as well as the cause of international peace).

The beauty of "Atoms for Peace," as conceived by Jackson and Strauss, its primary authors, was precisely that it would place Russia in an awkward position and allow America to gain a psychological advantage on the stage of world opinion. As Jackson wrote to Eisenhower on October 2, 1953: "It must be of such a nature that its rejection by the Russians, or even prolonged foot-dragging on their part, will make it clear to the people of the world . . . that the moral blame for the armaments race, and possibly war, is clearly on the Russians."[16]

Analysis of the Text

Eisenhower's speech follows a three-part pattern progressing from the present danger, to past efforts toward reconciliation, to a vision for the future. Each section features an America striving after "peace," a term that occurs twenty-four times in the address.[17] One might logically expect a deliberative speech structured chronologically to proceed from past to present to future. Why does Eisenhower violate expectations by starting with the present? There are several reasons.

First, the primary purpose of the speech is psychological advantage rather than historical narration. The story is important only insofar as it provides the context for the perceived psychological gains. Four such gains are paramount: to warn the Russians against nuclear attack on the United States; to alert Americans to the potential destructiveness of a nuclear exchange; to position the United States as a peacemaker and friend in the eyes of the developing nations; and to place the Soviet Union in a policy dilemma by issuing to them a public challenge.

Second, had Eisenhower started with the past he would have encountered two disadvantages: He would have been forced to start with a recitation of failure that would have set the wrong tone for the speech by drawing immediate attention to Russian intransigence, thereby establishing an atmosphere of confrontation, precisely the opposite of what needed to be done if the psychological advantage were to be obtained. Further, by elevating the past to the position of primacy, the president would have been forced to bury the present in the middle portion of the speech. This, too, would have been disadvantageous inasmuch as one of the primary purposes of the address is to issue an implicit warning to the Russians who, it was held widely in military cirlces, would soon possess the requisite number of nuclear weapons to launch a pre-emptive strike against the United States. Eisenhower wanted to feature the warning, not bury it in the midst of an historical narrative.

Finally, by holding the past efforts at reconciliation until the middle portion of the speech, Eisenhower is able dramatically to juxtapose the failures of the past with his visionary plan for the future. The rhetorical disposition adopted adds argumentative force to the atoms-for-peace proposal by highlighting the significant departure from past plans represented by the new proposal for an international pool of fissionable materials dedicated to peaceful purposes. If the past was characterized by suspicions leading to fear, the future is presented as an opportunity leading to hope.

Atomic Strength of the United States

In the introductory paragraphs the term "hope" or its derivative occurs five times. "Never before in history," claims Eisenhower, "has so much hope for so many people been gathered together in a single organization. Your deliberations and decisions during these somber years have already realized part of those hopes."[18] After paying homage to the organization, Eisenhower asserts that it would not be "a measure of this great opportunity merely to recite, however hopefully, pious platitudes." He realizes, he says, "that if a danger exists in the world, it is a danger shared by all—and equally, that if hope exists in the mind of one nation, that hope should be shared by all."

Thus, in his opening statement, Eisenhower prepares the audience for a speech about the way out of the atomic dilemma that confronts humanity. At this point it would be easy to slip into a chronological pattern, starting with past efforts to solve the dilemma, the state of present negotiations, and, finally, his new plan for the future. A second alternative might be to review, in summary fashion, the hopes of the past and then to continue without pause into discussion of his plan. Eisenhower chooses a third way.

He begins by speaking of the present. "I feel impelled to speak today in a language that in a sense is new—one which I, who have spent so much of my life in the military profession, would have preferred never to use. That new language is the language of atomic warfare." Thus does Eisenhower launch the first part of the body, a section that might well be labeled "The Nuclear Capability of the United States of America," by confronting the audience with the paradox of a warrior who hates to speak of war, thereby distinguishing the persona of the general from that of the statesman. The general spoke the language of war; the president speaks the language of peace.

Though ostensibly a recitation of the extent to which nuclear weapons have proliferated both in size and number since 1945, the opening section is, in reality, a series of veiled warnings to the Soviet Union. Though ostensibly informative in intent, the opening section is really an exhortation whose central message is that the Soviet Union should reconsider any plans it might have for launching a pre-emptive strike against the United States.

The entire section is a series of warnings under the guise of a dispassionate report as demonstrated in the following chart:

1. *Explicit Argument:* Today, the United States' stockpile of atomic weapons, which, of course, increases daily, exceeds by many times the explosive equivalent of the total of all bombs and all shells that came from every plane and every gun in every theatre of war in all of the years of World War II.

Implicit Argument: Be assured that we are not reducing our weapons program despite reported cutbacks in the defense budget. We are building more nuclear weapons every day and will continue to do so as long as we must.

2. *Explicit Argument:* The development has been such that atomic weapons have virtually achieved conventional status within our armed services. In the United States, the Army, the Navy, the Air Force, and the Marine Corps are all capable of putting this weapon to military use.

Implicit Argument: If you think you can hope to prevail over us merely by knocking out our Air Force bases and missile silos, you are woefully mistaken. We are capable of launching a retaliatory nuclear strike against you with any branch of our services.

3. *Explicit Argument:* Our earlier start has permitted us to accumulate what is today a great quantitative advantage.

Implicit Argument: You may have enough nuclear devices to hurt us, but we have a lot more and can outlast you in any nuclear exchange.

4. *Explicit Argument:* The free world . . . has naturally embarked on a large program of warning and defense systems. That program will be accelerated and expanded.

Implicit Argument: Don't think for a moment that we are letting down our guard. We are prepared both militarily and psychologically.

5. *Explicit Argument:* But for me to say that the defense capabilities of the United States are such that they could inflict terrible losses upon an aggressor—for me to say that the retaliation capabilities of the United States are so

Implicit Argument: Think not that the land of Mother Russia will remain inviolate. It will not. We will inflict damage so great that it will make your losses in WW II seem like child's play.

great that such an aggressor's land would be laid waste—all this, while fact, is not the true expression of the purpose and the hope of the United States.

That the movement from exlicit to implicit argument was a conscious and intentional strategy is clear from the documentary history.   On October 23, 1953, for example, Secretary of State John Foster Dulles sent a "personal and private" memorandum to Eisenhower in which he advises that the speech should "make clear our determination, so long as this danger exists, to take the necessary steps to deter attack, through possession of retaliatory power and the development of continental defense."[19]

The speech drafts leading up to the December 8 address make it abundantly clear that the writers, principally Jackson and Strauss, are attempting to retain the threat of retaliation while, at the same moment, couching that threat in language that becomes successively less confrontative.   In other words, the rhetoric of the drafts proceeds from bold, outright threats to implied warnings couched in the language of peaceful intentions.   By comparing the last "Operation Candor" draft completed on or about October 1, 1953, by presidential speechwriter Emmet Hughes, with the final draft delivered by President Eisenhower on December 8, 1953, the movement from explicit to implicit argument can be clearly observed.

Candor Draft 10/1/53: We are today armed with bombs a single *one* of which—with an explosive equivalent of more than 500,000 tons of TNT—exceeds by more than *30 times* the power of the first atomic bombs that fell in 1945. . . . Each *year* sees this mass increase with a power that is many times greater than that of *all* explosives dropped by the aircraft of *all* the Allied nations in World War II.

Wheaties Draft 12/8/53:   Today, the United States' stockpile of atomic weapons, which, of course, increases daily, exceeds by many times the explosive equivalent of the total of all bombs and all shells that came from every plane and every gun in every theatre of war in all the years of World War II.

Candor Draft 10/1/53: Any single *one* of the many air wings of our Strategic Air Command could deliver—in *one* operation—atomic bombs with an explosive equivalent greater than *all* the bombs that fell on Germany through *all* the *years* of World War II.

Any *one* of the aircraft carriers of our Navy could deliver in *one day* atomic bombs exceeding the explosive

Wheaties Draft 12/8/53: The development has been such that atomic weapons have virtually achieved conventional status within our armed services. In the United States, the Army, the Navy, the Air Force, and the Marine Corps are all capable of putting this weapon to military use.

equivalent of *all* bombs and rockets dropped by Germany upon the United Kingdom through *all* the years of World War II.

We have certain knowledge that we can not only increase greatly the power of our weapons but also perfect their methods of delivery and their tactical use.

These, then, are measures of the fantastic strength we possess.

Candor Draft 10/1/53: We possess detailed evidence of the progress, over the past four years, of the Soviet Union's development of atomic and thermonuclear weapons.

We know that in this period the Soviet Union has exploded six atomic devices—and quite recently, one involving thermonuclear reaction. We know, too, how the amassing of these weapons can be speeded by the implacable methods of police state and slave labor.

We know—above all else—this fact: Despite our own swift perfection of new weapons, despite our vast advantage in their numbers—the very nature of these weapons is such that their desperate use against us could inflict terrible damage upon our cities, our industries and our population.

Candor Draft 10/1/53: The second decision is to devise for America a defense system unmatched in the world. Such a system—entailing the most developed use of radar, interceptor aircraft, anti-aircraft artillery and guided missiles—is in the making.

The building of this defense will be pressed with uncompromising vigor.
. . . Our defenses will be built with vision, care, common sense—and a frank readiness to spend whatever money or energy such a logical program demands.

Candor Draft 10/1/53: . . . we declare clearly that if—and wherever—the United States forces are involved in repel-

Wheaties Draft 12/8/53: Our earlier start has permitted us to accumulate what is today a great quantitative advantage.

Wheaties Draft 12/8/53: The free world . . . has naturally embarked on a large program of warning and defense systems. The program will be accelerated and expanded.

Wheaties Draft 12/8/53: But for me to say that the defense capabilities of the United States are such that they could

ling aggression, these forces will feel free to use atomic weapons as military advantage dictates.

Any such use of atomic weapons would be strictly governed by a clear order of priority.

(1) They would be used immediately against military forces operating against us or our allies.

inflict terrible losses upon an aggressor—for me to say that the retaliation capabilities of the United States are so great that such an aggressor's land would be laid waste—all this, while fact, is not the true expression of the purpose and the hope of the United States.

The evolution of the speech drafts from early October to early December evidences a shift away from straightforward assertion to implicative argumentation. That the implications are, in most cases, similar or identical to the authorial intentions of the original Candor draft can be seen by comparing the October 1, 1953, draft with the implicit arguments found in the December 8 address.

That the Soviets are likely to have understood the argumentative implications in ways roughly similar to the reconstructions above is a function both of timing and of access. For four months prior to the December 8 address, the American media ran story after story about governmental, military, and scientific concerns about a possible nuclear confrontation. Not only were such concerns easily picked up through environmental cues, but the Soviets were also given advanced warning about the December 8 speech and instructed to pay close attention and to take seriously what the President said.

In a top secret cable sent from Chip Bohlen, U.S. Ambassador to the Soviet Union, to Secretary of State John Foster Dulles, Bohlen apprised the secretary of his talk with Russian foreign minister Vyacheslav Molotov: "The purpose of my visit to him," cabled Bohlen, "was to draw the attention of Soviet Government in advance to great importance which my Government attached to this speech. . . . I concluded by saying there was no need to stress to him (Molotov) the immense importance of whole question of atomic weapons and repeated the hope that Soviet Government would receive this suggestion as seriously as it was made."[20]

In addition to the special visit of Bohlen to Molotov, the Soviet Union's representative to the United Nations, Andrei Vishinsky, was provided an advance copy of the entire address. Vishinsky, as one reporter noted, "appeared to be the only delegate with a copy of the speech."[21] Thus, through both public and private sources, the Soviets were encouraged to listen closely to "Atoms for Peace."

The dichotomy between the arguments as explicitly stated and those same arguments' implications is matched by the dichotomous audiences created by each argumentative level. The audience created by the explicit argument is the world at large, the nonnuclear powers who, as spectators in the deadly game of superpower politics, have a legitimate interest in the state-of-the-standoff as perceived by the U.S. president.

A secondary audience for this explicitly argued content is the American public. Operation Candor was originally planned as a series of addresses to the domestic audience, and Eisenhower explicitly states at the outset of the address that these are "thoughts I had originally planned to say primarily to the American people." Though no longer the primary target audience, the American public will still be informed of the terrible destructive capacity of the U.S. arsenal, and thus Eisenhower is able to accomplish multiple goals simultaneously.

But while the audience for the explicit content is clearly the world at large, the target for the implicitly argued content can be none other than the Soviet Union. Why, in a speech ostensibly devoted to "peace," should Eisenhower spend fully twenty percent of his time issuing veiled warnings to the USSR? The reasons are many.

According to CIA estimates the Russians would, within a matter of months, have enough nuclear weapons to launch a pre-emptive strike against the United States. Knowledgeable sources within the scientific, political, and military establishments believed such an attack to be likely.[22] Furthermore, the USSR had exploded their first thermonuclear weapon and had immediately followed that test with a series of atomic tests lasting well into September. In the space of ninety days the Soviets had tested as many nuclear weapons as in the previous four years combined. Doubtless the sudden spate of activity could be read as a prelude to an all-out attack.

Hence, Eisenhower conceives his task not only to be the articulation of the atomic pool idea, but also the conveying of a strong warning, implicit though it is, that a "surprise attack" by an "aggressor in possession of the effective minimum number of atomic bombs" would be met with "swift and resolute" action. Though he informs the world of the terrible atomic might of the United States of America, he also exhorts the USSR to behave itself or suffer the consequences.

Western Deeds and Desires

Having given his "report" on the present state of United States atomic strength, Eisenhower then makes a long, almost Churchillian, transition into the second major section of the speech—the past record of the Western Alliance in both word and deed. To stop with the recitation of the atomic dilemma, says Eisenhower, "would be to accept helplessly the probability of civilization destroyed—the annihilation of the irreplaceable heritage of mankind handed down to us generation from generation—and the condemnation of mankind to begin all over again the age-old struggle upward from savagery toward decency, and right, and justice. . . . So my country's purpose is to help us move out of the dark chamber of horrors into the light."

But again, it is not the light of the future to which Eisenhower moves, not to the atoms-for-peace plan. Instead, the president turns to the recent past and a recitation of the actions undertaken by the United States and her allies in an effort, he claims, to restore peace and justice to the world. While the explicitly argued content again functions as a report to the world, the implications of the report, the "conclusions" to be drawn by the world audience, are that the Soviet Union has been intransigent.

"Let no one say that we shun the conference table," says Eisenhower. "On the record has long stood the request of the United States, Great Britain, and France to negotiate with the Soviet Union the problems of a divided Germany. On that record has long stood the request of the same three nations to negotiate an Austrian Peace Treaty. On the same record still stands the request of the United Nations to negotiate the problems of Korea."

Eisenhower's method is clear. He seeks to establish the willingness of the Western powers to negotiate, and thereby implies the intransigence and bad faith of the USSR. Moreover, by positioning the Soviets in the role of spoilers in the recent past, he increases the pressure on them to respond favorably to future entreaties, specifically the plan he is about to announce, a plan no peace-loving nation could reasonably refuse.

Eisenhower seeks to leave no route of escape as he concludes the second section by observing: "There is a record, already written, of assistance gladly given by nations of the West to needy peoples, and to those suffering the temporary effects of famine, drought, and natural disaster. These are deeds of peace. They speak more loudly than promises or protestations of peaceful intent." Once again, Eisenhower seeks to back the Russians into a corner. In effect, he is saying to them, as the whole world watches, "put up or shut up." In the final section of the speech he gives them their chance.

An International Atomic Energy Agency

Eisenhower introduces his atoms-for-peace proposal by quoting a portion of the United Nations resolution passed by the General Assembly only three weeks earlier: "that the Disarmament Commission study the desirability of establishing a sub-committee consisting of representatives of the Powers principally-involved, which should seek in private an acceptable solution . . . and report on such a solution to the General Assembly and to the Security Council not later than 1 September 1954."

By opening his final section with a quote from the United Nations, itself, Eisenhower accomplishes two goals: first, he establishes a frame of reference with which all delegates are familiar and, ostensibly, with which the vast majority agree; second, he invites the audience to understand his comments within the context of *disarmament*. This fact becomes particularly salient as one seeks to understand precisely what Eisenhower meant by his atoms-for-peace proposal. At the very least, it is clear that the president immediately invites his ostensible audience, the world at large, to believe that what he is about to say has something to do with nuclear disarmament, the subject of both the U.N. resolution and of the first section of the president's own speech.

That such an interpretation could not have been missed by the delegates is assured by the sentence immediately following: "The United States, heeding the suggestion of the General Assembly of the United Nations, is instantly prepared to meet privately with such other countries as may be 'principally involved,' to seek 'an acceptable solution' to the atomic armaments race."

Having committed himself to the exploration of arms control, Eisenhower makes a crucial transition that both shifts the ground from which he originally opened his final section of the speech and commences his challenge to the Soviet Union, a challenge which, whether accepted or rejected by the USSR, will, it is believed, result in a great psychological victory for the United States: "It is not enough to take this weapon out of the hands of the soldiers. It must be put into the hands of those who will know how to strip its military casing and adapt it to the arts of peace." Thus begins Eisenhower's argument for the development of atomic energy for peaceful purposes.

After proclaiming that "peaceful power from atomic energy is no dream of the future," but rather is "here—now—today," Eisenhower launches into the heart of the atoms-for-peace proposal: "The Governments principally involved, to the extent permitted by elementary prudence, to begin now and continue to make joint contributions from their stockpiles of normal uranium and fissionable materials to an International Atomic Energy Agency." This Agency, said Eisenhower, "could be made responsible for the impounding, storage, and protections of the contributed fissionable and other materials."

"The more important responsibility of this Atomic Energy Agency," he continues, "would be to devise methods whereby this fissionable material would be allocated to serve the peaceful pursuits of mankind. Experts would be mobilized to apply atomic energy to the needs of agriculture, medicine, and other peaceful activities. A special purpose would be to provide abundant electrical energy in the power-starved areas of the world."

The appeal is clearly to those nonnuclear nations represented in the U.N. audience, particularly those to whom power, and agriculture, and medicine are pressing needs. To the world audience of 1953 this would have included the vast majority of member states. The pledge is equally clear: to share of our abundance, in this case our nuclear know-how, with those nations less fortunate. But there is one condition attached.

"The United States would be more than willing," Eisenhower continues, "to take up with others 'principally involved' the development of plans whereby such peaceful use of atomic energy would be expedited. Of those 'principally involved' the Soviet Union must, of course, be one." The proposition could hardly have been put in a more explicit manner. Eisenhower challenges the Soviets to join in an international effort to aid U.N. member nations, and he does so right in front of them so there may be no mistake about his offer. The challenge shifts the burden of poof squarely onto the shoulders of the Soviets. If they really are interested in peace, then here, says Eisenhower, is the perfect chance to demonstrate their commitment.

The International Agency, Eisenhower pledged, would have four tasks:

1. To "encourage world-wide investigation into the most effective peacetime uses of fissionable material";
2. To "begin to diminish the potential destructive power of the world's atomic stock-piles";
3. To "allow all peoples of all nations to see that . . . the great powers of the earth . . . are interested in human aspirations first, rather than in building up the armaments of war";
4. To "open up a new channel for peaceful discussion, and initiate at least a new approach to the many difficult problems that must be solved."

"Against the dark background of the atomic bomb," he concludes, "the United States does not wish merely to present strength, but also the desire and the hope for peace. . . . To the making of these fateful decisions, the United States pledges before you—and therefore before the world—its determination to help solve the fearful atomic dilemma." The section ends, as it had begun, with allusions to atomic disarmament. Indeed, the implicit message to the assembled delegates is that atoms for peace, in addition to helping nonnuclear nations reap the benefits of nuclear energy, is a step toward and a mechanism for converting the means of war into instruments of peace. It is a different approach to the whole disarmament problem and the "awful arithmetic" to which Eisenhower had earlier referred.

The implied content of this final section is directed exclusively toward world opinion. The implications to be drawn by the worldwide audience are roughly as follows:

1. The United States is making a serious offer to share its nuclear materials and expertise with the international community.
2. The United States is doing this because it wants to reduce the risks of war and increase international cooperation.
3. If the "principally-involved" parties all cooperate, then there will be an advance in the quality of life all over the globe.

4. The powers of nuclear energy are near miraculous and the cures mentioned by Eisenhower are immediately available if only the Soviets will cooperate.

The explicit message directed to the Soviet Union is this: Here's the plan; it will benefit the entire world community whose eyes now rest on you. Will you cooperate? Eisenhower places a challenge squarely before the Soviets and dares them—in front of the whole world—to accept the challenge or suffer the consequences that will be wrought, not by the military might of the United States, but by the psychological weight of world opinion turned sour.

EXTERNAL REACTION

As Eisenhower finished his speech there was a "burst of applause" that swelled to a crescendo.[23]   Even Soviet representative Andrei Vishinsky joined in the chorus. The next day Eisenhower's proposal was bannered across the nation's leading newspapers, and the effort to decipher precisely what he meant began.

Thomas Hamilton, writing on the front page of the *New York Times*, observed that "implicit in the president's speech was the realization that the United Nations would have to make a new start if the seven-year-old deadlock on international atomic control was ever to be broken."[24] Hamilton recalled the failure of the Baruch Plan in 1946, and linked Eisenhower's atoms-for-peace proposal to that earlier effort.   In Hamilton's opinion the speech clearly was aimed at moving disarmament talks off dead center.

The editorial page of the *Washington Post* also viewed Eisenhower's proposals as precursors to disarmament: "If the nations of the world—meaning Russia and the Western Allies—could cooperate on the diversion of nuclear materials for peaceful purposes, the groundwork might be laid for cooperation on genuine disarmament."[25] The proposal was viewed as being part of the long-term process of disarmament.

Reaction on Capitol Hill was, if anything, even more infused with apocalyptic visions of peace. Representative James E. Van Zandt (R-Pa.) claimed that Eisenhower had "sounded the clarion call to all nations to beat the atomic sword of destruction into plowshares by harnessing the power of the atom for peaceful pursuits."[26] Similar reactions were voiced throughout the corridors of official Washington.

Such reactions, in themselves, should not be surprising in light of the fact that the "correct" interpretation of the speech was carefully orchestrated and planted in the various media organs by none other than C. D. Jackson. It was Jackson who provided advance copies of the speech, then classified top-secret, to Ernest K. Lindley of *Newsweek*, Roscoe Drummond of the *New York Herald Tribune*, and James Shepley of *Time* magazine.[27]   It was Jackson, who, in his capacity as a member of the Operations Coordinating Board, designed the campaign to "exploit" the speech, a campaign that included use of "leaders of opposition parties," the Voice of America, Radio Free Europe, the CIA, and other "non-attributable instrumentalities."[28] The message, regardless of medium, was the same: "Atoms for Peace" is a serious peace proposal that could lead to control of the atomic armaments race.

Despite Jackson's best efforts, not all opinion leaders bought into the official "line" on the speech. One such group was the leadership of the Canadian government. Reporting from Ottawa, a correspondent for the *New York Times* noted that "as the speech was interpreted here, President Eisenhower's proposal for an international body and a common stockpool of fissionable material was limited to peaceful uses of atomic energy and could not have any decisive effect on the question of the use of atomic weapons in war."[29]

Here was the crucial point: was the atoms-for-peace proposal a serious effort to take the first step toward disarmament or was it not? If it was not intended as a step toward disarmament, why was it given in the first place, and why was it placed within the general context of nuclear destruction and within the specific context of the ongoing disarmament debate at the U.N.? Clearly, the structuring of the speech invites the listeners to associate "Atoms for Peace" with the general disarmament debate.

INTERNAL DEBATE

If Eisenhower's precise meaning was, despite Jackson's best efforts, a matter of some speculation on the international scene, it was no less obscure within the administration's own inner circles. The debate over what the president meant to say started even before the speech was delivered. As early as mid-October there was fierce disagreement between Jackson and the State Department over the advisability of making any speech at all. As Candor evolved into Wheaties, early in November, the disagreements within the administration began to crystalize.

Jackson chronicled the struggle in his personal log. On November 17, 1953, he wrote: "Meeting in Foster Dulles' office with Lewis Strauss. Unfortunately Bob Bowie invited in. Subject—Wheaties, and UN appearance on December 8. Dulles went into reverse, ably needled by Bowie—he didn't like UN idea; he didn't like Strauss' proposal; he didn't like anything. Bowie kept repeating that this was not the way to do things—quiet, unpublicized negotiations were the only thing that would get anywhere with Ruskies."[30]

But quiet diplomacy was anything but what Jackson had in mind. On November 21, 1953, Jackson wrote to Sherman Adams concerning "what we have in mind for December 8," and warning that "if this is *not* properly orchestrated, and these things are dribbled out without organized impact, we will fritter away what is probably the greatest opportunity we have yet had."[31] Jackson suggested six specific steps to Adams for insuring proper orchestration. One of these was that "every single one of the Departmental and Agency PR heads should be constantly worked with to see that they keep the news coming out of their departments beamed on a pre-determined frequency."[32] Jackson's concern was the psychological victory to be gained and the supposed benefits flowing therefrom. But the State Department had not yet rested its case.

On November 23, 1953, Bob Bowie sent his criticisms of the latest Wheaties draft (draft #4) to Secretary Dulles: "I question whether the proposal on atomic contributions by the United States and the Soviets will have its intended effect. Many people, and probably the Soviets, will treat it as a propaganda tactic rather than a serious proposal if it is made in this way. If serious results were hoped for, many would expect us to attempt private discussions with the Soviets as a beginning."[33] Bowie's reservations came to fruition two days later at a "big meeting in Foster Dulles' office." According to Jackson's log, "red lights started blinking all over the place. Joint Chiefs and Defense have laid their ears back."[34] After a one-day Thanksgiving break, the group met again in Dulles' office. The "real problem," as Jackson recorded in his log, "is basic philosophy—are we or are we not prepared to embark on a course which may in fact lead to atomic disarmament? Soldier boys and their civilian governesses say no. Foster Dulles doesn't say yes or no, but says any atomic offer which does not recognize ultimate possibility is a phoney and should not be made. Strauss and I say we won't be out of the trenches by Christmas, or next Christmas or the next one, but let's try to make a start and see what happens. Foster considers this mentally dishonest (he should talk!)."[35]

Dulles was not the only one with reservations. His Policy Planning Staff head, Robert Bowie, was also deeply disturbed. As he wrote to Dulles on November 30, 1953: "The only serious point of substance is the one about which we have talked: whether the United States wishes to achieve full-scale atomic disarmament if that should prove possible. My own view is that we definitely should. But unless this is our view I do not think this speech should be made."[36] Bowie's opinion was not heeded. Eisenhower made the speech with no consensus among his inner circle as to precisely what, if anything, the United States would do if confronted with the possibility of disarmament.

CONCLUSION

The speech, as delivered, reflected the Jackson-Strauss position which held that disarmament, while desirable, was not an immediately realizable goal. The purpose for giving the speech was, therefore, not to establish a framework for talks about control of nuclear weapons, but instead was an effort to position the United States with respect to the peaceful uses of atomic energy and to bid the Soviets in a public forum to adopt that position, thereby gaining a psychological victory whatever the Russian response might be.

Jackson's memo to the Operations Coordinating Board on December 9, the day following the speech, is instructive: "It will be particularly important to impress upon world opinion the sincerity with which the United States seeks international security through the reduction of the arms burden, while at the same time avoiding any premature stimulation of false optimism regarding immediately realizable disarmament, which cannot be fulfilled under present conditions of international tensions."[37]   From Jackson's point of view there was no doubt that the speech, though clothed in the language of disarmament, was not itself a vehicle for such disarmament, at least not at the present time.

That Eisenhower's speech raised the hope of turning weapons into plowshares can hardly be denied. That the majority of those in the inner circle who crafted the speech intended that nothing more than hope be offered can also hardly be denied. Though the public exploitation of the speech emphasized peace and negotiation, the backroom decision was that the United States would not "be drawn into separate negotiations with the Soviets on the elimination or control of nuclear weapons alone. For our part," says a summary of a top-secret meeting held on January 16, 1954, "we intend to discuss only the peaceful uses of atomic energy."[38]

The summary of the January 16, 1954 meeting goes on to note that "Secretary Dulles reiterated that we should try through these discussions to get across to friendly nations the idea that the disagreement over the control of the atomic weapons was not a bilateral difference of opinion between the United States and the USSR, but rather was a split between the USSR and the remainder of the free world."[39]   If this could be accomplished, if the Soviet Union could be isolated as the foe who refused to cooperate with the rest of the world, then the psychological victory would be won. This was the great, and arguably the primary, purpose for the "Atoms for Peace" speech of December 8, 1953.

By employing both implicit and explicit argumentative techniques, Eisenhower was able to accomplish his goals. He warned the Soviet Union against a pre-emptive strike; he portrayed the United States as the friend and benefactor of the developing world; and, most importantly, he placed the Soviet Union in a policy dilemma by challenging the USSR to accept his atoms-for-peace proposal. Throughout the speech and the subsequent campaign to exploit it, the administration portrayed the December 8 speech as a serious offer to negotiate the problems of the nuclear age with any potential adversary. That the speech was, in reality, not such an offer at all testifies to the ease with which human agents can shape language and guide perception in accordance with their own purposes.

Language is not self-explanatory. It is a reflection of the goals, motives, and values of those who choose to use it as an instrument by which to realize their ends. This study demonstrates how a particular group of rhetors used language to address multiple audiences for divergent purposes while, at the same moment, maintaining that the audience was one and the purpose straightforward. Criticism, at this level, is the study of how language is used by humans to channel response, and is, in the case examined, a paradigm both of linguistic deception and strategic posturing at the highest levels of government.

NOTES

1. Letter from C. D. Jackson to Merlo Pusey, 5 February 1955. C. D. Jackson Papers, Box 24, Dwight D. Eisenhower Library.

2. Robert J. Donovan, *Eisenhower: The Inside Story* (New York: Harper and Brothers, 1956), 184.

3. Louis J. Halle, *The Cold War as History* (New York: Harper and Row, 1967), 312.

4. Memo from C. D. Jackson to Robert Cutler, 4 March 1953. C. D. Jackson Papers, Box 37, Dwight D. Eisenhower Library.

5. W. W. Rostow, *Europe After Stalin: Eisenhower's Three Decisions of March 11, 1953* (Austin: University of Texas Press, 1982), 7.

6. Ibid., 7.

7. Ibid., 4.

8. Konrad Adenauer cited in Rostow, 50.

9. According to Robert A. Devine, "on August 12, 1953, American officials detected the first Soviet hydrogen explosion. . . . What neither Eisenhower nor Strauss revealed, however, was that the Russian device had used dry hydrogen isotopes that did not require unwieldy refrigeration. The Soviets now appeared not only to have caught up with American nuclear technology but to have moved closer than the United States to a deliverable hydrogen bomb." See Devine, *Blowing on The Wind: The Nuclear Test Ban Debate 1954-1960* (New York: Oxford University Press, 1978), 16-17.

10. Memo from C. D. Jackson to Gordon Arneson, 2 September 1953. White House Central Files, Confidential File, Box 12, Dwight D. Eisenhower Library.

11. Stewart Alsop, "Candor Is Not Enough," *Washington Post*, 18 September 1953, 23.

12. Memo from James M. Lambie to R. Gordon Arneson, Edmond Gullion, Brig. Gen. P. T. Carroll, Emmet J. Hughes, Abbott Washburn, Roy McNair, William V. Watts, Ralph Clark, Ray Snapp, W. B. McCool, Jack DeChant, George "Pete" Hotchkiss, Edward Lyman, Maj. Gen. A. R. Luedecke, George Wyeth, Lt. Col. Edwin F. Block, William H. Godel, Fred Blachly, Mrs. Jeanne Singer, William Rogers, 28 September, 1953, White House Central Files (WHCF), Box 12, Dwight D. Eisenhower Library.

13. Given the chronology of development of the *idea* for "Atoms for Peace," it seems likely that Eisenhower picked up the general concept from a series of articles appearing in the *New York Times* August 12-14, 1953. The three-part series written by William L. Laurence included the following lines: "The first international conference on atomic energy for industrial power voted unanimously at its closing session today in favor of establishing an international nuclear energy association, open to nuclear scientists of all the nations of the world, including the Soviet Union and other countries behind the Iron Curtain. . . . The purpose of the association would be to promote the peaceful uses of atomic energy through the exchange of knowledge by the various participating countries on subjects not related to military applications." See Laurence, "Atom Scientists Favor World Pool of Ideas," *New York Times*, 14 August 1953, 1.

14. For an initial attempt to explain the rhetoric of these eleven drafts see my "Ghostwritten Speeches: Ethics Isn't the Only Lesson," *Communication Education* (1987): 241-249.

15. Dwight D. Eisenhower, *Mandate for Change* (Garden City, N.Y.: Doubleday, 1963), 254.

16. Memo from C. D. Jackson to Eisenhower, 2 October 1953. C. D. Jackson Papers, Box 24, Dwight D. Eisenhower Library.

17. The total count of twenty-four includes "peace" and its derivatives "peaceful" and "peacetime."

18. All quotations from Eisenhower's "Atoms for Peace" address are from the text as printed in *Public Papers of the President of the United States, 1953* (Washington, D.C.: U.S. Government Printing Office, 1954), 813-822.

19. Memo from John Foster Dulles to Eisenhower, 23 October 1953. John Foster Dulles Papers, Box 1, Dwight D. Eisenhower Library.

20. Cablegram from Chip Bohlen to John Foster Dulles, December, 1953. John Foster Dulles Papers, Box 1, Dwight D. Eisenhower Library.

21. Michael James, "President's Plan Stirs Doubts in U.N.," *New York Times*, 9 December 1953, 3.

22. Gregg Herken, *The Winning Weapon: The Atomic Bomb in the Cold War 1945-1950* (New York: Alfred A. Knopf, 1980), 325; Jules Menken cited in "Briton Warns U.S. of Atomic Attack," *New York Times*, 12 August 1953, 15; Harold C. Urey cited in Lewis L. Strauss, *Men and Decisions* (Garden City, N.Y.: Doubleday, 1962), 228.

23. Thomas J. Hamilton, "Eisenhower Bids Soviets Join United States in Atomic Stockpile for Peace," *New York Times*, 9 December 1953, 1-2.

24. Hamilton, "Eisenhower Bids Soviets," 1.

25. "The Choice on the Atom," *Washington Post*, 9 December 1953, 10.

26. Cited in "Ike's Speech Praised Generally on 'Hill,'" *Washington Post*, 9 December 1953, 16.

27. Marie McCrum, Oral History Interview, 15 May 1975, Dwight D. Eisenhower Library.

28. Memo from C. D. Jackson to members of the Operations Coordinating Board, 16 January 1954. White House Central Files, Confidential File, Box 13, Dwight D. Eisenhower Library.

29. "Canadians Await Details," *New York Times*, 9 December 1953, 3.

30. Jackson log entry, 17 November 1953. C. D. Jackson Papers, Box 56, Dwight D. Eisenhower Library.

31. Memo from Jackson to Sherman Adams, 21 November 1953. C. D. Jackson Papers, Box 23, Dwight D. Eisenhower Library.

32. Ibid.

33. Memo from Robert R. Bowie to John Foster Dulles, 23 November 1953. John Foster Dulles Papers, Box 1, Dwight D. Eisenhower Library.

34. Jackson log entry, 25 November 1953. C. D. Jackson Papers, Box 56, Dwight D. Eisenhower Library.

35. Jackson log entry, 27 November 1953. C. D. Jackson Papers, Box 56, Dwight D. Eisenhower Library.

36. Memo from Robert R. Bowie to John Foster Dulles, 30 November 1953. John Foster Dulles Papers, Box 1, Dwight D. Eisenhower Library.

37. Memo from C. D. Jackson to members of the Operations Coordinating Board, 9 December 1953. C. D. Jackson Records, Box 1, Dwight D. Eisenhower Library.

38. Summary of Operations Coordinating Board meeting, 16 January 1954. White House Central Files, Confidential File, Box 12, Dwight D. Eisenhower Library.

39. Ibid.

4

Rhetorical Portraiture: John F. Kennedy's March 2, 1962, Speech on the Resumption of Atmospheric Tests

Martin J. Medhurst

The difficulty, as we all know, is to decide what to do. The somewhat sombre thoughts which I have developed can have no purpose unless they are intended to lead to at least some proposals to find "a way out" of the maze in which we are set. It may be that there is no way out. It may be that we are condemned, like the heroes of the old Greek tragedies, to an ineluctable fate from which there is no escape; and that like those doomed figures we must endure it, with only the consolation of the admonitory and sometimes irritating commentaries of the chorus, the fore-runners of the columnists of today.[1]

Prime Minister Harold Macmillan to President John F. Kennedy
January 5, 1962

No single topic occupied more of John F. Kennedy's time as president than the effort to bring nuclear weapons under some semblance of control. From his first presidential news conference in January, 1961, in which he announced the formation of a special group charged with the task of drafting a *complete* arms control treaty, to the actual signing of a *limited* nuclear test ban treaty in October, 1963, Kennedy put arms control at the top of his presidential agenda.

But it must be remembered that the success represented by the limited nuclear test ban treaty was the direct result of many moments of failure, moments stretching back into the Truman and Eisenhower administrations and extending throughout most of Kennedy's brief tenure. No moment of failure was more pronounced than that of August 30, 1961—the day on which the Soviet Union announced its intention unilaterally to resume nuclear testing in the earth's atmosphere. From that moment until March 2, 1962—the day Kennedy announced his plans for resuming U.S. atmospheric tests—the Cold War began to warm.

In this essay, I want to examine Kennedy's March 2, 1962, speech. I will analyze the speech as a piece of strategic discourse, which is to say, a piece of a much larger whole designed to accomplish certain pragmatic purposes and strategic ends. Specifically, I shall argue that Kennedy's speech on the evening of March 2, 1962, was an exercise in portraiture, a picture intentionally creating in the minds of the listeners a particular image of the president. This picture, though drawn with words, painted a vivid portrait of Kennedy as a certain kind of decision maker—a man caught in the midst of a great historical drama, who chooses to play his part, though without enthusiasm or trepidation. This portrait was formed through the selection and skillful combination of individual images that clustered together to form a composite whole, a portrait of Kennedy the president.

I shall argue that, by painting this self-portrait for his audience, Kennedy was able both to accommodate the strategic military and geopolitical exigencies of the moment while simultaneously preserving for himself the rhetorical space to act differently, to make different choices, in the future. The rhetorical artistry of the speech lay in its ability to address the exigencies and constraints of past, present, and future without seeming self-contradictory or foreclosing future rhetorical or strategic options. By examining the speech as delivered, I will demonstrate how this strategic portrait was formed and discuss the potential effects that such a portrait likely had upon the audiences to which it was directed.

THE RHETORICAL SITUATION

To understand Kennedy's March 2 address, one must return to the summer of 1961 and the rhetorical situation that prevailed as the president prepared for his Vienna summit with Nikita Khrushchev on June 3 and 4 of that year. Since the fall of 1958 both superpowers had voluntarily refrained from testing atomic weapons in the atmosphere. Yet, for nearly three years little progress had been made in the effort to arrive at a test ban treaty acceptable to both sides. Even so, one effect of the cessation was to keep the atmosphere free of such nuclear carcinogens as iodine 131 and strontium 90, and to the public at large that advantage, in itself, was seen as worthy of preservation. But upon assumption of the presidency, Kennedy had to take into consideration all of the situational factors, not merely the fear of radioactive fallout.

Even before he had formally assumed office, Kennedy had been advised by his predecessor, Dwight Eisenhower, of the necessity to resume nuclear testing. Had Richard Nixon won the 1960 election, Eisenhower intended to announce such a resumption himself in order to spare his successor the opprobrium that would likely follow such an announcement. But now, with a member of the opposite party set to take over the reigns of government, Eisenhower contented himself with offering strategic advice to the president-elect, advice that Kennedy, for his own reasons, would reject.

Upon assumption of office, however, Kennedy found that Eisenhower was not the only source in favor of resuming nuclear testing. According to Jacobson and Stein, "as early as February [1961], the Joint Chiefs of Staff had urged the President to resume testing if agreement were not reached within sixty days of negotiations."[2] The Atomic Energy Commission, certain elements in the Defense Department, and key members of the congressional Joint Committee on Atomic Energy were also urging reconsideration of the testing moratorium. But Kennedy, having made a nuclear test ban treaty a key element in his presidential campaign, did not want to be the first to resume testing.

The first round of Geneva negotiations under the Kennedy administration was no more successful than the last round under Eisenhower had been. Thus, when Kennedy traveled to Vienna for a summit with Khrushchev on June 3, 1961, he went with the intention of sizing up his opponent and of determining for himself whether the Soviet leader really wanted a test ban treaty. By all accounts, the summit was a profoundly disturbing experience for Kennedy. According to Glenn Seaborg, chair of the Atomic Energy Commission under Kennedy, "his meeting with Chairman Khrushchev seemed to be somewhat of a turning point. I do not believe it was ever . . . a right angle change of direction, but I do have the impression that after this meeting he was more inclined to think that the resumption of testing was inevitable."[3]

Though Khrushchev had assured Kennedy "that the USSR would not resume nuclear testing until the United States did,"[4] a message that had also been conveyed to Secretary of State Dean Rusk by Soviet Foreign Minister Andrei Gromyko, the whole tone of the summit had left Kennedy somewhat shaken by the seemingly recalcitrant attitude displayed by Khrushchev. The failure of the summit also prompted other government officials to renew their call for immediate resumption of testing. Foremost among these was Representative Chet Holifield, chair of the Joint Committee on Atomic Energy. On June 14, 1961, Holifield issued a statement that said, in part: "Thus in reappraising our position on the test-ban, I believe the United States must assume the possibility or probability that the Soviets have been testing or will be shortly. In any event we cannot continue to gamble our destiny, when we base such a gamble on ignorance of our opponent's action."[5] Events would shortly prove Holifield to be prophetic, but in June of 1961 Kennedy did not wish to be put in the untenable position of ordering a resumption of tests when he had just received assurances from Khrushchev that the Soviet Union would observe the moratorium while negotiations continued.

Nevertheless, in part to satisfy his congressional critics and in part to secure the latest expert consensus, Kennedy announced the appointment of a select panel drawn from his Science Advisory Committee and charged with the task of determining whether the Soviets were likely to be conducting secret tests. Appointed on June 24, 1961, under the chairmanship of Professor Wolfgang K. H. Panofsky, this special panel was also asked to report on what progress the United States could make if it should decide to resume testing of nuclear weapons. Panofsky delivered the panel's findings to the White House where they were discussed in a meeting between Kennedy and his advisors on August 8. According to Seaborg, "the meeting on August 8 apparently persuaded the president that there was no urgent need for an immediate resumption of testing."[6] No plans were made to prepare for resumption of tests; not, that is, until three weeks later.

The Soviet Announcement

The Soviet announcement, on August 30, 1961, of the USSR's intention to resume immediately the atmospheric testing of atomic weapons came as a surprise to most Americans, though the Foreign Broadcast Information Service had, two days earlier, monitored a Soviet transmission warning aircraft to stay away from a specific area over Siberia—a sure sign of an impeding nuclear test. This advance warning gave Kennedy time to prepare a statement for issue immediately upon reception of the Soviets' official announcement. The Soviet announcement was a long and rambling statement that placed the blame for resumption squarely on the United States:

The Soviet Government considers it its duty to draw special attention of the peoples of the world to the fact that now in the United States there is much ado about projects for developing a neutron bomb, such a bomb which would kill everything living but at the same time would not destroy material things. Only aggressors dreaming of plunder, of capturing foreign lands and foreign property can mobilize the efforts of scientists for the development of such weapons.

Exterminating people, they want to use the fruits of labor of the victims killed by them, the riches created by those people. This is the morality of monsters. The plans of development of a neutron bomb expose the inhuman essence of modern imperialism, which is no longer satisfied with merciless exploitation of working people and which is ready for the sake of profit to commit crimes which would eclipse by their monstrosity the recollection of gas chambers and murder vans of the Hitlerite hangmen.[7]

In reply, the White House issued a short statement that said, in part: "The Soviet Union bears a heavy responsibility before all humanity for this decision, a decision which was made in complete disregard of the United Nations. The termination of the moratorium on nuclear testing by the Soviet unilateral decision leaves the United States under the necessity of deciding what its own national interests require."[8] After consultation with the British, Kennedy decided that the best interest of the United States lay in trying to stop the Soviet tests before they got very far along. On September 1, 1961, the Soviets detonated their first explosion. Two days later, Kennedy and Prime Minister Harold Macmillan issued a joint proposal calling for an uninspected ban on atmospheric testing:

The President of the United States and the Prime Minister of the United Kingdom propose to Chairman Khrushchev that their three governments agree, effective immediately, not to conduct nuclear tests which take place in the atmosphere and produce radioactive fallout.

Their aim in this proposal is to protect mankind from the increasing hazards from atmospheric pollution and to contribute to the reduction of international tensions.[9]

Khrushchev rejected the proposal calling, instead, for "general and complete disarmament,"[10] which had been the Soviets' standard litany for three years.

On September 5, Kennedy announced that the United States would resume underground testing unless the Soviets heeded the call to stop immediately. In phrases that would appear again in his March 2, 1962, speech, Kennedy said:

In view of the continued testing of the Soviet Government, I have today ordered the resumption of nuclear tests, in the laboratory and underground, with no fallout. In our efforts to achieve an end to nuclear testing, we have taken every step that reasonable men could justify. In view of the acts of the Soviet Government, we must now take those steps which prudent men find essential. We have no other choice in fulfillment of the responsibilities of the United States Government to its own citizens and to the security of free nations. Our offer to make an agreement to end all fallout tests remains open until September 9.[11]

Thus began the sequence of events that would lead, some six months later, to the announcement of the U.S. decision to resume atmospheric testing. The events of the six months from early September, 1961, to March 2, 1962, are important not so much for purposes of historical continuity, but rather for an accurate understanding of the situational constraints with which Kennedy had to deal when he finally announced to the American people his decision to resume atmospheric tests. Four constraining factors were paramount: the need to position the United States with respect to world opinion; the need to maintain a united front with the Western allies, especially the British; the need to maintain a domestic political base for whatever decisions might be made; and the need to avoid overreaction so as not to foreclose forever the possibility of an eventual test ban treaty. These constraints would interact with the dominant exigence of the moment—the fact that the Soviet Union was learning important information about the design and utilization of atomic weapons and the United States was not. How best to respond in both word and deed was the problem Kennedy faced in the fall of 1961.

Positioning the United States

Kennedy's first reaction to the news of an impeding Soviet test series was anger that he had been deceived. He would later learn that the Soviet series had been under preparation for at least a year—throughout the winter negotiations in Geneva as well as the summit in Vienna. The Soviets had been stalling, using talk as a smokescreen for secret preparations. According to Theodore Sorensen, Kennedy's first reaction was "unprintable."[12] His second reaction was to call a meeting of his top advisors to consider how best to respond to the situation.

Several advisors, including Rusk, met with the president on August 31 and counseled an immediate resumption of testing by the United States. Others, led by Edward R. Murrow, head of the U.S. Information Agency, argued for a more reasoned reaction. According to Seaborg, who was present at the meeting, "Murrow argued strongly for waiting perhaps as much as a few weeks before making any statement that we had decided to test in order to let the Soviet action have its maximum unfavorable effect on public opinion around the world. He felt that this would tend to isolate the Communist bloc."[13] Thus, from the outset, strategic dimensions were part of the debate—when to take certain actions, how to announce them, and how best to package them for world consumption.

The Kennedy-Macmillan proposal of September 3, 1961, was part of the strategy—an attempt to draw world attention to the basic unwillingness of the Soviet Union to accept any moratorium, even an unpoliced one. The intention, Seaborg noted, "was that the proposal would embarrass him [Khrushchev] and swing world opinion more heavily to our side."[14] However, world opinion, insofar as such an amorphous entity could be measured at all, seemed to swing only slightly toward the United States. There were not, as had been hoped, widespread public denunciations of the Soviets from the world community, only calls for a return to the status quo ante.

One such call came from the Conference of Nonaligned Countries meeting in Belgrade, Yugoslavia. On September 6, the conference issued a statement proclaiming it "essential that an agreement on the prohibition of all nuclear and thermonuclear tests should be urgently concluded."[15] The statement did not contain a condemnation of the Soviets' unilateral resumption, nor did many of the speeches made on the floor of the United Nations.

Having waited a few days for an expected propaganda boost that never came, Kennedy, under great pressure from the Atomic Energy Commission, Defense Department, and Congress, announced his decision to resume underground testing. Ten days later, on September 15, the first American underground test since 1958 was detonated. The race had begun once again, but it would still be some weeks before the decision to pursue *atmospheric* tests would be taken. There were several reasons for this delay.

First, Kennedy feared the reaction of public opinion, both at home and abroad. He did not wish to lose, immediately, what little propaganda gain may have been realized by the Soviet unilateral action. Second, Kennedy himself was both intellectually and emotionally opposed to further poisoning the environment. He believed fallout to be a significant health danger and was determined to avoid adding to the danger until the last possible moment. Third, Kennedy could not have conducted a meaningful series of atmospheric tests in September or October, 1961, even if he had wished to do so. According to Jacobson and Stein, "there appears to have been little preparation in the United States' weapons laboratories during the moratorium for resumed atmospheric testing. Moreover, the skills and morale of the laboratories appear to have deteriorated to some extent during this period."[16] Finally, Kennedy seems to have had a very difficult time making up his mind with respect to resumption of U.S. atmospheric tests. Even after key decisions had supposedly been made, Kennedy would backtrack, reconsider, and seek further assurances from his advisors. As Seaborg recalled: "I am bound to say that while I did not in general find Kennedy to be an indecisive man, he did vacillate on issues related to nuclear testing, contributing to some difficult situations."[17]

The months of September, October, and November, 1961, were particularly difficult, for as more data from the Soviet tests were analyzed the realization crystallized that the USSR was making significant gains. The tests had "allowed the Soviets to reduce weight-to-yield ratios, increase the absolute yield of warheads, reduce the size of the fission trigger, and test new weapon designs under simulated combat conditions."[18] Even in the face of this increasing evidence and the advice of Seaborg, Rusk, and the Secretary of Defense MacNamara, Kennedy hesitated. It was only with the explosion on October 30, 1961, by the Soviet Union of a 58-megaton bomb—the largest weapon ever exploded—that the president finally decided to move to atmospheric testing. He announced his intention to so test on November 2, and once again struck several themes that would be repeated in his March 2, 1962, address. Tests, said Kennedy, "will be undertaken only to the degree that the orderly and essential scientific development of new weapons has reached a point where effective progress is not possible without such tests—and only within limits that restrict the fall-out from such tests to an absolute minimum. In the meantime, as a matter of prudence, we shall make necessary preparations for such tests so as to be ready in case it becomes necessary to conduct them."[19]

Throughout the fall, Kennedy kept the constraint of world opinion firmly in mind. Even when he finally decided to prepare for atmospheric tests, he still phrased his announcement with public opinion—and public fears—clearly in mind. But it was not the general public that would present the most challenging situational constraint. That designation would belong to the attempt to maintain a united front with the Western allies, especially Great Britain.

Maintaining a United Front

From the outset of his administration, Kennedy had tried to make nuclear policy a matter of Western rather than solely American concern. The British had participated in discussions about the new American negotiating position as early as February, 1961. When the first complete treaty was tabled at Geneva in April, 1961, it was tabled jointly by the United States and the United Kingdom. Thus, from the outset, Kennedy's strategy for peace was a joint product, reflecting British input and approval. But the Soviets' resumption of testing threatened to sever the cooperative atmosphere between the two dominant Western powers.

Public opinion in Great Britain was heavily opposed to the resumption of U.S. testing. Macmillan, though a Tory, was as deeply committed to arms control as was his Labor Party counterpart, Hugh Gaitskell. Macmillan had already gone on record with Parliament that no further tests would be conducted unless required by military necessity. The pressures being brought to bear on Kennedy to resume atmospheric tests did not have an English equivalent. Indeed, as Macmillan would later write: "It is clear that the President is as unhappy as I am about the whole situation. But, of course, he is under great pressure, from the Pentagon and from Congress. Here all the pressure is the other way."[20]   The flash point between the Western powers came in December, 1961, and January, 1962, and revolved around the issue of Christmas Island—a British possession that was the desired location for U.S. atmospheric tests. After exchanging correspondence on the developing situation, Kennedy and Macmillan held a summit conference at Bermuda on December 21 and 22, 1961. In a joint communiqué, the principals noted "that pending the final decision preparations would be made for atmospheric testing to maintain the effectiveness of the deterrent."[21] The language obscured the fact that, from the British point of view, no "final decision" had been reached. Macmillan promised only to discuss the use of Christmas Island with his cabinet.

On January 5, 1962, Macmillan wrote to Kennedy: "A decision to resume tests and to make British territory available for the purpose will not be readily understood unless it is accompanied by some public indication that we were making a new move to influence events. For that reason I would want to be able to announce at the same time the broad lines of this proposal and the decision to make available facilities at Christmas Island."[22] There was, in other words, to be a quid pro quo: use of Christmas Island in return for another round of negotiations with the Soviets.

On January 14, Kennedy replied: "Whatever may be your final decision about Christmas Island, or mine about American atmospheric testing, I can assure you that we are ready to examine with you the possibilities for new efforts toward disarmament."[23] Kennedy made clear that he and only he would make the final decision about resumption of U.S. testing—with or without Christmas Island. Macmillan, apparently sensing this bristling on the part of Kennedy, took the complete correspondence between himself and the president to a cabinet meeting on January 18, from which the decision to allow use of Christmas Island emerged. In deference to his British allies, Kennedy agreed to add an escape clause to his resumption announcement that provided for a halt to U.S. plans should the Soviets agree, in the interim, to the joint U.S.-U.K. plan tabled the preceding April. There was, as several commentators have noted, virtually no chance that the Soviets would take this final offer since the USSR had "already rejected an inspected test cessation."[24] Nevertheless, such an escape clause was crucial, both to the maintenance of allied solidarity and to the establishment of Kennedy's rhetorical portrait, a portrait that would present Kennedy as a man trying his best to avoid testing in the atmosphere.

Maintaining a Political Base

No less important than the maintenance of a solid alliance with Great Britain was the preservation of Kennedy's domestic political base. Having campaigned on the promise to apply more vigor, creativity, and flexibility to arms control problems,[25] Kennedy suddenly found himself in the uncomfortable position of having to do what Eisenhower and Nixon had advocated—resume nuclear testing. Worse yet, he found himself having to contradict his own publicly stated position that any resumption of U.S. tests in response to a Soviet resumption should be confined to those tests that would "prevent a further increase in the fallout menace;"[26] to wit, to underground testing only.

Though a July, 1961, Gallup Poll had registered a "more than two-to-one public support for the United States unilaterally resuming testing,"[27] a more detailed analysis by Samuel Lubbel, conducted in December, 1961, "showed that those who had supported Kennedy in the 1960 election followed the position he took in the campaign and opposed resumption of testing. Conversely, those who had voted for Nixon adopted his campaign line and supported resumption of testing."[28]   So while the majority supported resumption of testing, most of that majority were not Kennedy supporters.

The president found himself in a difficult situation. From a purely strategic point of view, he had to resume atmospheric testing. From a purely political standpoint such action had the potential of significantly eroding his base of support. His speech would have to be fashioned in such a manner as to emphasize the forces that compelled decision—a decision that would be pictured as being at odds with his own desires and attitudes. Such a portrait would be necessary if Kennedy was to avoid completely alienating his own base of support.

Avoiding Overreaction

The final constraining factor was Kennedy's own freedom of action subsequent to announcing the renewal of atmospheric tests. A delicate balance had to be struck between emphasizing the need to test (and thus minimizing the risks of fallout) on the one hand, and not minimizing the hazards to such a degree that some future arms agreement might seem superfluous. Sorensen, the chief architect of the speech, noted that Kennedy "refused to sound so reassuring on the possible dangers of fallout that a future test-ban treaty would seem unimportant."[29]

So the rhetorical challenge was to fashion a speech that would justify American testing, but do so in such a way as to make that need clearly subsidiary to the larger goal of long-term arms control. Seaborg, one of the six cabinet or agency heads to help edit the final draft of the speech, noted: "One of our guidelines was that there be nothing in the statement that would be inconsistent with continued negotiation of a test ban treaty."[30] This goal, along with the other constraining factors, shaped the final form of the address, and it was the form—the drawing of a rhetorical portrait—that marked the March 2, 1962, address as a masterpiece of strategic oratory.

DRAWING THE PORTRAIT

Kennedy's rhetorical portrait was composed of four interlocking image clusters, each of which interacted with the others to form a composite whole. These image clusters were: (1) Kennedy as actor within an ongoing historical drama; (2) Kennedy as defender of America's freedom and security; (3) Kennedy as a man of reason, rationality, and restraint; and (4) Kennedy as the protector of American ideals—ideals that now forced him to act. By examining how these four clusters of images were rhetorically constructed and how each shaped and modified the others, I will demonstrate how Kennedy used the portrait to address the exigencies and constraints of the situation.

Constructing the Images

The first image formed was that of an actor in a great, ongoing drama. The image emerged from the clustering of eight phrases that built sequentially from the past to the immediate present. The key elements in the cluster were:

* "seventeen years ago . . . "
* "throughout the years that have followed, under three successive Presidents
  . . . "
* "this Nation has long urged . . . "
* "in 1958 we voluntarily subscribed . . . "
* "But on September first of last year . . . "
* "I authorized on September fifth . . . "
* "This week, the National Security Council . . . "
* "I have today authorized . . . "[31]

In the first seven minutes of the speech Kennedy moved from 1945 ("seventeen years ago") to March 2, 1962 ("I have today authorized"). In so doing he contextualized his actions within the historical drama of the nuclear age, an age that started before he came on stage and that developed a life of its own long before he came into office.

The effect of this opening was to provide a sense of historical momentum—a force almost beyond the control of any one person to stop or reverse. The contemporary action—"I have today authorized the Atomic Energy Commission and the Department of Defense to conduct a series of nuclear tests . . . to take place in the atmosphere over the Pacific Ocean"—was but a part of those larger historical forces and was, in fact, called into being by them.

It was because "on September first of last year . . . the Soviet Union callously broke its moratorium with a two month series of tests of more than 40 nuclear weapons" that the United States had now to respond with its own test series. Such a series was to be undertaken after "competent scientists" had "carefully reviewed" all the factors and given "careful attention" to those tests that were "essential to our military and scientific progress." Kennedy assured his listeners that the United States had made "complex preparations" that had been "thoughtfully weighed," "carefully considered," and had received "unanimous recommendations."   The images of reason, rationality, and restraint were woven in and out of the speech at various places, signalling that past and present—as well as future—would be marked by reasoned judgment.

The other image clusters—defender of freedom and protector of American ideals—were also present within the first seven minutes of the speech.   Indeed, at the very outset Kennedy noted: "For of all the awesome responsibilities entrusted to this office, none is more somber to contemplate than the special statutory authority to employ nuclear arms in the defense of our people and freedom."   Freedom, said Kennedy, required strength.   "Only through such strength," said he, "can we in the free world . . . face the tragedy of another war with any hope of survival."

The defense of freedom was dependent upon the listeners' ability to actualize one of the most contemporary of cultural values—technological progress.   It was in the name of progress that Kennedy called for the resumption of testing, linking it with the maintenance of strength and freedom: "And that deterrent strength, if it is to be *effective* and *credible* when compared with that of any other nation, must embody the most *modern*, the most *reliable* and the most *versatile* nuclear weapons our *research* and *development* can produce.   The testing of *new* weapons and their effects is necessarily a part of that *research* and *development* process. Without *tests*—to *experiment* and *verify*—progress is limited" (emphasis added).

Kennedy, as representative and protector of the American ideal of technological progress and defender of American freedom, was pictured as acting in character with his role.   As he said, "no American President—responsible for the freedom and the safety of so many people—could in good faith make any other decision."   The historical forces, combined with the need to defend freedom and ensure progress, led the president to make a cool, calculated, and fully rational decision to resume atmospheric testing.

If the purpose of the speech was merely to announce the decision and provide a brief justification to the American people, Kennedy could well have ended it at this point, but he did not.   Instead, he went on for another twenty-two minutes.   Why?   Because the speech was not addressed solely to the American audience and did not have as its sole purpose the making of an announcement.   In addition to these basic purposes, Kennedy also needed to address the situational constraints of positioning the United States with respect to world opinion, maintaining a united front with the British, bolstering his own political base, and creating a rhetorical space for future actions that could be different, even opposite, of the action he was announcing.   The rhetorical advantages Kennedy accrued by first sketching his portrait before addressing the constraining factors will become clear as we turn to the last two-thirds of the speech.

Addressing the Strategic Needs

Following the sketching of the rhetorical portrait, Kennedy moved directly into a discussion of what the Soviets had learned from their tests and what the United States, by refusing to test in similar ways, was not learning.   The president spoke of the Soviets' "highly sophisticated technology" that was based on "novel designs and techniques" that led to "substantial gains in weaponry." "I must report to you in all candor," said Kennedy, "that further Soviet tests, in the absence of further Western progress, could well provide the Soviet Union with a nuclear attack and defense capability so powerful as to encourage aggressive design."

As he did in the earlier part of the address, Kennedy rhetorically aligned progress with tests. To test was to make progress; to refuse to test was to fall behind. Not only was such an action opposed to a deeply held cultural ideal, but it also risked the loss of freedom, for freedom, said Kennedy, was predicated on strength and strength came through the ability to deter aggression. He said: "Were we to stand still while the Soviets surpassed us . . . the Free World's ability to deter, to survive and to respond to an all-out attack would be seriously weakened."

The equation being developed in the speech was clear: Progress equaled testing; testing equaled strength; and strength constituted the vanguard of freedom.   To fail to test was to impede progress and to risk the loss of our strength and freedom.

To bolster this scenario, Kennedy called upon another dimension of his rhetorical portrait—the commitment to reason, rationality, and restraint. Key terms in this cluster were "fact," "research," "information," "experiments," "data," "efficiency," "measure," and "scientific." Progress was not only a military necessity, but an intellectual and moral imperative. "The fact of the matter," said Kennedy, "is that we cannot make similar strides without testing in the atmosphere."   Thus, it was necessary to conduct "research" and "experiments" that could generate "new data" on the "complex effect of a nuclear explosion."

"If we are to be alert to new breakthroughs, to experiment with new designs—if we are to maintain our scientific momentum and leadership," said Kennedy, "then our weapons progress must not be limited to theory." Improvement, progress, and efficiency were the code words of this part of the portrait. They functioned to lend both an intellectual and moral imperative to the maintenance of nuclear strength and deterrence.

That there was in fact a moral dimension to this aspect of the portrait became evident when Kennedy moved from talking about what the Soviets had done to what the United States intended to do: "While we will be conducting far fewer tests than the Soviets, with far less fallout, there will still be those in other countries who will urge us to refrain from testing at all. Perhaps they forget that this country long refrained from testing, and sought to ban all tests, while the Soviets were secretly preparing new explosions. Perhaps they forget the Soviet threats of last autumn and their arbitrary rejection of all appeals and proposals, from both the United States and the United Nations. But those free peoples who value their freedom and their security, and look to our relative strength to shield them from danger—those who know of our good faith in seeking an end to testing and an end to the arms race—will, I am confident, want the United States to do whatever it must do to deter the threat of aggression."

The moral superiority of the United States lay in three dimensions: It had tried to ban all tests (implicitly referring back to the great historical drama); it had operated in good faith as evidenced by the fact that the Soviets not only broke the moratorium, but did so in a sneaky, secret way; and it had responded, even when forced, in a moderate and less dangerous way ("fewer tests" and "less fallout"). The maintenance of strength and the preservation of freedom demanded progress—and to progress was presented as the morally right thing to do.

In addition to lending a righteous aura to the decision, this portion of Kennedy's speech functioned to disarm those critics, both within the United States and abroad, who opposed the decision. By framing the opposition as "those in other countries," Kennedy was able to articulate his stance to the domestic opposition—many of whom were his own support-ers—without seeming to attack them. Kennedy adopted a rhetorical stance that seemed to assume that all Americans would be behind his decision when he knew very well that such was not the case. He framed the question in an us-versus-them manner in order to use the foreign audience as a rhetorical fiction for addressing domestic opposition. What loyal American, after all, would want to identify with the foreign "them" versus the native "us"? Kennedy thus attempted to disarm his opposition, but indirectly.

Moreover, Kennedy explicitly identified with the hopes of this opposition, placing himself squarely on the side of advocates of disarma-ment: "I have no doubt that most of our friends around the world have shared my own hope that we would never find it necessary to test again—and my own belief that, in the long run, the only real security in this age of nuclear peril rests not in armament but in disarmament." Here Kennedy was attempting to reassure those supporters, both at home and abroad, that he was still an advocate of their cause—that he did believe in the pathway of disarmament and except for the forces of history and circumstance that compelled this decision, would have acted differently. Again, the statement served the dual purposes of positioning the United

States as a great power wanting peace and portraying a president still in line with the aspirations of his political supporters.

Just as Kennedy used the device of "other countries" to address his domestic opposition, so he used the Soviet Union as the rhetorical foil for addressing world opinion. Instead of telling the world at large what the United States had decided to do on its own, Kennedy contextualized U.S. moves as a response to Soviet provocations. Kennedy asked the audience a series of questions: "With such a one-sided advantage, why would they change their strategy, or refrain from testing, merely because we refrained? Why would they want to halt their drive to surpass us in nuclear technology? And why would they ever consider accepting a true test ban or mutual disarmament?" The strategy was clear: Demonstrate to the listening audience that it was not to their advantage to allow Soviet hegemony over nuclear weapons. Indeed, by supporting the U.S. countermove other countries would be strengthening "the prospects for peace" and fighting against the "steady decrease in the security of us all."

This nod to world opinion allowed Kennedy to move smoothly into the final section of the speech—the promise to advance yet another Geneva proposal and the offer to cancel the United States' test series in exchange for a signed, verifiable treaty. This portion of the speech functioned both to reassure the British that the effort to reach agreement was not dead (and to fulfill the promise that Kennedy had made to Macmillan) and to secure the rhetorical space Kennedy needed for any future actions on arms control. "We shall," said Kennedy, "in association with the United Kingdom, present once again our proposals for a separate comprehensive treaty—with appropriate arrangements for detection and verification—to halt permanently the testing of all nuclear weapons, in every environment." By making this pledge, Kennedy sent a signal to his British allies that he was not intending to go it alone or to abandon the quest for real arms reduction. The statement also had the effect of picturing Kennedy as going the extra mile. Even though the United States had been the victim of "deception" and "secret preparations"—Kennedy managed to mention this five times—it was still willing to press forward on the negotiating front. Merely by announcing further negotiations at the same time that he announced resumption of atmospheric testing, Kennedy secured for himself further room for action. By picturing the resumption as a step along the way to total disarmament, the president reserved for himself the option of acting differently.

As an effort to improve the public relations position of the United States vis-à-vis world opinion, Kennedy's offer to cancel the test series before it had even begun was a masterstroke of realpolitik. "If the Soviet Union should now be willing to accept such a treaty, to sign it before the later part of April, and apply it immediately," said Kennedy, "if all testing can thus be actually halted—then the nuclear arms race would be slowed down at last—the security of the United States and its ability to meet its commitments would be safeguarded—and there would be no need for our tests to begin." It was, in short, an effort to call the Soviet Union's bluff, with no expectation at all that the USSR would accept such a proposal. Nevertheless, it was an important part of the image-building function of the speech, for it reinforced the portrait of Kennedy as a man who really wanted peace but who, because of the recalcitrance of the Soviets and the momentum of historical circumstance, was forced to take actions that he found "deeply regrettable." As he said: "If they [USSR] persist in rejecting all means of true inspection, then we shall be left with no choice but to keep our own defensive arsenals adequate for the security of all free men."

CONCLUSION

The rhetorical portrait drawn by Kennedy in his March 2, 1962, speech functioned to achieve several strategic objectives, most importantly, to provide a rhetorical justification for resumption of U.S. atmospheric tests, tests that were going to be made whether or not they were perceived by the world at large as justified. The speech succeeded in contextualizing the U.S. decision within the broader domains of Soviet progress and the ongoing search for viable means of arms control. It thus removed or deflected much of the opprobrium that otherwise would have accompanied such an announcement.

By first sketching a rhetorical portrait and then using the features of that portrait to emphasize the ethical character of the speaker—a man of good will, good sense, and high purpose—Kennedy was able to address each of the situational constraints in a positive fashion. He successfully positioned the United States with respect to world opinion, maintained a cooperative relationship with the British, pacified his domestic opposition, and created for himself rhetorical space in which further action *in the opposite direction* was possible. By preserving such a space, Kennedy was able to continue the pursuit of an arms control agreement without seeming disingenuous or inconsistent. The kind of man pictured in the portrait of March 2, 1962, was in fact compelled to continue the search. That the effort was rewarded in October, 1963, with the signing of a limited nuclear test ban treaty was due, in part, to the space created some twenty months before.

Writing in 1981, Seaborg noted that "occasionally what a politician says and how he says it are so significant as to have the effect of an important action."[32] The address of March 2, 1962, was one such instance.

NOTES

1. Harold Macmillan, *At the End of the Day, 1961-1963* (London: Macmillan, 1973), 158-159.

2. Harold Karan Jacobson and Eric Stein, *Diplomats, Scientists, and Politicians: The United States and the Nuclear Test Ban Negotiations* (Ann Arbor: University of Michigan Press, 1966), 277.

3. Glenn T. Seaborg, *Kennedy, Khrushchev, and the Test Ban* (Berkeley: University of California Press, 1981), 68.

4. Jacobson and Stein, *Diplomats, Scientists, and Politicians*, 276.

5. Holifield cited in Earl H. Voss, *Nuclear Ambush: The Test-Ban Trap* (Chicago: Regnery, 1963), 463.

6. Seaborg, *Kennedy, Khrushchev*, 76.

7. "Statement by the Soviet Government on the Resumption of Nuclear Weapons Tests, August 30, 1961," in *Documents on Disarmament 1961*, United States Arms Control and Disarmament Agency (Washington, D.C.: U.S. Government Printing Office, 1962), 342-343.

8. "White House Statement on the Resumption of Soviet Tests, August 30, 1961," in *Documents on Disarmament 1961*, 350.

9. "Proposal by President Kennedy and Prime Minister Macmillan for a Ban on Atmospheric Tests, September 3, 1961," in *Documents on Disarmament 1961*, 351.

10. "Statement by Premier Khrushchev Regarding the Proposed Ban on Atmospheric Tests, September 9, 1961," in *Documents on Disarmament 1961*, 390.

11. "Statement by President Kennedy on the Resumption of Underground Tests, September 5, 1961," in *Documents on Disarmament 1961*, 355.

12. Theodore C. Sorensen, *Kennedy* (New York: Harper and Row, 1965), 619.

13. Seaborg, *Kennedy, Khrushchev*, 82.

14. Ibid., 86.

15. "Statement and Declaration by the Belgrade Conference of Non-aligned Countries, September 6, 1961," in *Documents on Disarmament 1961*, 381.

16. Jacobson and Stein, *Diplomats, Scientists, and Politicians*, 343.

17. Seaborg, *Kennedy, Khrushchev*, 124.

18. Lincoln P. Bloomfield, Walter C. Clemens, Jr., and Franklyn Griffiths, *Khrushchev and the Arms Race: Soviet Interests in Arms Control and Disarmament 1954-1964* (Cambridge, Mass.: MIT Press, 1966), 156.

19. "Statement by President Kennedy on Nuclear Tests, November 2, 1961," in *Documents on Disarmament 1961*, 567.

20. Macmillan, *At the End*, 173-174.

21. "Bermuda Communiqué by President Kennedy and Prime Minister Macmillan, December 22, 1961," in *Documents on Disarmament 1961*, 743.

22. Macmillan, *At the End*, 161.

23. Kennedy cited in Macmillan, *At the End*, 164.

24. John W. Spanier and Joseph L. Nogee, *The Politics of Disarmament: A Study in Soviet-American Gamesmanship* (New York: Praeger, 1962), 159.

25. In a campaign speech on June 14, 1960, for example, Kennedy said: "We must begin to develop new, workable programs for peace and the control of arms. We have been unwilling to plan for disarmament, and unable to offer creative proposals of our own, always leaving the initiative in the hands of the Russians" (John F. Kennedy, *The Strategy of Peace*, ed. Allan Nevins [New York: Harper and Brothers, 1960], 11).

26. The phrase is a direct quote from Kennedy's November 2, 1959 speech at UCLA. See Seaborg, *Kennedy, Khrushchev*, 32.

27. Jacobson and Stein, *Diplomats, Scientist, and Politicians*, 277.

28. Seaborg, *Kennedy, Khrushchev*, 122.

29. Sorensen, *Kennedy*, 623.

30. Seaborg, *Kennedy, Khrushchev*, 138.

31. All quotations from the speech are from John F. Kennedy, "Radio and Television Address to the American People: Nuclear Testing and Disarmament," *Public Papers of the Presidents of the United States, 1962* (Washington, D.C.: U.S. Government Printing Office, 1963), 186-192.

32. Seaborg, *Kennedy, Khrushchev*, 212.

PART II

METAPHOR

5

Cold War Motives and the Rhetorical Metaphor: A Framework of Criticism

Robert L. Ivie

A critique of Cold War rhetoric can serve many useful purposes, but none is more important than improving our understanding of the motives perpetuating America's rivalry with the Soviet Union. Rhetorical motives for Soviet-American rivalry are as compelling and durable as any other source of sustained tension or potential conflict. They have evolved over four decades into powerful conventions of public discourse that diminish the political imagination, undermine the incentive to envision better alternatives, and thus reduce the scope of practical options available to leaders of both nations. In short, the received wisdom of the Cold War rhetor prescribes a narrow range of choices for managing international relations realistically. Yet, the stuff of which these durable motives are made is mere metaphor. The guiding perspective that motivates confrontation in the nuclear age consists of figures of speech elaborated and literalized over time into conventional visions of national peril. The critic who inspects these visions of national peril aims ultimately at enriching our political imagination. Thus, the purpose of the present discussion is to clarify a program of criticism that endeavors to enhance the rhetorical act it investigates.

An approach to rhetorical criticism that features metaphor as a key to understanding Cold War motives makes certain assumptions about sources of rhetorical invention, procedures of critical inquiry, and the goals of criticism. Critical inquiries conforming to such assumptions seek to uncover images that constrain the political imagination of Cold War leaders and their publics, images that otherwise would remain literalized beyond recognition as elaborated tropes and figures. An overview of these images and the critical perspective that leads to their deliteralization should help to clear a path of scholarship in the continuing quest for practical alternatives to rhetorical hostility.

Attending closely to Cold War metaphors reveals a variety of related vehicles that have structured America's perception of the Soviet threat.

Summarized briefly, these vehicles illustrate the rhetorical essentials of the logic of confrontation. The nation's adversary is characterized as a mortal threat to freedom, a germ infecting the body politic, a plague upon the liberty of humankind, and a barbarian intent upon destroying civilization. Freedom is portrayed as weak, fragile, and feminine—as vulnerable to disease and rape. The price of freedom is necessarily high because the alternatives are reduced symbolically to enslavement and death. A constant tension exists between great expectations and uncertain outcomes, a tension that converges on a recurrent vision of freedom's vulnerability in a hostile world: Birth anticipates death, experiments fail, flames flicker and eventually suffocate, and the preyed-upon risk being ensnared and killed. Images of freedom's vulnerability correspond to visions of the enemy's savagery, thereby propelling the MAD (Mutual Assured Destruction) logic of nuclear deterrence—a logic of peace through strength that assumes nuclear weakness invites aggression by a barbarian who only understands and respects force. Lady Liberty, weak and vulnerable, must protect herself by brandishing the nuclear club.

These vehicles of Soviet-American confrontation represent the unity of figurative and literal language in political rhetoric. We move from a perception of speaking metaphorically to a perception of speaking literally when we stop talking about one thing in terms of another and begin treating distinct terms ("savage" and "Soviet," for example) as virtual identities, as if one were the other. We are in the presence of literalized metaphor when we act upon the figurative as if it were real, not recognizing that two domains of meaning have been merged into one despite their differences. As Kenneth Burke might say, literalized metaphor is another term for motive. Deliteralizing the metaphor defuses one motive and paves the way for others by calling attention to their common dependence upon our linguistic imagination, or what Ernesto Grassi calls rhetorical *ingenium*.[1]

The motive for Cold War, like all other human motives, is entangled in metaphor's linguistic web. The more we struggle to break free of figurative language in search of literal and true characterizations of ourselves and our adversaries, and the more we deny the inevitable ambiguity and constitutive force of our linguistic choices, the less likely we are to put metaphor to good use in the search for practical alternatives. Thus, the critic is well advised to treat literalized metaphors as pragmatic fictions, exposing those that are no longer practical in the nuclear age and searching for others that may prove more functional as symbolic equipment for living.

Paul Cantor has discussed the "use and abuse of metaphor" in the world of politics by returning to the insights of Friedrich Nietzsche, a man who foresaw the need to break down "the clear distinction between literal and figurative language."[2] In Nietzsche's view, the difference between the literal and the figurative amounts merely to a distinction between the customary and the novel vehicles of discourse, a distinction based on "frequency and rarity" instead of reality and fiction.[3] Thus, "what is regarded as literal at one moment may become figurative at another, and vice versa."[4]

Nietzsche recognized an "imperialistic principle" in the operation of metaphor. As the figurative becomes literal, its meaning is constantly extended to encompass a widening range of experience within its domain: "man's capacity for metaphor is a special case of . . . his will to power."[5] Terms compete with one another to dominate the hierarchy of meaning by which our interpretations of political experience, and ultimately our political acts, are guided. There is no natural hierarchy of meaning, but our eventual choice of a master metaphor determines what we regard at any moment as the literal over the figurative. As F.C.T. Moore has written, "Today's metaphor is tomorrow's literal sense."[6] This terministic warfare for conceptual dominance, although arbitrary in its origin and conventional in its outcome, can lead to armed conflict if we mistake the conventions of human creativity for the fixed laws of nature.

The metaphorical origins of political motives, following Burke, can be understood usefully as the extension of a master image into a perspective or general framework of interpretation. A perspective, or overall orientation, emerges from realizing the heuristic potential of a guiding metaphor; it leads to the formulation of motives or interpretations of how to act in specific circumstances and situations. As Burke observes, a vocabulary of motives contains "a program of action" for responding to a situation.[7] We name one thing in terms of another, treat the name as a realistic perspective, and act as if it applies literally to a given situation.

Burke points out that rhetorical motives are made complex by their simultaneous dependence upon multiple metaphors. As various terms for act, scene, agent, agency, and purpose are drawn upon to name a particular situation, a diversity of vehicles is integrated into a coherent interpretation of political reality through the dominance of a single master metaphor. Yet, each metaphor subsumed under the authority of the master image contains the seeds of its own perspective. Each is a subperspective "needed to produce the total development" of one motive but straining also to establish its own motivational authority.[8] The critic's potential for engaging in an act of perspective by incongruity—of wrenching a term from its conventional category and applying it unconventionally to another category in order to redefine the situation usefully—is a function of each term's limited authority as the representative anecdote within a complex framework of interpretation.

Grassi underscores the metaphorical origins of rhetorical invention generally when he reminds us that the middle terms (or *topoi*) of enthymemes are grounded in analogies. Metaphors, as the source of arguments and first principles, provide the linguistic mechanism for grasping similarities among dissimilarities. In Grassi's words, "The concepts through which we come to understand and 'grasp' each situation come from our ingenious, metaphorical, fantastic capacities that convey meaning in the concrete situations with which we are confronted."[9]

Critics in search of the conceptual metaphors guiding rhetorical invention and forming Cold War motives find networks of such images by examining sets of messages in various contexts. The more critics familiarize themselves with both the texts and contexts of Cold War discourse, the better prepared they become to identify and interpret patterns of vehicles that reveal systems of conceptual metaphors. Additional vehicles are revealed with each new reading of a text until the point is reached where the critic perceives a pattern that integrates the meaning and constitutes the motive of the speaker's message.

Upon the first reading of a text, the critic encounters the terms that are most obviously figurative. These vehicles, in turn, point toward their more literalized cousins, which subsequent readings reveal to the persistent and observant critic. Marking the occurrence of each newly discovered vehicle prepares the critic to begin clustering vehicles into subgroups that share similar entailments of meaning, each subgroup representing a first approximation of one of the rhetor's principal conceptual images. As these clusters of vehicles become more refined, the critic begins to examine their interaction throughout the text to determine how they function as a system of conceptual metaphors—where clusters co-occur, how they accommodate one another, which dominates the others, and what lines of argument they inspire.[10]

Following such a procedure, critics are likely to encounter a number of recurring motives in Cold War rhetoric. The metaphor of savagery, for instance, and its supporting cast of decivilizing vehicles play a central role in constructing the image of a hostile and threatening enemy. Various terms characterize the enemy as irrational, coercive, and aggressive.[11] Ronald Reagan and others who have been in positions of power typically draw upon a variety of such decivilizing terms that categorize the enemy with natural menaces such as floods, tides, cold winds, and fire. They speak of the Soviets as if they were snakes, wolves, and other kinds of dangerous predators, and as if they were primitives, brutes, barbarians, mindless machines, criminals, lunatics, fanatics, and the enemies of God.[12] Various habits of discourse, including Harry Truman's plain-speaking style, condition us to accept these images as literal statements.[13]

Ironically, critics will discover similar patterns of conceptual imagery in the discourse of many who criticize cold warriors for their confrontational policies toward the Soviet Union. Individuals as diverse as Henry Wallace, William Fulbright, and Helen Caldicott have drawn upon conceptual metaphors such as sickness, force, pathology, and madness (including Caldicott's purposefully Freudian allusion to "missile envy") to condemn the conduct of American foreign policy since the end of World War II. Wallace, for instance, identified Truman's containment doctrine with the negative forces of tides, torrents, floods, conflagrations, pressure, bullying, criminality, mobs, shouting, and stampedes. His favorite vehicles of sickness included terms such as "fester," "infection," "rot," "neurotic," and "psychopathic."[14]

Of course, Americans are more accustomed to thinking of their enemies than themselves in depersonalizing and decivilizing terms. Joseph McCarthy, for instance, engaged in a form of demagoguery that associated the forces of darkness with Communist subversion. He spoke of subversives hiding behind the Constitution, calling them Fifth-Amendment Communists. They conspired and spied under cover of darkness. As the instruments of Communist "slave masters," they followed a trail of deceit, lies, murder, and treason which led the naive and the innocent into the chains of slavery.[15] McCarthy characterized his mission as one of uncovering traitors by digging them out of the dark recesses and exposing them to the light of day.

Critics following the leads provided by conceptual metaphors will discover further that the enemy is portrayed not only as barbarian but also as preying upon America's fragile freedom. Cold War rhetors talk variously of the beacon of liberty as a flickering flame, freedom as a frail body threatened by the cancer of Communism, as a defenseless quarry set upon by relentless predators, and so on. Liberty, perceived as unsafe in a world of brute force, depends upon its guardians to remain forever vigilant and prepared for a costly struggle.[16]

True to Burke's observations about hierarchical complexities, the predominant motive of protecting and preserving freedom in the Cold War era is complicated by competition between two metaphorical concepts—containment and liberation—for mastery over one another. For instance, the Truman administration's doctrine of containment featured an image of holding the Communist surge within current borders in order to prevent it from spreading further around the globe. Thus, the war in Korea was initially a limited war designed to keep the North Koreans from advancing world Communism beyond the 38th parallel. Soon, however, the administration succumbed to the temptation of liberating North Korea from Communism. After the Chinese entered the war to insure against North Korea's "liberation," Truman returned to a rhetoric of limited war and containment, causing him to part ways with General Douglas MacArthur, who continued to insist on the pursuit of total victory. Liberation became Secretary of State John Foster Dulles's dominant theme, even though the actual policy of the Eisenhower administration remained one of containment, a policy that led step-by-step to America's commitment in Vietnam.

After the Johnson administration decided to escalate America's involvement in the Vietnam War, it encountered again the difficulty of reconciling the competing motives of containment and liberation. Ultimately, the president and his advisors became entangled in a self-neutralizing system of conceptual metaphors that doomed them to rhetorical defeat. Containment of Communist aggression was emphasized above, but not to the exclusion of, giving birth to a free Vietnam—a tenuous hierarchy of terms that led to a gradual and cautious increase in U.S. military pressure but that weakened the potential rhetorical force of other influential images, including images of being firm, taking risks for freedom, and defeating the savage opponents of America's experiment in Vietnamese democracy.[17]

Further critical inquiry into these and other complexities of the Cold War mentality will help to deliteralize the conventional imagery that holds sway over our political imaginations, thereby increasing our collective potential for different kinds of rhetorical *ingenium*. Critics also can turn their attention profitably to identifying the conceptual metaphors guiding incipient rhetorics of détente, rhetorics such as those represented by Kennedy's address at American University. Kennedy's creative adaptation of the image of a new frontier, for instance, enabled him to draw upon the courage and spirit of an American pioneer who would walk the path of peace and coexistence while continuing to protect the frontiers of freedom. Others, such as George Kennan, have attempted to articulate an image of the Soviets that avoids the caricature of savagery and therefore the necessity of converting or defeating the Communist enemy in order to insure freedom's future. The network of conceptual metaphors embedded in efforts such as these contains clues for critics who seek alternative sources of invention with which to codify a realistic rhetoric of coexistence.

The goal of improving the human condition is no stranger either to scholarship in general or rhetorical criticism in particular. Research leads to theory not as an end in itself but instead as a means of reducing the potential for dysfunctional conflict. Knowledge as the result of critical inquiry serves to enhance our ability to act upon the world with positive effect. Thus, the critic's understanding of rhetorical motives is never value-free. While nothing is more practical than a good theory, it is also important to recognize that practicality has its priorities. Value-laden priorities influence the questions asked, the events examined, the information collected, and the interpretations rendered.

Burke demonstrated the link between knowledge and values when he undertook a study of Hitler's poisonous rhetoric for the purpose of immunizing Americans against its effects.[18] His was a strategic characterization of Hitler's *Battle* designed to defeat the rhetorical construction of genocidal motives in America. Description and analysis served the larger end of judgment and action, of constructing a new understanding and a political motive intended to serve more humane purposes. Anyone can read Hitler's *Battle* and Burke's criticism side-by-side to determine whether the criticism is accurate and honest, that is, whether the language to which Burke refers can be found in Hitler's text and whether Burke's charts and interpretations are justified in the context of Hitler's situation. Yet, even as the critic's characterizations meet the criteria of accuracy, replicability, and honesty, they do so from a partisan perspective and for a moral purpose—not from all points of view or for every purpose. Burke's analysis of Hitler makes sense in terms of Burke's purpose and perspective and to the extent that it serves as an antidote to poisonous rhetoric.

Failure to acknowledge the relationship between knowledge and judgment in rhetorical inquiry may pacify the scholar's desire to be perceived as objective rather than biased or ideological. Succumbing to such a desire, however, suppresses the critic's awareness of the values influencing description and inference. If the Holy Grail for which rhetorical scholars search is absolute knowledge analogous to universal laws of nature, a sort of omniscience unbounded by human purpose, then they surely will meet the frustration of other worldly crusaders who discover their motives are necessarily impure. As Paolo Valesio has observed, "No form of rhetorical criticism can be completely 'pure' with respect to the discourse it analyzes." Criticism cannot escape "from the circle of rhetoric," for "every rhetorical criticism embodies one or the other form of rhetoric."[19] The rhetoric of criticism is no less political than the political rhetoric criticized.

Just as criticism is a form of rhetoric, the critic is a practicing rhetor. Rhetor-scholars proceed carefully, rigorously, and honestly toward a serviceable language of discovery, a language that lends insight from the critic's perspective, motivates a response, and requires reconsideration when its ends no longer are salient or well served. Critics expose the rhetorical constructions of which they disapprove in order to diffuse their motivational force and thereby create an opening for better alternatives. Thus, critic-scholars who disapprove of overdrawn images of savagery on the grounds that they undermine attempts at realistic empathy between nuclear rivals are motivated to weaken the appeal of such images by deliteralizing and thereby reconstructing them as fictions and metaphors, as figures of speech disguised in literal garb, and as vehicles that caricature one's adversaries.

As the product of an interested and invested scholar, criticism remains an unfinished project until it is integrated with the ends it serves and assessed for its moral and rhetorical efficacy. The scholarly goals of explanation, prediction, and influence serve value-laden purposes. There can be no absolute measure of objectivity and validity without reducing rhetoric and criticism to a single ideology, and, as Valesio has observed, "ideology is decayed rhetoric."[20] No less than other rhetors, critics are partisans of various causes, but the goal they serve in common is to point toward ways of envisioning better realities. Within the present framework of criticism, that task consists of inspecting networks of Cold War metaphors for dysfunctional images while intensifying the search for fresh sources of rhetorical *ingenium*.

NOTES

1. Ernesto Grassi, *Rhetoric as Philosophy: The Humanist Tradition* (University Park, Pa.: Pennsylvania State University Press, 1980), 100.

2. Paul Cantor, "Friedrich Nietzsche: The Use and Abuse of Metaphor," in *Metaphor: Problems and Perspectives*, ed. David S. Miall (Atlantic Highlands, N.J.: Humanities Press, 1982), 71.

3. Ibid., 72.

4. Ibid., 74.

5. Ibid., 75.

6. F.C.T. Moore, "On Taking Metaphor Literally," in Miall, *Metaphor*, 3.

7. Kenneth Burke, *Attitudes toward History*, 2d rev. ed. (Boston: Beacon Press, 1961), 92.

8. Kenneth Burke, *A Grammar of Motives* (Berkeley: University of California Press, 1969), 512-516.

9. Grassi, *Rhetoric as Philosophy*, 100.

10. Robert L. Ivie, "Metaphor and the Rhetorical Invention of Cold War 'Idealists,'" *Communication Monographs* 54 (1987): 166-168.

11. Robert L. Ivie, "Images of Savagery in American Justifications for War," *Communication Monographs* 47 (1980): 279-294.

12. Robert L. Ivie, "Speaking 'Common Sense' about the Soviet Threat: Reagan's Rhetorical Stance," *Western Journal of Speech Communication* 48 (1984): 39-50.

13. Robert L. Ivie, "Literalizing the Metaphor of Soviet Savagery: President Truman's Plain Style," *Southern Speech Communication Journal* 51 (1986): 91-105.

14. Ivie, "Metaphor and the Rhetorical Invention," 168-173.

15. Robert L. Ivie, "Diffusing Cold War Demagoguery: Murrow vs. McCarthy on 'See It Now.'" Paper delivered at the Seventy-third Annual meeting of the Speech Communication Association, Boston, November 7, 1987.

16. Robert L. Ivie, "The Ideology of Freedom's 'Fragility' in American Foreign Policy Argument," *Journal of the American Forensic Association* 24 (1987): 27-36.

17. Robert L. Ivie, "Metaphor and Motive in the Johnson Administration's Vietnam War Rhetoric," in *Texts in Context: Critical Dialogues on Significant Episodes in American Political Rhetoric*, ed. Michael C. Leff and Fred J. Kauffeld (Davis, Calif.: Hermagoras Press, 1989), 121-141.

18. Kenneth Burke, "The Rhetoric of Hitler's 'Battle,'" in his *The Philosophy of Literary Form*, 3d ed. (Berkeley: University of California Press, 1973), 191-220.

19. Paolo Valesio, *Novantiqua: Rhetorics as a Contemporary Theory* (Bloomington, Ind.: Indiana University Press, 1980), 3, 99.

20. Ibid., 66.

6

Diffusing Cold War Demagoguery: Murrow versus McCarthy on "See It Now"

Robert L. Ivie

Edward R. Murrow's celebrated confrontation with Senator Joseph R. McCarthy on "See It Now" introduced network television to the ancient rhetorical genre of accusation and defense. Murrow's half-hour "report" on March 9, 1954, condemning McCarthy's indiscriminate campaign against so-called "Fifth-Amendment Communists," was the first instance of national television being used to attack an individual.[1] McCarthy defended himself a month later, on the April 6th edition of "See It Now," by accusing Murrow of being "the leader of the jackal pack which is always found at the throat of anyone who dares to expose Communists and traitors."[2] Their exchange set off a wave of viewer response, favoring Murrow as much as fifteen to one after the initial broadcast and continuing in his favor at the ratio of two to one even after McCarthy's well-publicized reply.[3] McCarthy's iron grip on public opinion had been broken. His fall from political power, hastened that spring by a miserable account of himself in the televised Army-McCarthy hearings, was complete in December when the Senate voted to censure their wayward colleague for "contemptuous, contumacious, denunciatory, unworthy, inexcusable and reprehensible" conduct.[4]

The rhetorical dynamics of Murrow's encounter with McCarthy were a function of each program's relationship to the other, for, as Halford Ross Ryan has argued, *kategoria* and *apologia* are interconnected genres best examined together in "speech sets."[5] Consistent with Ryan's model of speech sets, Murrow's accusation sought to affirm the image of McCarthy as a dangerous demagogue while McCarthy's apologia attempted to purify his public persona as a courageous crusader against Communist subversives. Thus, Murrow's condemnation of McCarthy's "unscrupulous," "bully-boy" tactics served as the controlling exigence of the senator's counterblast.[6] Furthermore, both broadcasts intertwined issues of character with a concern over questions of policy—how best to cope with the domestic threat to freedom—and each of the four stases of fact, definition, quality, and jurisdiction was touched upon in the exchange.

A number of studies confirm the utility of Ryan's three-dimensional model, which calls the critic's attention to (1) the motives of affirmation and purification, (2) the four stases, and (3) the interplay of each speaker's perception of the rhetorical situation.[7]   Implicitly, at least, such a perspective has led previous investigators to several important observations about the rhetorical strategies and techniques of the Murrow-McCarthy broadcasts, some of which are reviewed below.[8]   Yet, the immediate significance of this speech set is that it draws the critic's attention to a fourth dimension of symbolic action, a dimension that provided the rhetorical foundation of Murrow's strategy for neutralizing McCarthy's Cold War demagoguery, even in the midst of a domestic Red scare.

Each rhetor's strategy, as we shall see, rested on a common foundation of conceptual and archetypal imagery that was structured over time and within each broadcast to McCarthy's disadvantage, causing him to contribute to his own degradation. The form of this rhetorical foundation can be discerned from the observable pattern of metaphorical vehicles and associated terms displayed in both broadcasts.[9] Upon reconstruction, this underlying form reveals a symbolic predisposition within the exchange to identify both McCarthy and Communism with the destructive forces of darkness and death.

The influence of metaphorical substructure on rhetorical strategy can be seen most clearly within the context of previous investigations into the Murrow-McCarthy confrontation. A brief review of these earlier studies yields an account of the strategies and techniques relied upon by each speaker. It does not, however, provide a satisfactory explanation for why McCarthy's demagoguery backfired on "See It Now" when he employed the same methods that had destroyed or cowered so many previous opponents. For such an explanation, I will argue, we must turn ultimately to the speech set's symbolic substructure and look for the archetypal image that configured its conceptual vehicles into a prevailing pattern of interpretation.

RHETORICAL STRATEGY AND TECHNIQUE

Observations about Murrow's persuasive methods range widely from the strategic scheduling of his March 9th broadcast to the careful cultivation of his television ethos. They refer to his ability to project an objective tone and sophisticated demeanor in contrast to McCarthy's loutish and boorish conduct. They point to the selective editing of film in order to portray McCarthy at his worst and to Murrow's catching the senator in contradictions, criticizing his methods instead of his anti-

Communism, and seducing viewers through a sophisticated use of irony. Together these observations provide a representative view of Murrow's rhetoric at the level of strategy and technique.

The timing of Murrow's attack on McCarthy was carefully considered in order to strike an optimum balance between personal safety and political effect.[10] The senator was still popular in January (Gallop reporting 50 percent public approval and only 29 percent disapproval) and therefore remained a dangerous opponent even for a broadcaster of Murrow's stature. Thus, Murrow, who was very deliberate about the timing of the show and who knew his criticism of McCarthy was coming relatively late in the game, stalked his prey patiently, collecting material for his program until the anticipated moment of vulnerability finally arrived.

McCarthy's political power had peaked by mid-1953. Thereafter, a crescendo of criticism had begun to arise in the press and Senate, and by the turn of the year a previously reticent Republican administration was beginning to make noises of disapproval. Eisenhower himself had become publicly exasperated by McCarthy's attacks on the army. Even those who supported McCarthy were tiring of his tactics. On March 9, in an act of "cautious courage" that seemed heroic to many, Murrow mobilized the growing sentiment against a man who in many people's view had gone too far and gotten too rough.[11] While the program helped to intensify anti-McCarthy sentiment, its timing insured against Murrow being singled out for the full brunt of McCarthy's rage. The senator was too distracted by the impending Army-McCarthy hearings to do much more than take a few mean swipes at his opponent on television.

In addition to the program's strategic timing, Murrow was also careful to cultivate his ethos as a television celebrity and respected journalist. His weekly program "Person to Person," which had a larger audience than "See It Now," enabled him to be seen regularly in the homes of the rich and famous. Such positive exposure provided an added degree of credibility that allowed him to get away with more controversial program-ming on "See It Now," especially given his already well-established World War II reputation as the man who reported the fighting each night from London.[12] Murrow enhanced his credibility further by projecting an image of "sophistication, learning, and sincerity" in the March 9 broadcast.[13] In Michael Murray's judgment, he "sought the pretense of objectivity for the sake of effectiveness."[14]

By contrast, "See It Now" portrayed McCarthy in the worst possible light: "belching, picking his nose, contradicting himself, giggling at his own vulgar humor . . . and harshly berating witnesses."[15] Murrow's basic technique was to show the Senator making his typical charges and then to follow each accusation with a correction of the "facts."[16] Rather than tangle with the issue of Red hunting itself, which remained popular among the public, Murrow attacked where his opponent was most

vulnerable: the public's growing disapproval of the Senator's indiscriminate methods. Even Richard Nixon conceded, in a speech televised a few
days after Murrow's program, that although "Communists should be shot
like rats . . . you have to shoot straight, because when you shoot wildly
it not only means that the rats may get away more easily . . . but you
might hit someone else who's trying to shoot rats, too."[17]

The potential conflict between Murrow's studied image of objectivity
and his deliberate attempt to portray McCarthy in a negative light was
resolved by the program's seductive appeal to irony. Drawing upon
Wayne Booth's observation that irony gets its rhetorical power by inviting
audiences to participate in the reconstruction of texts (that irony promotes
a degree of self-persuasion as audience members attempt to resolve
apparent contradictions between their expectations and their encounters
with specific texts), Thomas Rosteck has argued that the first part of
Murrow's program was artfully designed to guide his viewers toward
interpreting what ostensibly was a report on McCarthy as actually a clever
argument against him. Thus, for example, Murrow played the game of
rhetorical irony, persuading by indirection, when he held uncomplimentary
close shots of McCarthy's facial expressions a few seconds longer than
newsfilm conventions would otherwise dictate, and when he quoted "left-
wing" newspapers such as the *Chicago Tribune*, which criticized
McCarthy for acting like an "avenging angel," a "demagogue," and a
"bully."[18]

McCarthy's basic strategy for defending himself against Murrow's
accusations was to denounce his detractor as a Communist agent. Relying
upon the well-tested technique of guilt by association, the senator listed a
number of alleged instances of Murrow's participation in Communist-
controlled organizations and then cited several examples of Communists
who supposedly had endorsed Murrow as if he were one of their own.
This time, however, the technique backfired, with various commentators
concluding that McCarthy's reply served mainly to dramatize the validity
of Murrow's charges.[19] Significantly, Murrow's detailed memorandum
of rebuttal to McCarthy's charges, released immediately after the April 6th
program had been aired, was published in full by a number of newspapers.
Thus, Murrow's mastery of the television medium had proved superior to
McCarthy's technique of intimidation. As William Bluem (paraphrasing
Gilbert Seldes) observes, "One man clubbed another and then passed him
the stick, knowing full well he could not use it so effectively."[20]

Beneath the level of either speaker's technique, however, there existed
an interpretive substructure that had formed prior to the exchange between
Murrow and McCarthy and that was beyond their power to change
substantially within the immediate situation. It was this substructure that
enabled Murrow's rhetorical strategy to work its intended effect and that
undermined McCarthy's attempt to defend himself.

INTERPRETIVE SUBSTRUCTURE

Resistance to McCarthy and McCarthyism had been building for years toward the threshold of rejection that finally was reached in the early months of 1954. In 1951, for instance, the cover of *Time* magazine's October 22nd issue featured the senator's picture with the caption "Demagogue McCarthy." In August of 1952, presidential candidate Adlai Stevenson spoke out at an American Legion convention against "sinister threats to the Bill of Rights" and "fear breed[ing] repression."[21] In June of 1953, President Eisenhower sent an open letter to the American Library Association, pointedly stating that "freedom cannot be served by the devices of the tyrant." Later that year he warned against "reckless, un-American methods of fighting Communism."[22] Many in the United States and abroad were beginning to equate McCarthy with Hitler and fascism.[23] H. V. Kaltenborn, NBC's radio news commentator, dropped his support of McCarthy on March 1, 1954, complaining that the Senator had hit below the belt once too often and that he had become "completely egotistical, arrogant, arbitrary, narrow-minded, reckless, and irresponsible."[24]

Murrow himself had been contributing to the developing language of anti-McCarthyism throughout the Cold War years in his many radio commentaries against infringements of civil liberties, especially freedom of association and expression.[25] He criticized the hearings of the House Un-American Activities Committee in 1947, arguing for the right of dissent as central to free speech and "fundamental to the existence of a democratic society."[26] Again, on June 9, 1949, he commented on the issue of "espionage, treason and subversive activity" associated with the Alger Hiss case, reminding his listeners that a man should not be convicted "unless the rules of evidence are followed" and deploring the fact that "individuals and some organs of opinion are disposed to convict people by association . . . before they have been tried."[27]

Beginning in 1950, Murrow's radio broadcasts mentioned McCarthy with increasing frequency.[28] On March 10th, he labelled McCarthy the symbol of the "un-American doctrine" of "guilt by association."[29] Little over a year later, on June 14th, he criticized McCarthy for quoting George Marshall out of context in order to accuse the secretary of defense falsely of being a traitor and "playing the Russian game all along."[30]

Thus, as Betty Winfield concludes, Murrow's words were not new when on March 9th he accused McCarthy over network television of brutally attacking civil liberties and ignoring due process of law in a misguided crusade against Communist subversion.[31] By that point, Americans had become increasingly accustomed to hearing of McCarthy within a negative symbolic context consisting of terms such as tyranny, brutality, witch-hunts, un-American methods, demagoguery, fascism, Gestapo methods, half-truths, guilt by association, arrogance, and recklessness—all of which cast a shadow over the nation's sense of fair play and commitment to democratic values. The many and diverse terms in this cluster were integrated into a negative view of McCarthy through the medium of an archetypal image of darkness that provided the interpretive substructure of both "See It Now" programs.

Method of Analysis

Systematic analysis of metaphorical vehicles in each program confirms the existence of such a substructure and enables us to see how archetypal imagery guided the interpretive turn against McCarthy. The basic, five-step procedure for identifying vehicles and organizing them into sets of conceptual metaphors has been explained elsewhere.[32] In addition, software is now available for expediting the basic procedure, which was originally limited by the word-search and block-and-file capabilities of typical word processing programs. The new software, which generates concordances using IBM AT or AT-compatible hardware with ten or more megabytes of hard disk storage, no longer necessitates the reduction of full texts to abridged versions for purposes of analysis.

A composite text of each broadcast was prepared by comparing three sources: (1) the transcripts in Murray's dissertation, (2) the transcripts in the Edward R. Murrow papers, and (3) films of the complete programs.[33] Both composite transcripts were stored as electronic text files and prepared for analysis using WordCruncher, the text indexing and retrieval program marketed by Electronic Text Corporation.[34]

Following a series of close readings to identify the metaphorical vehicles in each program, the WordCruncher program was used to locate and verify each occurrence of designated vehicles, to search the text for additional vehicles, and to check each vehicle's interpretation in its original context. In short, the WordCruncher program served as a supplement to and systematic check on (rather than a replacement for) direct analysis of the transcripts. It contributed to the thoroughness and consistency of analysis, providing a fast and uncompromising way of testing and revising tentatively held hypotheses about the metaphorical structure of the two broadcasts.

Murrow's Report on McCarthy

Both sets of negative vehicles featured in Murrow's report on McCarthy were consistent with the symbolic context established prior to the March 9 broadcast. One set came from McCarthy's characterization of Communism, as captured in the edited tapes and films of his speeches, press conferences, and committee hearings on Communist subversion. The other emerged from characterizations of McCarthy himself.

The first set of metaphorical vehicles represented Communism as "the raw, harsh, unpleasant fact" of 1954 (see chapter Appendix 1). McCarthy spoke of "Fifth-Amendment Communists" who proved their guilt by hiding behind Constitutional protections. They were subversives engaged in "conspiracy" and "traitors" who "covered up" their "espionage." One had to be "tipped off" and then "get rough" in order to "drag the truth" from Communists. Those who "coddled Communists" engaged in "mudslinging" against McCarthy and his committee. By sheer determination, McCarthy had "dug out of the dark recesses" and "exposed to public view" Communist activities that were "never supposed to see the light of day."   In short, Murrow's edited version of McCarthy symbolized Communism as a dark force that had to be confronted directly and exposed to the light, even if that meant ignoring technicalities such as constitutional protections about which the "bleeding hearts scream and cry."

The second set of negative metaphorical vehicles represented McCarthy as the man who "dons his war paint," "goes into his war dance," "emits his war whoops," "goes forth to battle and proudly returns with the scalp of a pink Army dentist" (see chapter Appendix 2). He was portrayed as a "demagogue" who "assaults" his foes, uses "bully boy tactics," and "feeds" on his victims' "meat" after they have been "terrorized," "bull whipped," "smeared," and had their public necks wrung. The "staples of his diet" were "Congressional immunity" and "the half-truth." Hiding behind the immunity accorded his "one-man committee," McCarthy confused "investigating" with "persecuting," "exploited fear," "summoned" witnesses, made unsupported "claims," "accusations," and "charges," and perpetrated a "hoax" that was "confusing the public mind." His aggression had caused "a domestic Munich." In short, the senator's savagery was associated with the dark forces of brutality and irrationality. Terror lurked where truth had been shrouded by unreason.

Whereas McCarthy shared the image of darkness with his declared foe, Communism, Murrow linked himself, the Republic, and its citizens to more enlightened attitudes and aspirations (see Table 3). The purity and innocence of the nation was reflected in Murrow's observation that Americans, "defenders of freedom," had come into their "full inheritance at a tender age." They had evolved beyond a primitive "age of unreason." They would not be "driven by fear" to "desert [freedom] at home," for they were "not descended from fearful men." Their commitment was to "proof," "evidence," and "due process of law," to an open and rational society confident of its enlightened "heritage."

These metaphorical clusters implicitly identified McCarthy with the darkness into which he himself had cast Communism, thereby opposing the tyranny of his demagoguery to the enlightenment of freedom for which Murrow and the republic stood. Together, these clusters conformed to and reinforced the negative symbolic context of McCarthyism that had emerged prior to the broadcast. The metaphorical substructure of Murrow's accusation set up an interpretive formula which McCarthy's response served to validate: Communism = darkness = tyranny = McCarthy. The turn against McCarthy was constructed to take advantage of his own momentum.

McCarthy's Reply

Predictably, McCarthy's portrait of Communism and himself in his April 6 reply amplified and confirmed the picture painted in Murrow's earlier report (see chapter Appendices 4 and 5). "Fifth-Amendment Communists" were portrayed as "notorious," "professional burglars" who "conspired" and "connived" in "cleverly calculated" acts of "subversion." These "spies" of the "night" were "seeping down" and "undermining" the foundations of freedom, attempting through black "propaganda," frenzied "shouting," and insidious "indoctrination" to "capture" and "enslave" the world. These subversives were the mindless "instruments" of "slave masters" who laid down the "Communist line" and followed "a trail of deceit, lies, terror, murder, treason, [and] blackmail" that led inevitably to the "chains" of "slavery."

Murrow was accused of being the "cleverest" leader among this "jackal pack" of "vicious" "traitors." He covered up the truth by "shouting" Communist "propaganda" and "attacking" anyone "exposing Communists." Murrow was "giving aid and comfort to the enemy" and therefore was "praised by Communists" for "following the Communist line."

Although opposed by the dark force of Communist subversion, McCarthy made little attempt in his reply to sound like the voice of enlightenment. Instead, he associated himself with acting like a "well-trained watchdog" and "digging out Communists." "Heads [were] rolling" because of his "plodding exposure of Communists." Exposing Communism to the light was his goal, but burrowing after them underground was his preferred method.

The shades of darkness in McCarthy's self-portrait reconfirmed the validity of Murrow's formula for linking the Senator to tyranny and Communism, a formula that made good sense within the established symbolic context of anti-McCarthyism. At the same time, McCarthy's attempt to identify Murrow with Communism appeared as yet another brutal exercise in guilt by association, one of the senator's darkest methods for bypassing the principle of free speech and the canons of evidence that are essential to the survival of an enlightened democracy.

Murrow's subtextual formula, and McCarthy's conformity to it, made it possible for viewers to reject the senator's black methods without endorsing the evils of Communism. Communists were still "rats" from the underworld, as Richard Nixon said, but the hunter himself had been shooting blindly, threatening the survival of those he claimed to defend. Thus, the interpretive turn against McCarthy was premised on the archetypal imagery of darkness, an enduring "bedrock" of rhetorical symbolism, as Michael Osborn has explained.[35]

INTERPRETIVE SUBSTRUCTURE AND RHETORICAL STRATEGY

The superiority of Murrow's technique over McCarthy's was a function largely of each speaker's rhetoric conforming to a pre-established substructure of interpretation. McCarthy had a hand in his own defeat prior to, during, and after his exchange with Murrow because of his insensitivity to that substructure and subsequent failure to modify his counterproductive presentation of self and others. The political opportunist turned true believer was blinded by ideological fervor and therefore suffered the consequences of rhetorical insensitivity.[36]

Over the course of several years, the force of his rabid and progressively undiscriminating attacks—on Communists, fellow travellers, Communist sympathizers, Fifth-Amendment Communists, liberals, ordinary people, Democrats, presidential candidates, members of the State Department, generals, fellow senators, and Republicans in the executive branch who were not tough enough on Communism (including even Eisenhower)—rebounded in an equally intense but more focused rejection of McCarthyism. The language of this rejection was essentially metaphorical to the extent that it increasingly compared McCarthy and his conduct to demagoguery, brutality, fascism, irrationality, and other dark images of tyranny rather than to the heroic deeds of a courageous crusader against domestic subversion.

Murrow knew the importance of showing his opponent in action, "browbeating witnesses at congressional committee hearings, contradicting himself without any regard to truth, resorting to innuendo and slander, playing the bully. And he did."[37] McCarthy, on the other hand, did not seem to understand that his vicious reply served to literalize before millions of viewers earlier images of his demagoguery. As Leo Bogart concludes, the senator's "appearance before the television cameras may only have heightened the impression left by the original broadcast."[38] That impression was most essentially one of darkness contrary to the values of an open society, values which Eisenhower had reiterated on national television as recently as November 23, 1953—just three and a half months before Murrow's report on McCarthy. As the president explained, "In this country, if someone dislikes you or accuses you, he must come up in front. He cannot hide behind the shadow. He cannot assassinate you or your character from behind without suffering the penalties which an outraged citizenry will inflict."[39]

McCarthy magnified his blunder by repeating his loutish behavior in committee hearings after Murrow's March 9th broadcast. On March 16, "See It Now" featured McCarthy browbeating the elderly Annie Lee Moss before his committee, a seemingly innocent victim who had been accused by an unseen witness of engaging in subversive activity. His performance in the televised Army-McCarthy hearings, beginning on April 22 and continuing into June, served only to blacken his image beyond repair.

The structure of the interpretive formula (Communism = darkness = tyranny = McCarthy) never changed after it had been used to identify the Senator's brand of tyranny with the tyranny of Communism, both of which posed a bleak threat to the principle of democracy. The effect of Murrow's strategy turned on his ability to capitalize on the symbolic dynamics that had already structured his rhetorical situation. His strategic timing, waiting to strike at a moment of vulnerability after the language of anti-McCarthyism had begun to consolidate, enabled "See It Now" to serve as a further catalyst of public opinion. His carefully nurtured ethos as a solid member of the democratic establishment served him well in an interpretive formula that rejected McCarthy's countercharges by equating them with the tyranny of half-truths and the irrationality of guilt by association. Murrow's deliberate editing to show McCarthy at his worst and the ironic twist of the persuasive report could not have met with success without a foundation of symbolic reality on which to base the credibility and coherence of each technique. Murrow's obvious bias otherwise would have been grounds for dismissing his charges and missing his attempt at irony.

CONCLUSION

By attending to this fourth dimension of symbolic action, the interpretive substructure of conceptual and archetypal imagery, we gain a more complete understanding of why strategies of accusation and defense are more or less well adapted to their rhetorical situations. To the extent the subtext of a speaker's accusation (or defense) is better adapted than an opponent's to the audience's symbolic context of interpretation, the strategy and technique of the accusation (or defense) will be that much more likely to succeed. It is even possible, as illustrated in McCarthy's case, that the effect of the speech will be further enhanced by an opponent's insensitivity at the level of rhetorical invention just below strategy and technique.

Furthermore, attention to this dimension of symbolic action improves our understanding of how McCarthy's demagoguery could be defused without also lowering the intensity of Cold War paranoia, which continued unabated after the senator's demise. Neither Murrow nor anyone in the mainstream attacked McCarthy's anti-Communism. Instead, they attacked the twin forces of darkness—McCarthyism and Communism—both of which were perceived as threatening to undermine the foundations of freedom.   McCarthyism was associated implicitly with Communism through diverse sets of metaphorical vehicles that nevertheless shared the black connotations of tyranny and disrespect for democratic institutions. Thus, Murrow's rhetoric necessitated no reconsideration of Cold War assumptions and may instead have inadvertently reinforced them as a consequence of identifying, even indirectly, the Communist threat with McCarthy's demagoguery.

Finally, the exchange between Murrow and McCarthy indicates the centrality and flexibility of dark-light imagery as a rhetorical resource of the Cold War.   Although an archetypal image, it operates more like a variable than a linguistic determinant.   Just as McCarthy was able to capitalize on it in his condemnation of Communist subversives, Murrow and others were able to turn it against McCarthy. Others, too, on both sides of the ideological divide between hawks and doves, or realists and idealists, have associated their enemies with the forces of darkness. The idealist Henry Wallace, for instance, drew heavily on images of darkness to condemn America's "get tough policy" toward the Soviet Union in the early years of the Cold War.[40]   More recently, the realists at AIM (Accuracy in Media) produced a counter-documentary on the Vietnam War that drew heavily on the dark imagery of death and distortion in order to make a case for strengthening America's Cold War resolve against the Russians.[41] Whomever might be identified as the real prince of darkness, however, freedom itself remains symbolically at risk because of its continuing association with the fragile light of a flickering flame.[42] The guardian of that flame, whether it be a Murrow or a McCarthy, can be counted upon to rally the rest of us against demons lurking in the night.

APPENDIX 1

McCarthy's Image of Communism as Presented on
"See It Now," March 9, 1954

Speaker	Excerpt (Key Vehicles Highlighted)

McCarthy: The **raw, harsh**, unpleasant fact is that Communism is an issue and will be an issue in 1954.

Murrow: On one thing the Senator has been consistent. Often operating as a one-man committee, he has traveled far, interviewed many, terrorized some, accused civilian and military leaders of the past administration of a great **conspiracy** to turn over the country to Communism. . . . He has interrogated a varied assortment of what he calls **"Fifth Amendment** Communists."

McCarthy: Nothing is more serious than a **traitor** to this country in the Communist **conspiracy**.

McCarthy: And wait 'til you hear the **bleeding hearts scream** and **cry** about our methods of trying to **drag** the truth from those who know, or should know, who **covered up** a **Fifth Amendment** Communist Major. But they say, "Oh, it's all right to uncover them but don't get rough doing it, McCarthy."

McCarthy: Apparently—apparently, the President and I now agree on the necessity of getting rid of Communists. We apparently disagree on how we should handle those who protect Communists. When the **shouting** and the **tumult** dies the American people and the President will realize that this unprecedented **mud slinging** against the Committee by the extreme left wing elements of press and radio was caused solely because another **Fifth Amendment** Communist was finally **dug out** of the **dark recesses** and **exposed** to the public view.

McCarthy: Well, may I say that I was extremely shocked when I heard that Secretary Stevens told two Army officers that they had to take part in the **cover-up** of those who promoted and coddled Communists.

APPENDIX 2

The Image of McCarthy on "See It Now,"
March 9, 1954

Source	Excerpt (Key Vehicles Highlighted)
Murrow:	He has **interrogated** a varied assortment of what he calls "Fifth Amendment Communists." Republican Senator Flanders of Vermont said of McCarthy today: "He **dons war paint**; he goes into his **war dance**; he emits his **war whoops**; he goes forth to battle and proudly returns with the **scalp** of a pink Army dentist."
Murrow:	Other critics have accused the Senator of using the **bull whip** and **smear**.
Chicago Tribune:	McCarthy will better serve his cause if he learns to distinguish the role of investigator from the role of **avenging angel**.
New York Times:	The unwarranted interference of a demagogue—a domestic **Munich**.
Herald Tribune:	McCarthyism involves **assaults** on basic Republican concepts.
Evening Star:	It was a bad day for everyone who resents and detests the **bully boy** tactics which Senator McCarthy often employs.
World Telegram:	**Bamboozling, bludgeoning, distorting**.
St. Louis Post Dispatch:	**Unscrupulous**, McCarthy **bullying**.
Murrow:	And upon what **meat** doth Senator McCarthy **feed**? Two of the **staples** of his **diet** are the investigations (protected by immunity) and the half-truth.
Murrow:	Now—a sample investigation. The witness was Reed Harris . . . . The Senator **summoned** him and questioned him about a book he had written in 1932.

Harris: I resent the tone of this inquiry very much, Mr. Chairman. I resent it, not only because it is my **neck** (my public **neck**) that you are, I think, very skillfully trying to **wring** . . .

Murrow: Two years ago Senator Benton of Connecticut accused McCarthy of apparent perjury, unethical practice, and perpetrating a **hoax** on the Senate.

Murrow: It is necessary to investigate before legislating, but the line between investigating and **persecuting** is a very fine one and the junior Senator from Wisconsin has stepped over it repeatedly. His primary achievement has been in **confusing** the public mind, as between the internal and the external threat of Communism. We must not confuse dissent with disloyalty. We must remember always that **accusation** is not proof and that conviction depends upon evidence and due process of law. We will not walk in fear, one of another. We will not be driven by fear into an age of **unreason**.

APPENDIX 3

Murrow's Image on "See It Now," March 9, 1954

Speaker	Excerpt (Key Vehicles Highlighted)
Murrow:	. . . we are not **descended** from fearful men—not from men who feared to write, to speak, to associate and to defend causes that were, for the moment, unpopular.
Murrow:	We can deny our **heritage** and our history, but we cannot escape responsibility for the result. There is no way for a citizen of a republic to **abdicate** his responsibilities. As a nation we have come into our full **inheritance** at a **tender age**. We proclaim ourselves, as indeed we are, the **defenders** of freedom, wherever it continues to exist in the world, but we cannot defend freedom abroad by **deserting** it at home.

APPENDIX 4

McCarthy's Image of Communism and Murrow
on "See It Now," April 6, 1954

Speaker	Excerpt (Key Vehicles Highlighted)

McCarthy: And, you know, it's interesting to note that the **viciousness** of Murrow's attacks is in direct ratio to our success in digging out Communists.

McCarthy: I am compelled by the facts to say to you that Mr. Edward R. Murrow, as far back as twenty years ago, was engaged in **propaganda** for Communist causes.

McCarthy: Mr. Murrow sponsored a Communist school in Moscow. In the selection of American students and teachers who were to attend, Mr. Murrow's organization acted for the Russian **espionage** and **propaganda** organization known as Voks (V-O-K-S) and many of those selected were later exposed as Communists. Murrow's organization selected such **notorious** Communists as Isadore Gegun, David Zablodowsky.

McCarthy: Now, Mr. Murrow, by his own admission, was a member of the IWW. That's the Industrial Workers of the World—a **terrorist** organization cited as **subversive** by an Attorney General of the United States, who stated that it was an organization which seeks (and I quote) "to alter the Government of the United States by unconstitutional means."

McCarthy: They openly wrote (nothing secret about it!) that, in their efforts to gain power they would be justified in doing anything—that they would be justified in following the **trail of deceit, lies, terror, murder, treason, blackmail.** All these things were elevated to virtues in the Communist rule book. If a convert to Communism could be persuaded that he was a citizen of the world, it of course would be much easier to make him a **traitor** to his own country.

McCarthy: In every country they, of course, had to find **glib, clever** men like Edward R. Murrow who would sponsor invitations to students and teachers to attend indoctrination schools in Moscow, exactly as Murrow has done. They trained Communists in every country in the world. Their sole purpose was: **infiltrate** the government.

McCarthy: Now let us look at the map of the world as it was twenty years ago. At that time there was one country with 180,000,000 people in Communist **chains.** Now let us look at a map of the world as of tonight, this sixth day of April, Nineteen Hundred and Fifty-four: over one-third of the earth's area under Communist control and 800,000,000 people in Communist **chains,** in addition to the 800,000,000 in Communist **chains** in Europe and Asia. Finally, the Communists have gained a foothold and a potential military base here in our half of the world, in Guatemala, with the Communists **seeping** down into Honduras.

Unnamed: Because of those people, **night** has fallen upon my nation and **slavery** upon my people.

McCarthy: Now, my good friends, if there were no Communists in our government, would we have consented to and **connived** to turn over all of our Chinese friends to the Russians?

APPENDIX 5

The Image of McCarthy on "See It Now," April 6, 1954

Speaker	Excerpt (Key Vehicles Highlighted)
McCarthy:	The Senate Investigating Committee has **forced** out of government, and out of important defense plants, Communists engaged in the Soviet conspiracy. And, you know, it's interesting to note that the viciousness of Murrow's attacks is in direct ratio to our success in **digging out** Communists.
McCarthy:	. . . Murrow is a symbol—the leader and the cleverest of the jackal pack which is always found at the throat of anyone who dares to **expose** individual Communists and traitors.
McCarthy:	Of course you can't measure the success of a committee by a box score, based on the number of Communist **heads** that have **rolled** from secret jobs. It is completely impossible to even estimate the sort of the effects on our government of the day-to-day **plodding exposure** of Communists. And that is, of course, why the Murrows **bleed.**
McCarthy:	Now attempts to evaluate the efforts of the work of an investigating committee would be about as impossible to attempt to evaluate the effects of well-trained **watchdogs** upon the activities of professional burglars.

NOTES

1. Michael D. Murray, "Persuasive Dimensions of See It Now's 'Report on Senator Joseph R. McCarthy,'" *Today's Speech* 23 (Fall 1975): 18.

2. Michael Dennis Murray, "See It Now vs. McCarthyism: Dimensions of Documentary Persuasion," Ph.D. diss., University of Missouri, 1974, Appendix B, 216. Murray's transcripts of the two broadcasts are hereafter referred to as "Murrow's Report" and "McCarthy's Reply" respectively.

3. Edwin R. Bayley, *Joe McCarthy and the Press* (Madison: University of Wisconsin Press, 1981), 195; Fred W. Friendly, *Due to Circumstances beyond Our Control* (New York: Random House, 1967), 43, 58.

4. A[nn] M. Sperber, *Murrow: His Life and Times* (New York: Freundlich Books, 1986), 471.

5. Halford Ross Ryan, "*Kategoria* and *Apologia*: On Their Rhetorical Criticism as a Speech Set," *The Quarterly Journal of Speech* 68 (1982): 254-261.

6. Murray, "Murrow's Report," 208-209.

7. Ryan, "*Kategoria* and *Apologia*"; Halford Ross Ryan, "Baldwin vs. Edward VIII: A Case Study in *Kategoria* and *Apologia*," *The Southern Speech Communication Journal* 49 (1984): 125-134; also Halford Ryan, ed., *Oratorical Encounters: Selected Studies and Sources of Twentieth-Century Political Accusations and Apologies* (Westport, Conn.: Greenwood Press, 1988).

8. One early study of Murrow's technique is Murray R. Yaeger, "An Analysis of Edward R. Murrow's 'See It Now' Television Program." (Ph.D. diss., University of Iowa, 1956).

9. Robert L. Ivie, "Metaphor and the Rhetorical Invention of Cold War 'Idealists,'" *Communication Monographs* 54 (1987): 165-182.

10. Murray, "See It Now vs. McCarthyism," 88-89; also Friendly, *Due to Circumstances*, 30.

11. Bayley, *McCarthy and the Press*, 193. Also see Sperber, *Murrow*, 427-31, 440; Thomas C. Reeves, *The Life and Times of Joe McCarthy: A Biography* (New York: Stein and Day, 1982), 384, 429, 452, 493, 523-524, 529, 535, 556, 563.

12. Sperber, *Murrow*, 426; Bayley, *McCarthy and the Press*, 199.

13. Reeves, *Life and Times*, 564.

14. Murray, "Persuasive Dimensions," 18.

15. Reeves, *Life and Times*, 564; see also Daniel J. Leab, "*See It Now*: A Legend Reassessed," in *American History, American Television: Interpreting the Video Past*, ed. John E. O'Connor (New York: Frederick

Ungar Publishing Co., 1983), 17; and Phillip Meyer, *Precision Journalism* (Bloomington, Ind.: Indiana University Press, 1973), 8.

16. Friendly, *Due to Circumstances*, 40.

17. Reeves, *Life and Times*, 578.

18. I am indebted to Thomas Rosteck for sharing a draft of his chapter on this program as he neared completion of his Ph.D. dissertation at the University of Wisconsin under the direction of Michael Leff. I first became acquainted with his work on Murrow through the paper he presented at the Speech Communication Association convention in 1986, entitled "Synecdoche and Audience in Television Documentary: 'The Case of Milo Radulovich, AO589839.'" See Thomas Rosteck, "Irony, Argument, and Reportage in Television Documentary: *See It Now* versus Senator McCarthy," *Quarterly Journal of Speech* 75 (1989): 277-298.

19. Murray, "See It Now vs. McCarthyism," 150; Bayley, 199; Leo Bogart, *The Age of Television* (New York: Frederick Ungar Publishing Co., 1972), 225.

20. A. William Bluem, *Documentary in American Television: Form, Function, Method* (New York: Hastings House, 1965), 98.

21. Reeves, *Life and Times*, 429.

22. Ibid., 496, 529.

23. Sperber, *Murrow*, 427, 433.

24. Quoted in Bayley, *McCarthy and the Press*, 190.

25. Betty Houchin Winfield, "Edward R. Murrow, Radio and the Cold War." Paper delivered at the 51st Annual Meeting of the Southern Historical Association, Houston, November 1985, 11.

26. Edward Bliss, Jr., ed., *In Search of Light: The Broadcasts of Edward R. Murrow, 1938-1961* (New York: Alfred A. Knopf, 1967), 120.

27. Ibid., 151.

28. Winfield, "Murrow, Radio," 13.

29. Bliss, *Search of Light*, 157-158.

30. Ibid., 190.

31. Winfield, "Murrow, Radio," 16-17.

32. Ivie, "Metaphor and the Rhetorical Invention," 166-168.

33. Murray, "See It Now vs. McCarthyism," 204-222; Edward R. Murrow Papers, Washington State University Library, Reel 40: 367; 1,574-1,582, Reel 41: 377, 752-758; films of the two broadcasts are available through the University of Wisconsin.

34. Electronic Text Corporation, 5600 North University Ave., Provo, Utah 84604.

35. Michael Osborn, "Archetypal Metaphor in Rhetoric: The Light-Dark Family," *Quarterly Journal of Speech* 53 (1967): 115.

36. Reeves, *Life and Times*, 202.

37. Leab, "See It Now," 17.

38. Bogart, *The Age of Television*, 225.

39. Quoted in Murray, "See It Now vs. McCarthyism," 135.

40. Ivie, "Metaphor and the Rhetorical Invention," 168-173.

41. Robert L. Ivie, "Cold War 'Realism' in AIM's Counter-Documentary on the Vietnam War." Paper delivered at Annual Meeting of the Western Speech Communication Association, San Jose, Calif., February, 1986.

42. Robert L. Ivie, "The Ideology of Freedom's 'Fragility' in American Foreign Policy Argument," *Journal of the American Forensic Association* 24 (1987): 27-36.

7

Metaphor and the Rhetorical Invention of Cold War "Idealists"

Robert L. Ivie

Since the beginning of the Cold War, those who have spoken out against Soviet-American confrontation have appealed foremost to the fear of nuclear holocaust, replete with visions of civilization destroyed. Their principal argument has been that the two sides must learn to cooperate in the abolition of nuclear weapons or risk extinction of the species.[1] E. P. Thompson's metaphor of "exterminism" captured for many the essence of the survival motive on which contemporary peace advocates have heavily relied.[2] Yet, fear of total annihilation has failed so far to produce public pressure sufficient even to slow the arms race, let alone reverse it.

Assessing their losses (or at least their lack of satisfactory progress), proponents of nuclear disarmament have acknowledged that support for the movement has been undercut by the prevailing image of the Soviet threat. Thus, Ground Zero attempted to "educate" the public on such matters with the publication of *What About The Russians—and Nuclear War?*[3] As Molander and Molander write in their foreword to the book:

"What about the Russians?" has long been a stock response to the notion that the United States set limits on its nuclear weapons program. Whether the proposals be for unilateral action or for bilateral action . . . the question is the same. . . . The policies of the Soviet Union, whether we like them or not, are fundamental when we think about American security. For too long, those who have proposed curtailment of the U.S. weapons buildup by arms negotiations or other means have given too little thought to that basic question in the minds of so many Americans: "What about the Russians?"[4]

Just as Ground Zero's book, written "to provide the public with strictly nonpartisan, nonadvocacy educational materials," was designed to correct false images of the Soviet adversary and thereby establish a political atmosphere more conducive to arms negotiations, many other voices have been raised to protest historic Cold War antagonisms and challenge visions, in George Kennan's words, "of the totally inhuman and totally malevolent adversary." According to Kennan, those in government who hold such an "unreal" view of the Soviets have been largely responsible for undermining progress toward better relations between the two great rivals.[5]

Henry Wallace, J. William Fulbright, and Helen Caldicott must be counted, at various stages of the Cold War, among the most vociferous critics of the persistent enemy-image. They, among others, have attempted mightily to dispel the myth of Soviet savagery that goaded the nation into supporting Harry Truman's "get tough" policy, Lyndon Johnson's "Americanization" of the Vietnam War, and Ronald Reagan's program of "peace through strength." Yet, today the essential problem remains: Americans are forced to choose between radically opposing and potentially disastrous views of the Russians. One view, advocated by "realists," threatens them with extermination should the arms race touch off a nuclear war. The other view, advanced by "idealists," threatens them with loss of national power and personal freedom should the Russians take advantage of a disarmed America. As Lifton and Falk have observed:

The vector of nuclear intentions is, of course, the Soviet Union. More and more Americans grasp the tragic flaws bound up with nuclearism and yet they support the nuclearist path as the lesser of evils. Pushed, the majority of Americans would rather take their chances with nuclear war than expose the country, or even its world position, to Soviet aggression. A rigidifying either/or mentality that can only envisage pacifism as an alternative to nuclearism confines choice and creates a national and species destiny.[6]

Thus, the advocates of superpower accommodation have achieved little more than a negative critique of the implacable-foe image, leaving those they have convinced with only a pacifist's alternative.

My goal in this paper is to identify sources of rhetorical invention that have undermined efforts so far to transcend the choice between chauvinism and pacifism. By examining the structure of metaphor, primarily in the rhetoric of Wallace, Fulbright, and Caldicott, I intend to show the roots of their collective failure. On a more hopeful note, I believe the analysis also reveals a recurring opportunity for rhetorical transcendence created, ironically enough, by the confrontation of "realists" and "idealists." In order to reveal the sources both of failure and opportunity, I turn next to a brief discussion of my method of analysis.

IDENTIFYING KEY METAPHORS

I begin with the premise that metaphor is at the base of rhetorical invention. Elaborating a primary image into a well-formed argument produces a motive, or interpretation of reality, with which the intended audience is invited to identify. The form of the argument actualizes and literalizes the potential of the incipient figure.[7] In the most important uses of metaphor, as a source of rhetorical invention, a term (or "vehicle") from one domain of meaning acts upon a subject (or "tenor") from another domain. Their "co-presence" routinely yields a meaning "which is not attainable without their interaction," and in certain cases the tenor becomes so closely identified with its vehicle that it "is imagined 'to be that very thing which it only resembles.'"[8] In such instances, the vehicle and its "system of associated commonplaces" organize our view of the tenor much like a filter determines which particles will be selected out and a mold defines a final shape.[9] This kind of metaphor serves as a nomenclature that "necessarily directs the attention into some channels rather than others" and thus establishes what Kenneth Burke has called a "terministic incentive."[10]

Given the assumption that metaphors are routinely elaborated into motivating perspectives, it stands to reason that vestiges of these generating images will regularly appear in speeches (or texts) as the speaker's favorite vehicles. As Lakoff and Johnson say, "Since metaphorical expressions in our language are tied to metaphorical concepts in a systematic way, we can use metaphorical linguistic expression to study the nature of metaphorical concepts and to gain an understanding of the metaphorical nature of our activities."[11] The pattern of vehicles revealed in a corpus of discourse, then, leads directly back to master metaphors, which more often than not are the essential terms of the speaker's "terministic screen."[12] Speaking of one thing in terms of another is the norm rather than the exception in rhetorical discourse. For, as Richards has written, "metaphor is omnipresent in speech"; our "pretence to do without metaphor is never more than a bluff waiting to be called."[13]

The value of locating underlying metaphors is in revealing their limits or untapped potential as sources of invention, something that is far more difficult to accomplish when a generating term is allowed to operate without being explicitly acknowledged as such. Speakers lose sight of alternatives when they become accustomed to routine extensions of images no longer serving their original purposes. Stripping away the outer layers of literalized metaphors exposes them to closer scrutiny and possible reconstruction.[14]

Five basic steps provide a rudimentary procedure for identifying key metaphors. First, familiarizing oneself with the speaker's text and context is essential to interpreting any particular selection of his or her discourse. Critics achieve this objective in various ways, but whatever their preferred method, they attempt to create a sense of the complete experience before attending to its particulars. They gather information from sources contemporaneous with the speaking event—reviewing a broad sample of speeches, counter-speeches, audience reactions, etc.—and supplement their primary materials by consulting relevant scholarship—e.g., histories, theories, and previous works of criticism.

Second, representative texts are selected for a series of close readings undertaken to identify and mark vehicles employed by the speaker. Typically, each reading yields previously overlooked vehicles as the critic becomes more sensitized to figurative terms disguised initially by their seemingly literal usage. Marked vehicles are then filed along with their immediate contexts, amounting usually to a paragraph or less for every occurrence of a vehicle (or for every concurrence of two or more vehicles). Anyone working with word processing equipment may find it convenient to mark each vehicle in bold letters while keying paragraphs for entry into the document file designated for the particular speech or text being analyzed. Whatever storage system is utilized, however, the result is to reduce the original text to an abridged version that comprises only marked vehicles and their immediate contexts.

The third step is to arrange the complete set of marked vehicles into subgroups by clustering those with similar "entailments." Each cluster, it can be tentatively assumed, represents one of the "metaphorical concepts" featured in the speaker's discourse, and the clusters together indicate the speaker's "system of metaphorical concepts."[15]

Fourth, a separate file of vehicles and their immediate contexts is compiled for each cluster of terms, i.e., one file for every metaphorical concept. The most extreme procedure is to search the abridged text until all occurrences of the vehicles in a given cluster have been identified and placed in a single file. Word processing equipment makes the task relatively easy by the use of word-search commands and block-and-file operations. These "concept" files, however they are compiled, display the speaker's various applications of vehicles within a given cluster, as well as concurrences with vehicles from other clusters.

Finally, the "concept" files compiled in step four are analyzed one-by-one for patterns of usage within and between clusters, thereby revealing the speaker's system of metaphorical concepts. Attention is focused on prevailing patterns, assuming that the critic may have inaccurately assigned a few of the vehicles in each cluster and that the speaker may have drawn upon certain vehicles in isolated instances to meet special purposes. With this fifth step completed, the critic is in a position to assess both the limits and untapped potential of the metaphorical system guiding the speaker's rhetorical invention.

The matter of immediate interest, of course, is the rhetorical invention of Cold War "idealists." What can the procedure outlined above reveal about their failure to supplant the vision, advanced by tough-minded "realists," of a barbarian foe bent upon destroying the United States? A case study of three Cold War "idealists," each at a different stage of the

Soviet-American rivalry, provides at least a partial answer to this question, for the vehicles at work in their rhetoric reveal self-defeating metaphorical concepts.

HENRY A. WALLACE AND THE "GAME OF POWER POLITICS"

The story of Harry Truman's underdog campaign and stunning victory over Thomas Dewey in 1948 is legendary. Yet few remember the name of the third-party candidate in that race who, under the banner of world peace, expected to draw as much as 10 percent of the total vote, mostly at the expense of an already hard-pressed incumbent. Henry A. Wallace risked his public career "to bring about understanding between Russia and the Western World before it was too late" but managed as the Progressive Party candidate to attract only 1,157,140 votes, just over two percent of the total.[16] Although he was the "most prominent critic of America's 'get-tough' posture toward the Soviet Union," Wallace was abandoned during the campaign by liberals and nearly everyone else, except the Communists.[17] Opponents branded the "prophet of peace" an "apologist for Russia," banishing him to the fringes of American politics and ending any chance of softening the administration's hard line on foreign policy.[18] As Richard Walton has observed: "The campaign [of 1948] was the last time that the basic assumptions of American foreign policy were questioned until the mid-1960s. Not until five presidential elections later did American voters begin to re-examine the anti-Communism that had been the motivating force of American foreign policy since the death of Franklin D. Roosevelt in April 1945."[19] Wallace fought hard but failed even to dent the iron-curtain mentality of the early Cold War era.

Five texts furnish a good sample of Wallace's rhetoric on issues developed prior to and during the campaign of 1948: (1) his memorandum as secretary of commerce to President Harry S. Truman on the subject of foreign policy, dated July 23, 1946;[20] (2) his Madison Square Garden speech on September 12, 1946, which led a week later to his dismissal from the cabinet;[21] (3) his radio broadcast of December 29, 1947, declaring himself an independent candidate for the presidency;[22] (4) his speech of July 24, 1948, accepting the Progressive party's presidential nomination;[23] (5) his campaign book, *Toward World Peace*.[24]

Analysis of these texts reveals seven clusters of vehicles that appear consistently throughout Wallace's speaking and writing on the Cold War. First is the GAME cluster comprising terms such as "game," "race," "cards," "competition," "play," "vie," "pawn," and "team." Wallace spoke of "the game of power politics" as a "competition [that] should be put on a friendly basis."[25] Presently, he argued, the United States was relying on coercive tactics and violating the rules of fair play in its "card game" of atomic negotiations with the Russians:

> Realistically, Russia has two cards which she can use in negotiating with us: (1) our lack of information on the state of her scientific and technical progress on atomic energy and (2) our ignorance of her uranium and thorium resources. These cards are nothing like as powerful as our cards—a stockpile of bombs, manufacturing plants in actual production, B-29s and B-36s, and our bases covering half the globe. Yet we are in effect asking her to reveal her only two cards immediately—telling her that after we have seen her cards we will decide whether we want to continue to play the game.
>
> Insistence on our part that the game must be played our way will only lead to deadlock. . . . We may feel very self-righteous if we refuse to budge on our plan [the Baruch plan] and the Russians refuse to accept it, but that means only one thing—the atomic armament race is on in deadly earnest.[26]

The United States must avoid an "atomic bomb race," he insisted, because "Russia can play the present game as long as the United States."[27] We must stop "playing with matches," "conniving," and "scheming" and start "play[ing] ball with the Russians," for "our lives depend on it."[28] In short, Wallace called for playing by the rules in a friendly game of power politics, letting "the results of the two [competing economic] systems speak for themselves";[29] violating the rules, he insisted, would divide the world into "two armed camps" and lead ultimately to "the civilized world . . . go[ing] down in destruction."[30]

The second cluster, featuring FORCE, contained many vehicles, including "tide," "drive," "pressure," "grind," "torrent," "flood," "conflagration," "upper hand," "bow," "ruthless," "tough," "outposts," "bully," "fight," "march," "Gideon's Army," "slam," "flexed muscles," "showdown," "steal," "clubs," "grip," "split," "rob," "hammer," "drag," "tug," "criminal," "stampede," "mob," "shout," "cry," "tantrums," and "force." Two kinds of force were emphasized: negative force and positive force. Negative force was that which violated rules and laws and consequently was destructive. Wallace complained, for instance, that "far too often, hatred and fear, intolerance and deceit have had the upper hand over love and confidence, trust and joy. Far too often, the law of nations has been the law of the jungle; and the constructive spiritual forces of the Lord have bowed to the destructive forces of Satan."[31]

Negative force, Wallace warned, included "ruthless economic warfare" that was "headed straight for boom, bust, and worldwide chaos," "criminal" talk about World War III by a "little handful of warmongers" who might "stampede" the "bulk of our people," Americans being used as "fire fighters armed with matches and gasoline," thus increasing the "danger of world conflagration," and "preach[ing] force and deceit" that leads to a worldwide "faith in force as the ultimate arbiter."[32] Relying on negative force, such as the "get tough" policy, would only "spawn" a "get tougher" policy by the Russians: "'Getting tough' never brought anything real and lasting—whether for schoolyard bullies or businessmen or world powers. The tougher we get, the tougher the Russians will get."[33]

Negative force, the force of Satan, represented a mindless submission to trends, stampedes, drives, or tides of hate, fear, intolerance, deceit, and destruction. The "tide of American public opinion" was "again turning against Russia";[34] power was "gravitat[ing]" to the few instead of the many;[35] the world had "ricocheted from crisis to crisis," and the "drive" to buy arms was continuing "to push us toward war."[36]

Positive force, on the other hand, was the constructive force of the Lord. It was active, renewing, and full of fight but blessed with love, joy, and hope. "In recent years," Wallace wrote, "there has been . . . a vast awakening, a stirring of new hope, new demands."[37] Americans, liberals especially, could no longer afford to "turn over on their backs and wave their four paws in the air while the special interests tickle[d] their fears of Communism"; they had to choose "either to sell their souls or stand up and fight."[38] Wallace had assembled a "Gideon's Army, small in number, powerful in conviction, ready for action" that would lead the people on a "march" for "peace, progress and prosperity" and against "the powers of evil."[39] His army would "capture the imagination of all religious people" in order to alert the world that "quick profits on war prospects are suicidal."[40] His "crusade to rediscover the spirit of America" was designed to build public support for "establishing an atmosphere of mutual trust and confidence" between the United States and the Soviet Union.[41] He would "unleash [a] creative force beyond the power of man to imagine."[42]

Thus, in Wallace's lexicon, playing the *game* of power politics properly—i.e., in a friendly manner and consistent with the rules of fair play—was a corollary of activating *positive force*; a spiritual awakening of love and trust among humankind would bring forth peaceful competition with the Russians. Conversely, unfair competition, coercion, and ultimately war were a function of succumbing passively to *negative force*, of submitting mindlessly to the forces of hatred and fear. This basic metaphorical concept, created by the interface of GAME and FORCE, was solidified by five reinforcing clusters: DARK-LIGHT, SICK, MONEY, BREED-PLANT, and PREACH.

Vehicles in the DARK-LIGHT cluster included "down," "dark," "fog," "blind," "shadow," "nightmare," "frozen," "distorted," "astigmatic," "thick," "smoke," "chaos," "abyss," "dawn," "light," "torchbearers," "x-ray," "vision," "dreams," "awakening," "stirring," "ray," and "wake." Images of darkness were associated with the negative force of coercion, distrust, fear, and death. Negative force, in short, was condemned as the dark force. Wallace complained "the atmosphere" between the U.S. and USSR had become "thick" so that any gesture of goodwill was "lost and stifled by the smoke of manufactured hate, of groundless fear."[43]   He argued that "when people are afraid, they are blinded to the good in each other," that "fearmongers" should not be allowed to "distort and becloud the issue by name calling," and that Americans "must understand the real Russia and not be guided by the distorted picture" presented daily "in our press."[44]   He warned that the threat of military domination was "stealing up on us" and insisted "negotiations on the establishment of active trade might well help to clear away the fog of political misunderstanding."[45]

Images of light projected the sense of positive force onto Wallace's proposals for world peace.   In his words, "The party of hope needs workers to bring light to the dark corners where the afflicted are oppressed by the parties of Hatred, Despair, Scarcity, Exploitation, Hunger, and War."[46]   An "atmosphere of mutual trust and confidence" would solve "many of the problems relating to the countries bordering on Russia."[47]   He spoke glowingly of Franklin Roosevelt who "looked beyond the horizon and gave us a vision of peace. . . . It was a dream that all of us had."[48]

Wallace further denigrated negative force by associating it with vehicles in the SICK cluster, including "neurotic," "symptoms," "sick," "afflicted," "obsessed," "psychopathic," "fester," "infection," "rot," "suicide," and "graveyard."   Wallace spoke derisively of candidates in "the graveyard parties," Democrats and Republicans, who "flexed their muscles" and "declared their intention to continue the cold war."[49]   He warned of a "neurotic, fear-ridden, itching-trigger psychology" in a world of several nations armed with atomic bombs and wrote that pursuing the Truman Doctrine was "the surest way of committing a long, slow, painful national suicide."[50]   Furthermore, trouble spots around the world were said to be "festering" to the point of being "shot through with social and economic infection that could lead to spreading conflict."[51]   Quite simply, the world was "desperately sick," spiritually, economically, and politically.[52]

Wallace also relied upon the negative connotations of MONEY terms to denigrate negative force.   His favorite vehicles in this category included, "price," "cost," "bought," "bankrupt," "cheap," "buy," "pay," "coin," "sold," "investments," "liquidate," "sell," and "money." He spoke of "cheap lies," "ruthless profiteering," "trying to buy the world . . . cheaply," and "social and moral bankruptcy."[53]   He referred to "the temples of the money changers and the clubs of the military."[54]   He warned that "those whom we buy politically with our food" would soon desert us; they would "pay us in the basic coin of temporary gratitude and then turn to hate us because our policies [were] destroying their freedom."[55]

Vehicles in the BREED-PLANT cluster included "incubate," "stagnate," "breed," "cesspool," "cultivate," "circulate," "fertilize," "seed," "fruit," and "harvest."   The BREED terms portrayed negative force as degenerative, spawning evil and its residue of war. Wallace warned that "hatred breeds hatred," that "stagnant pools of capital breed unemployment and degeneracy," that "money, like water, [could] be kept pure only by circulation," and that the Truman Doctrine had been "incubated in certain minds."[56]

PLANT terms, on the other hand, reinforced Wallace's commitment to positive force by intensifying the image of renewal. The United Nations never would get off "dead center" until it developed "the courage to fertilize the thought of the world"; the time had come for "a modern Johnny Appleseed animated by the missionary spirit to go into all the world and preach the gospel to every creature. Broadcast the seeds of investment, science, technology, and productivity to all peoples."[57]

Finally, Wallace advanced positive force as the key to world peace by drawing upon vehicles in the PREACH cluster, including "missionary," "minister," "spirit," "preach," and "crusade." He promised to lead "the forces of peace, progress and prosperity" in a "great fight" against "the powers of evil" by assembling a "Gideon's Army."[58]   In his view, "'Nationalism' [had] not given a sufficiently satisfying answer to the deep spiritual cry of man for a supreme allegiance"; therefore, he proclaimed "a crusade to rediscover the spirit of America."[59]   Wallace's crusade would bring positive force to bear on the resolution of the Cold War and its root causes. He would awaken, enlighten, and plant the world out of its suicidal submersion in the cesspool of shortsighted economic greed. His crusade would unleash the power of faith in humankind and commitment to human welfare that would allow America to play the game of power politics fairly, ultimately winning the competition with Russia without resorting to violence.

Overall, then, Wallace's critique of the Cold War was driven by an ideal image, or metaphorical concept, of a spiritually awakened America engaging the Soviet Union in peaceful competition to heal an economically sick world and eventually to win the allegiance of humankind. His metaphors placed the blame for the problem and the responsibility for its solution almost exclusively on the United States, which was associated with a sick, dark, and deceitful "get tough" policy designed to overpower the Russians and serve the evil interests of "reactionary capitalism."[60]   In his words, the "Wall Street-military control in Washington" was "so obsessed with fear and hatred of Russia" that it was "certain, sooner or later, to make war."[61]   Not surprisingly, the public simply was unwilling to accept any such analysis that focused the guilt on their nation alone. Thus Wallace was easily dismissed as Russia's naive apologist.

Not only was Wallace's ideal image rhetorically flawed by its preponderant criticism of the United States, blaming the American government and reactionary capitalists almost exclusively for the Cold War, but it also lacked a characterization of the Russians that was well suited to their designated role as responsible players in the friendly game of power politics. Wallace said hardly anything to assure the public of Russia's inherent goodwill and commitment to fair competition. Instead, he warned of "red hysteria" in the United States, and allowed that Communism itself had emerged in Russia only because of a "grinding poverty" caused by the exploitation of the Czars in cooperation with Western capitalists.[62] Just as hatred had bred hatred, he reasoned, friendly competition initiated by the United States would be reciprocated by the Soviets. America could make of its opponent whatever it chose: either an unbeatable rival in war or a cooperative opponent in peaceful competition. Faith in the inherent goodness of human nature and a willingness to act upon that faith were all that were required to bring about world peace and happiness. Yet the public's image of Soviet savagery, reinforced by the Cold War rhetoric of Wallace's critics, allowed for little faith in the inherent goodness of an atheistic and barbarian foe.

American voters were not the only ones to reject Wallace's vision of peace. Wallace himself recanted only a few years later in an article entitled, "Where I Was Wrong." He had failed to take into account, he now believed, "the ruthless nature of Russian-trained Communists." Russia was "still on the march," Wallace wrote, determined "to enslave the common man morally, mentally and physically for its own imperial purposes." He was now convinced by developments in Czechoslovakia, Korea, and elsewhere that "Russian Communism in its total disregard of truth, in its fanaticism, its intolerance and its resolute denial of God and religion is something utterly evil."[63]

Wallace ultimately fell victim to the inadequacies of his own rhetorical invention. His system of metaphorical concepts proved to be self-defeating because it did not enable him to explain Soviet initiatives without either continuing to blame the United States for creating the conditions that forced the Soviets to compete unfairly or deciding eventually that the Soviets were actually Satan's surrogates. As the vehicles of light and darkness, breeding and planting, sickness and greed, and ministering and crusading combined to reinforce Wallace's faith in peaceful competition, they undermined his ability to perceive the rhetorical limits of a vision that failed both to account for Soviet imperialism and to characterize the Russians as good sportsmen in the game of power politics. The only alternative, finally, was to adopt the opposing metaphor of Soviet savagery that, within Wallace's metaphorical system, made Communism itself a dark, degenerative, negative force—the source of all evil. As we shall see, Cold War idealists who spoke out long after Wallace's defeat proved unable to avoid similar weaknesses in their own systems of rhetorical invention.

J. WILLIAM FULBRIGHT AND THE "PATHOLOGY OF POWER"

Ironically, the same senator who had concluded as early as 1946 that Soviet totalitarianism was an immoral, aggressive force, and who had criticized Henry Wallace in 1947 for delivering a speech that sounded "just as though it had been written in the Kremlin," was himself the author thirty years later of a powerful attack on U.S. Cold War doctrine.[64] "Few modern books on foreign policy have been so influential," conceded one of his critics, "as Senator J. William Fulbright's classic lectures, *The Arrogance of Power*. To find a world of comparable impact on American opinion one has to go back to Mahan."[65] Although signs of Fulbright's reassessment of Soviet-American relations were present in his *Old Myths and New Realities*, published in 1964, the transition was not complete until two years later.[66] His "arrogance thesis" emerged in the midst of growing frustration over American involvement in Vietnam and was restated prior to American disengagement from the war in *The Crippled Giant*.[67] Thus, my analysis of the senator's leading metaphorical concepts emphasizes vehicles displayed in his two principal works during the Vietnam era.[68]

Unlike Wallace, Fulbright rejected the GAME metaphor which, in his assessment, led to a "conception of politics as warfare":

Even the most dazzling success in the game of power politics does nothing to make life more meaningful or gratifying for anybody except the tiny handful of strategists and geopoliticians who have the exhilarating experience of manipulating whole societies like pawns on a chessboard.[69]

Fulbright believed the Johnson administration had made the mistake of fighting a "mindless game of power politics" in Indochina and the Nixon administration was repeating the error by "playing the spheres-of-influence game in a world of power politics."[70] In his view, power was not a game to be played correctly but instead a "narcotic, a potent intoxicant" that had taken the nation on a "trip."[71] Power conceptualized as a game put too much emphasis on winning and losing, trivializing war "into a mindless contest to prove that we are 'Number One.'"[72] Conceptualized as a narcotic, however, power was more easily recognized as an "addiction" that "nourished our vanity," drove us to acts of "arrogance," and created "a psychological need" to prove we are "bigger, better, or stronger than other nations."[73]

Also unlike Wallace, Fulbright rejected the CRUSADE metaphor. In the senator's view, "The crusading spirit" of great nations throughout history had "wrought havoc" on others as well as themselves.[74] America's involvement in Vietnam, he believed, resulted from viewing "Communism as an evil philosophy" and "ourselves as God's avenging angels."[75] Such misguided moralism had its roots in a history of "intolerant puritanism" that "coexisted uneasily" with "a dominant strand of democratic humanism."[76] Warning the United States not to pursue the "anti-Communist crusade," Fulbright relentlessly attacked vehicles associated with an arrogance of power (including "saints," "preaching," and "missionary"), denigrating them with the oxymoron "war prayer" and related vehicles such as "pontificating," "fanaticism," and "zealotry."[77] Fulbright rejected the CRUSADE concept in order to condemn American missionary zeal, even though he had drawn upon the same language himself since 1946 to denounce "the crusading spirit of the Russians."[78] By retaining, but also negating, the very terminology that had guided him between 1946 and 1963, Fulbright succeeded in freeing himself of an image that until then had defined the enemy as Soviet aggressive totalitarianism.

The senator's principal concept, however, was similar to the SICK cluster used by Wallace to denigrate negative force. Just as Wallace had emphasized "neurosis," "obsession," "suicide," and "psychopathology" among the various forms of physical and mental sickness, Fulbright primarily drew upon a cluster of PSYCHOLOGY vehicles, including essentially negative terms such as "psychotic," "delusions of grandeur," "projection," "pathology," "confuse," "arrogance," "irrational pressures," "drive," "instinct," "insane," "nervous breakdown," "paranoid fears," and "inferiority complex," as well as more positive terms such as "rehabilitation," "grow up," "empathy," "reconciliation," "mature," and "come of age."

In Fulbright's opinion, "The causes and consequences of war may have more to do with pathology than with politics, more to do with irrational pressures of pride and pain than with rational calculations of advantage and profit."[79] Americans viewing Communism as an "evil philosophy" were looking through a "distorting prism," seeing "projections" of their "own minds rather than what is actually there."[80] The "unfathomable drives of human nature" created a "psychological need" for dominance, and "competitive instincts" led to "dehumanizing" antagonists."[81] Excessive pride was "born of power," undermining "judgment" and "planting delusions of grandeur in the minds of otherwise sensible people and otherwise sensible nations."[82] If war were to be avoided, America had to learn to control its competitive instincts, "confining them to their proper sphere, as the servant and not the master of civilization."[83]

Thus, according to Fulbright, "the reconciliation of East and West [was] primarily a psychological problem, having to do with the cultivation of cooperative attitudes and of a sense of having practical common objectives."[84] As he explained, "Perhaps the single word above all others that expresses America's need is 'empathy.'"[85] The nation must "mature," "come of age," and regard itself as a "friend, counselor, and example for those around the world who seek freedom."[86] The United

States must learn to regard Communist countries as "more or less normal states with whom [it] can have more or less normal relations," and it must "encourage Communist imitation of [its] own more sensible attitudes."[87] Americans and Russians could "form the habit of working together as international civil servants" through "projects of direct cooperation."[88]

Although Fulbright's system of metaphorical concepts differed significantly from Wallace's, it suffered from some of the same flaws. Most importantly, the senator's metaphorical system stressed the culpability of the United States almost exclusively, accusing it of an anti-Communist obsession, an underlying lack of confidence in itself, an exaggerated fear of failure, an arrogance of power, and a crusading puritan spirit manifested as ideological warfare.[89] This American psychosis had driven the nation's policy makers to "irresponsible behavior."[90] The trouble between the United States and the Soviet Union was a function of misperception rooted principally in America's confusion of power with virtue. China's "paranoid fears" of American hostility were distorted and exaggerated but "not pure invention."[91] Russia's "paranoiac suspiciousness" and "inferiority complex" had been worsened by America's Cold War crusade: "by treating them as hostile, we have assured their hostility."[92] It was up to the United States to heal itself of psychotic, destructive tendencies, to mature as a great power and seek reconciliation with the Communists. Under no circumstances should America try to justify its own truculence as a response to Communist intransigence, zealotry, subversion, intervention, and ideological warfare, for tolerance and accommodation are far better and more likely to resolve differences than "imitating the least attractive forms of Communist behavior."[93]

Such idealism hardly took into account any better than Wallace's game metaphor the sources of Soviet behavior that could be expected to promote accommodation over confrontation, cooperation over subversion, or tolerance over totalitarianism. Fulbright depended on a psychological principle, grounded in a single research finding of Muzafer Sherif who had studied patterns of conflict and cooperation between two groups of eleven-year-old American boys in an experimental camp, to conclude that there "may be great promise for strengthening world peace in limited, practical projects of cooperation" between the U.S. and USSR.[94] He advocated "practicing psychology in international relations," but his dependence on PSYCHOLOGY as the dominant metaphorical concept was, at best, overdeveloped for the United States and underdeveloped for the Soviets.[95]

Even though Fulbright was convinced "that Russia can now properly be regarded as a conservative power in international relations, as a nation whose stake in the status quo is a far more important determinant of her international behavior than her philosophical commitment to world revolution," there was little in the PSYCHOLOGY cluster to explain such a development. His conclusion was rooted in an allusion to revolutions passing through normal stages of development, as did the French Revolution, until "a conservative reaction supplants extremism."[96]

Although undeveloped, this "stages-of-revolution" vehicle could have been linked perhaps to certain of Fulbright's PSYCHOLOGY vehicles, such as "maturity," "growing up," and "coming of age," and to other seemingly related but infrequently used terms in his lexicon, terms such as "development," "gradual change," and "tide of change."[97] Certainly, the potential of such an extension was not explored by the senator, and no other concept in his metaphorical system could yield arguments that might pacify the fear of a barbarian foe. Again, Americans were expected to accept the full burden of guilt for the Cold War and to take on faith that the enemy would respond in kind to their leadership by example and acts of friendship.

HELEN CALDICOTT AND "NUCLEAR MADNESS"

About the same time as Senator Fulbright published *The Crippled Giant*, Helen Caldicott emerged as an anti-nuclear activist in Australia, arousing her countrymen to protest French atmospheric testing in the South Pacific and then organizing Australian labor unions against the mining and selling of their nation's uranium on the international market. A pediatrician, the founder of Physicians for Social Responsibility and a former faculty member at Harvard Medical School, Caldicott earned recognition as the mother of the nuclear freeze movement.

Caldicott published her first book, *Nuclear Madness: What You Can Do!*, in 1978, presented her standard anti-nuclear lecture in a controversial and award-winning film in 1983, *If You Love This Planet: Dr. Helen Caldicott on Nuclear War*, and published her second book, *Missile Envy: The Arms Race and Nuclear War*, in 1984.[98] Together, these materials advanced the message she had brought to countless audiences for over a decade, warning them of imminent danger and urging everyone to take action.

Caldicott's quest for a non-nuclear world, however, has been long on courage and energy but short on rhetorical invention. Her nearly total dependence on the MADNESS metaphor has left her unable to mollify America's fear of the enemy, even when she has attempted to answer directly that haunting question:

But what about the Russians? Every time the Pentagon needs more money, the Russian spectre is called up. The reality is that if both superpowers, together with the lesser powers, continue on this mad spiraling arms race, building more and more atomic bombs, sooner or later they will be used. We cannot trust in the sanity and stability of world leaders. (In fact, great power tends to attract disturbed individuals.) . . . Someone must make the first move away from death and toward life. . . . I believe that the Russian people are so frightened of nuclear war that they would heave a momentous sigh of relief and would want their own leaders to follow America's moral initiative toward nuclear disarmament.[99]

Thus, her answer has been to dismiss the question as a dangerous illusion and to pursue the pacifist's alternative in order to save the human race.

MADNESS vehicles have pervaded Caldicott's rhetoric to a fault. Her favorites have been "crazy," "deranged," "madness," "insane," "pathogenesis," "pathological," "mad lust," "paranoia," "anxiety," "indignation," "anger," "frustration," "projection," "fantasy," "mental masturbation," "disease," "etiology," "psychic numbing," "missile envy," "suicide," "mental illness," "frantic desperation," "emotional cripple," "power-hungry," "egocentric," and "killing animus." As the list suggests, she has elaborated the concept well beyond Wallace's SICK cluster and even pursued more vehicles than were featured in Fulbright's PSYCHOLOGY cluster. So complete a commitment has magnified the concept's limitations.

The first problem is that the metaphor has been used to circumvent the enemy-image rather than encompass it in a transcendent image. In answer to her own question—"Why are Russia and America such bitter enemies?"—Caldicott has pointed to "the passionate hatred and paranoia harbored by Americans," emphasized America's "seemingly implacable hatred and dislike of Russia," explained that "the nation's pathological reactions are rooted deep in the past," and charged that "the Russian menace has been dragged out of the closet to justify either personal or political ambitions or new weapons development." She has posed the question—"But what about the Russians?"—and then finessed it by suggesting "the question is a mechanism of psychic numbing, where the questioner refuses to emotionally integrate the facts . . . and a symptom of denial: 'If I can blame the Russians, I won't have to disintegrate emotionally if I contemplate the end of the earth.'"[100]   In short, the pattern has been to associate the United States with MADNESS, focusing attention on the sources of American culpability and dismissing fear of the Russians as a pathological condition, "the primitive mechanism of blaming the Russians."[101]   The Soviet Union has been presented essentially as the victim of America's craziness. In Caldicott's view, "As America has led the arms race, so Russia has inevitably and inexorably copied and followed." Russian fears are justified; their leaders "have every cause to be realistically frightened and perhaps a little paranoid." The culprit is America who "has engineered her own suicide" through the mechanism of "paranoid projection."[102]

The second problem with the MADNESS metaphor is that it has led to a healing image that assumes a loving, supportive environment. Just like the parents who show no sign of emotion when told their child has leukemia, America needs a psychiatrist so that it can become appropriately passionate about the world's survival.[103]   Just like the terminally ill patient brought into the emergency room, our terminally ill planet must be admitted to the intensive care unit and treated with loving care if it is to have a chance of surviving.[104]   Just as Caldicott resolves conflict with her husband by "capitulating" on her own wants, becoming "vulnerable," and making "the first move" to "give love," the United States must forget its "selfish needs" and "make the first move" to insure "a future life-preserving relationship" with the Soviet Union, for "the superpowers are married to each other on this planet."[105]   America must "reach out to," "make friends with," and "learn to love the Russians."[106]   If only the United States could bring itself to take this "simple, obvious, and easy" path of dropping its "ancient need for a tribal enemy," Russia "would cease to be an enemy and the weapons would become anachronistic."[107] Educating the American public and politicians, who have been so terribly ignorant of the nuclear threat, is the key to therapy, for the human being's strongest instinct is survival.   Because the Russians are "people like ourselves," they will respond in kind to our informed initiatives for peace.[108]

Reduced to the level of the individual and the couple, the doctor and the patient, the parent and the child, such advice for healing the rift between ideological and nuclear rivals seems idealistic at best. Worse yet, from the perspective of "realists," Caldicott's solution could lead directly to war if taken seriously, for any sign of weakness would only incite the enemy's savage instinct to attack. It would be hard enough, probably impossible, for Americans to shoulder the full burden of guilt for their nuclear pathology, but the call to capitulate out of love for an enemy makes the analogy absurd.

Caldicott has offered Americans little reason to accept the Soviet Union as a supportive marital partner and has attempted even less to acknowledge Soviet ambitions. Thus, as George Moffett recently reported, "forty years after the dawn of the cold war . . . the task of finding a balance between toughness and compromise remains as elusive as ever." Disagreement continues "among policymakers and public alike" over "the nature of the Soviet threat and how to deal with it." Polls consistently have shown that "the American people want arms control but don't trust the Soviets to honor the terms. The public is concerned about the rapid growth of nuclear arsenals, but also fears falling behind in the arms race."[109]   The image of Soviet savagery continues to haunt Americans even as they contemplate compromise and wish for arms control. As Lifton and Falk have concluded, "The Soviet menace is generally perceived as real and must be addressed" if the peace movement is to avoid being dismissed as "naive, pacifist, or utopian."[110]

TRANSCENDING THE IMAGE OF SAVAGERY

The metaphorical concepts guiding "idealist" rhetoric throughout the Cold War have been self-defeating largely because they have promoted a reversal, rather than transcendence, of the conventional image of a barbarian threat to civilization. Americans traditionally have exonerated themselves of any guilt for war, hot or cold, by decivilizing the image of their adversaries. This "victimage ritual," enacted with generic regularity, has sanctified the ideals of peace, freedom, and democracy. It has legitimized total victory over a foe caricatured as irrational, coercive, and aggressive, i.e., a foe who is totally uncivilized and therefore perfectly evil.[111]

Contrary to tradition, Cold War "idealists" have attempted to decivilize America's image rather than the enemy's. By relying upon metaphorical concepts such as MAD, PATHOLOGY, SICK, and FORCE, they have portrayed the United States as the irrational, coercive, and aggressive agent of extermination, urging Americans to follow instead the path of love, friendship, trust, and empathy. Thus, they have called for a redeeming act of self-mortification by a nation accustomed to condemning scapegoats, asking in effect that it purge itself of savagery without benefit of the principle of substitution.[112] The victimage ritual has been turned inward upon a self-righteous nation, intensifying its guilt and ultimately increasing its need to sacrifice an external enemy "so powerful and cunning that his suffering and death will be a total purgation."[113]

This error of turning savagery inward, instead of transcending it, has provoked "realists" to regress further into decivilizing imagery. One such realist was Walt Rostow, special assistant for national security affairs, whose memorandum to Lyndon Johnson on February 8, 1968, proposed a strategy for a speech to "slay the credibility-gap dragon with one blow." Feeling the pressure of "those who talk peace" and reeling from the Tet offensive, Rostow argued that it was time "to take on the peace issue squarely"—i.e., that it was "time for a war leader speech instead of a peace-seeker speech"—and he attached a draft of a speech designed to accomplish that end. The most striking feature of Rostow's proposed speech was the predominance of explicit savagery symbols. The draft was laced with one reference after another to "the savage assault" on a defenseless civilian population "during the heart of the lunar New Year's celebration," to "a savage and vicious attack upon civilian populations with a callous and total lack of concern for the welfare of civilian lives," to attacks that were "savage in execution," to "the savagery of the past week," to "last week's savagery," to an "enemy who specialized in savagery," and to reminders that "we have known savagery before."[114] Clearly, Rostow's inclination was to retreat to the basic symbol of national peril at a time when the administration's Vietnam policy was under siege and the public needed to be rallied to war.

Regardless of how compelling any metaphor may be, however, its limitations eventually are encountered in its application. Savagery, whether applied to the United States or its enemies, has been no exception. Thus, a cycle of adoption, extension, criticism, and reversal has been established and perpetuated throughout the Cold War.

American involvement in the Vietnam War, for instance, was largely a function of extending the early Cold War image of Soviet and Communist savagery to events in Southeast Asia.[115] The Johnson administration never reassessed the enemy image that led to Americanizing the war in 1965 and the emergence of a strong anti-war movement soon thereafter. The metaphor's compelling but essentially unstable opposition between the forces of civilization and savagery had been literalized by administration rhetoric from Truman through Eisenhower and Kennedy to Johnson.[116] Such a long-term extension eventuated in an unpopular war and revealed flaws in the simple opposition between a savage enemy and a civilized savior. Peace advocates responded by portraying the enemy as the victim of American aggression. The administration's stubborn, uncompromising insistence on Communist savagery and American innocence forced the issue to the point where an unstable opposition was partially reversed long enough for the United States to withdraw from the war and pursue détente with the Communist world. This temporary modification of the savagery versus civilization equation soon encountered its own opposition as détente proved illusive, Soviet "adventurism" became more difficult to ignore, and America's post-war malaise subsided.[117] Reagan's election consummated a return to the original equation of America threatened by a barbarian and evil foe.

Huntington has advanced one suggestion for coping with this cycle, arguing that it should be conceptualized as a series of waves. In his view, "The détente wave slowly gathered force during the 1960s, became stronger, peaked in 1972, broke, reached its high point on the beach a year later, and then began to recede, as the renewed hostility wave began to move in and overlapped with the receding wave of détente." In Huntington's most "hopeful" extension of his wave metaphor, moderation in practice is seen as the child of extremism in rhetoric. That is, administrations that ride the wave of rhetorical hostility "are likely to come under significant pressures to moderate their stance and may be led to a middle-of-the-road, balanced policy in practice." The risk, of course, is that a wave of rhetorical hostility may thrust us onto the jagged rocks of nuclear war if political leaders lack "unusual insight and skill."[118]

A better solution is to break the cycle by superseding the traditional opposition of savagery versus civilization. At the point where reversal normally occurs, an opportunity exists for replacing savagery with a metaphor that encompasses the superpowers within the same system and identifies a common external enemy. The replacement metaphor must take into account the evidence that both parties are rational and irrational, aggressive and pacific, competitive and cooperative, independent and interdependent. It cannot ignore, for instance, established perceptions that the Soviets are obsessed with a paranoid desire for security, that they are secretive, xenophobic, and distrustful, that they suffer from an inferiority complex and are ruthless, imperialistic, authoritarian (even totalitarian), militaristic, and anti-capitalist. It cannot deflect attention, though, from other less threatening observations about the Soviets: that they possess a rich culture, suffer from limited resources and an inefficient economy, are basically conservative managers and technologists; that their revolutionary climate is localized (not a symptom of or inspiration for world revolution), that they are seeking to achieve limited objectives and to avoid war with the United States, that they endorse cooperative, communal, and altruistic ideals, that they are a patriotic people and a stable society, that they share with America a frontier heritage, and that they are officially atheistic but culturally religious.[119] The replacement metaphor must serve the goal of coexistence by redefining the ideal of global freedom (or world Communism) to one of mutual security and continued competition.

A replacement metaphor is needed to integrate mixed images of both superpowers in a manner that will promote arms reduction and manage conflict between them. The solution is not, as so many have suggested, a matter of eschewing abstractions and educating ourselves in the details and complexities of U.S.-Soviet relations.[120] It requires more than recognizing our habit of demonizing the Soviets through an "endless series of distortions and oversimplifications."[121] Understanding is a function of conceptualization, not just information, and the best way to undermine a dysfunctional metaphorical concept "is to choose a new one."[122] As Lifton and Falk have observed, "moving beyond nuclearism" and war requires "the displacement of Machiavellianism by a holistic world picture."[123] The whole must be large enough to bind the United States and the Soviet Union together by mutual interests, a common threat, and continued corrivalry.

Unfortunately, "we live in a period of transition, the old ways no longer work, but new ways have not yet become available."[124] Although the time for rhetorical transcendence has arrived, the mechanism of invention has yet to be discovered largely because attention has been fixed on extending a set of self-defeating metaphorical concepts without sufficient awareness of their operational significance.

"Spaceship earth," "hostages on a terminally ill planet," and "rowboat earth"—i.e., "recognizing that we are all in the same boat together" in "stormy seas" and that "we cannot make our end safer by making their end tippier"—are the vehicles to which some have tentatively turned.[125]

These vehicles, though, are limited in their application, undeveloped as a metaphorical concept for international relations, and inconsistent with some of the criteria for a replacement metaphor mentioned above; viz., they emphasize interdependence and survival but ignore the motive of competition, and they encompass the U.S. and USSR within the same holistic system but offer no basis, beyond the existence of a common threat, for trusting or tolerating each other. Détente failed in the 1970s partly because Nixon and Kissinger were determined through linkage to tame the Soviet monster rather than co-exist with a worthy competitor.[126] Certainly, a sense of world stewardship and common interest in the survival of the species must be encouraged, but not without also finding a metaphor that legitimizes collaboration between antagonists. Each must have something to lose from the other's demise and something to gain from the other's survival, and there must be recognized limits of competition beyond which neither can go without sacrificing their mutual self-interest. In short, some kind of a SYMBIOSIS metaphor must be identified and elaborated in order to move beyond the peril of pre-nuclear thinking in the nuclear age.

NOTES

1. For example, Jonathan Schell, *The Fate of the Earth* (New York: Alfred A. Knopf, 1982); and Jonathan Schell, *The Abolition* (New York: Alfred A. Knopf, 1984).

2. E. P. Thompson, *Beyond the Cold War: A New Approach to the Arms Race and Nuclear Annihilation* (New York: Pantheon, 1982), 41-79.

3. Ground Zero, *What About the Russians—and Nuclear War?* (New York: Pocket Books, 1983).

4. Ibid., xi.

5. Ground Zero, *What About the Russians*, xii; George F. Kennan, *The Nuclear Delusion: Soviet-American Relations in the Atomic Age* (New York: Pantheon, 1982), 33, 57, 65.

6. R. J. Lifton and R. Falk, *Indefensible Weapons: The Political Case Against Nuclearism* (New York: Basic Books, 1982), 208.

7. Robert L. Ivie, "The Metaphor of Force in Prowar Discourse: The Case of 1812," *The Quarterly Journal of Speech* 68 (1982): 240-241; Michael Leff, "Topical Invention and Metaphoric Interaction," *The Southern Speech Communication Journal* 48 (1983): 219, 222-223.

8. I. A. Richards, *The Philosophy of Rhetoric* (New York: Oxford University Press, 1965), 100-101.

9. M. Black, "Metaphor," in M. Johnson, ed., *Philosophical Perspectives on Metaphor* (Minneapolis: University of Minnesota Press, 1981), 73-75.

10. Kenneth Burke, *Language as Symbolic Action: Essays on Life, Literature, and Method* (Berkeley and Los Angeles: University of California Press, 1968), 45.

11. G. Lakoff and M. Johnson, "Conceptual Metaphor in Everyday Language," in M. Johnson, ed., *Philosophical Perspectives on Metaphor* (Minneapolis: University of Minnesota Press, 1981), 290.

12. Kenneth Burke, *Permanence and Change: An Anatomy of Purpose* (Indianapolis: Bobbs-Merrill, 1965), 95; Burke, *Language as Symbolic Action*, 46; Lakoff and Johnson, "Conceptual Metaphors," 312.

13. Richards, *Philosophy of Rhetoric*, 92-93.

14. C. M. Turbayne, *The Myth of Metaphor*, rev. ed. (Columbia, S.C.: University of South Carolina Press, 1970).

15. Lakoff and Johnson, "Conceptual Metaphor," 289-292.

16. Henry A. Wallace, "Where I Was Wrong," *New York Herald Tribune*, 7 September 1952, p. 46.

17. J. S. Walker, *Henry A. Wallace and American Foreign Policy* (Westport, Conn.:   Greenwood Press, 1976), 3; A. L. Hamby, "Henry A. Wallace, the Liberals, and Soviet-American Relations," *The Review of Politics* 30 (1968): 153-169; N. D. Markowitz, *The Rise and Fall of the People's Century: Henry A. Wallace and American Liberalism, 1941-1948* (New York: The Free Press, 1973).

18. E. L. Schapsmeier and F. H. Schapsmeier, *Prophet in Politics: Henry A. Wallace and the War Years, 1940-1965* (Ames, Ia.:   Iowa State University Press, 1970), 180.

19. J. W. Walton, *Henry Wallace, Harry Truman, and the Cold War* (New York: Viking Press, 1976), 1.

20. Henry A. Wallace, "Henry A. Wallace to Harry S. Truman," in *The Price of Vision: The Diary of Henry A. Wallace, 1942-1946*, ed. J.M. Blum (Boston: Houghton-Mifflin, 1973), 589-601.

21. Wallace, "The Way to Peace," in Blum, *The Price of Vision*, 661-669.

22. Henry A. Wallace, "I Shall Run in 1948," *Vital Speeches of the Day*, 1 January 1948, 172-174.

23. Henry A. Wallace, "My Commitments," *Vital Speeches of the Day*, 1 August 1948, 620-623.

24. Henry A. Wallace, *Toward World Peace* (New York: Reynal and Hitchcock, 1948).

25. Wallace, "Wallace to Truman," 599; Wallace, "Way to Peace," 666.

26. Wallace, "Wallace to Truman," 593-594.

27. Wallace, *Toward World Peace*, 3-4; Wallace, "Wallace to Truman," 594.

28. Wallace, *Toward World Peace*, 71, 114; Wallace, "Way to Peace," 666.

124   Robert L. Ivie

29. Wallace, "Way to Peace," 666.

30. Wallace, "I Shall Run," 173; Wallace, "Wallace to Truman," 590.

31. Wallace, "Wallace to Truman," 661.

32. Wallace, "Way to Peace," 663; Wallace, "I Shall Run," 173; Wallace, *Toward World Peace*, 89; Wallace, *Toward World Peace*, 117-118.

33. Wallace, "My Commitments," 620; Wallace, "Way to Peace," 664.

34. Wallace, "Wallace to Truman," 596.

35. Wallace, *Toward World Peace*, 83.

36. Wallace, "My Commitments," 620; Wallace, *Toward World Peace*, 33.

37. Wallace, *Toward World Peace*, 90.

38. Ibid., 86.

39. Wallace, "I Shall Run," 174.

40. Wallace, *Toward World Peace*, 33-34.

41. Ibid., 119; Wallace, "My Commitments," 620.

42. Wallace, "My Commitments," 622.

43. Wallace, *Toward World Peace*, 113.

44. Ibid., 113, 174, 15.

45. Wallace, "Wallace to Truman," 599.

46. Wallace, *Toward World Peace*, 121.

47. Wallace, "Wallace to Truman," 600.

48. Wallace, "My Commitments," 620.

49. Ibid., 622.

50. Wallace, "Wallace to Truman," 592; Wallace, *Toward World Peace*, 115.

51. Wallace, *Toward World Peace*, 101-102.

52. Ibid., 19-20.

53. Wallace, "I Shall Run," 173; Wallace, "My Commitments," 623; Wallace, *Toward World Peace*, 39, 30.

54. Wallace, "My Commitments," 622.

55. Wallace, "I Shall Run," 174.

56. Wallace, "Way to Peace," 662; Wallace, *Toward World Peace*, 41, 10.

57. Wallace, *Toward World Peace*, 45.

58. Wallace, "I Shall Run," 174.

59. Wallace, *Toward World Peace*, 20, 119.

60. Ibid., 83.

61. Ibid., 68.

62. Ibid., 9, 51.

63. Wallace, "Where I Was Wrong," *New York Herald Tribune*, 7 September 1952, Sec. 7, pp. 7, 47.

64. Quoted in K. Tweraser, *Changing Patterns of Political Beliefs: The Foreign Policy Operational Codes of J. William Fulbright, 1943-1967*

(Beverly Hills, Calif.: Sage, 1974), 29; J. William Fulbright, *The Arrogance of Power* (New York: Random House, 1966).

65. E. V. Rostow, *Peace in the Balance: The Future of American Foreign Policy* (New York: Simon and Schuster, 1972), 179.

66. J. William Fulbright, *Old Myths and New Realities* (New York: Random House, 1964).

67. J. William Fulbright, *The Crippled Giant* (New York: Random House, 1972).

68. Fulbright, *Arrogance* and *Crippled Giant*.

69. Fulbright, *Crippled Giant*, 9, 12.

70. Ibid., 92, 96.

71. Ibid., 100.

72. Ibid., 87.

73. Fulbright, *Arrogance*, 5; Fulbright, *Crippled Giant*, 99-100.

74. Fulbright, *Arrogance*, 138, see also 248.

75. Ibid., 107.

76. Ibid., 250.

77. Fulbright, *Crippled Giant*, 160; Fulbright, *Arrogance*, 138, 203, 245-251.

78. Quoted in Tweraser, *Changing Patterns*, 29.

79. Fulbright, *Arrogance*, 7.

80. Ibid., 107.

81. Ibid., 5, 161, 165.

82. Ibid., 130.

83. Ibid., 162.

84. Ibid., 204.

85. Ibid., 197-198.

86. Ibid., 221-222, 257.

87. Ibid., 254, 257.

88. Fulbright, *Crippled Giant*, 168; Fulbright, *Arrogance*, 204.

89. Fulbright, *Arrogance*, 5, 250-251; Fulbright, *Crippled Giant*, 18, 26-27.

90. Fulbright, *Crippled Giant*, 27.

91. Fulbright, *Arrogance*, 170.

92. Ibid., 221; Fulbright, *Crippled Giant*, 10, 20.

93. Fulbright, *Arrogance*, 254.

94. Ibid., 166-168.

95. Fulbright, *Old Myths*, 168.

96. Fulbright, *Arrogance*, 80.

97. Ibid., 202, 211.

98. Helen Caldicott, *Nuclear Madness: What You Can Do!*, rev. ed. (New York: Bantam Books, 1980); Caldicott, *If You Love This Planet: Dr. Helen Caldicott on Nuclear War*, film transcript (Los Angeles: Direct

Cinema Limited, 1983); Caldicott, *Missile Envy: The Arms Race and Nuclear War* (1984; reprint, New York: Bantam Books, 1985).

99. Caldicott, *Nuclear Madness*, 78.

100. Caldicott, *Missile Envy*, 44-45, 70.

101. Ibid., 348.

102. Ibid., 103, 308, 313.

103. Caldicott, *Love This Planet*, 12.

104. Ibid., 14.

105. Caldicott, *Missile Envy*, 314.

106. Ibid., 363-365.

107. Ibid., 364.

108. Caldicott, *Nuclear Madness*, 69; Caldicott, *Missile Envy*, 350-353, 363.

109. George D. Moffett, "Keeping the Soviets in Line: Consistent Policy of 'Containment' Eludes US," *The Christian Science Monitor*, 26 September 1985, pp. 16-17.

110. Lifton and Falk, *Indefensible Weapons*, 210.

111. For studies exemplifying the process, see Robert L. Ivie, "Presidential Motives for War," *The Quarterly Journal of Speech* 60 (1974):   337-345; Robert L. Ivie, "Images of Savagery in American Justifications for War," *Communication Monographs* 47 (1980): 279-294; Ronald L. Hatzenbuehler and Robert L. Ivie, *Congress Declares War: Rhetoric, Leadership, and Partisanship in the Early Republic* (Kent, Ohio: Kent State University Press, 1982), 114-126; Robert L. Ivie, "The Metaphor of Force in Prowar Discourse: The Case of 1812," *The Quarterly Journal of Speech* 68 (1982): 240-253; and Robert L. Ivie, "Speaking 'Common Sense' About the Soviet Threat: Reagan's Rhetorical Stance," *Western Journal of Speech Communication* 48 (1984): 39-50.

112. Kenneth Burke, *The Rhetoric of Religion: Studies in Logology* (Berkeley and Los Angeles: University of California Press, 1970).

113. Hugh D. Duncan, *Symbols in Society* (New York: Oxford University Press, 1968), 146;   Hugh D. Duncan, *Symbols and Social Theory* (New York: Oxford University Press, 1969), 259.

114. Walt W. Rostow to Lyndon B. Johnson, LBJ Library, NSC Country File: Vietnam.

115. Larry Berman, *Planning a Tragedy: The Americanization of the War in Vietnam* (New York: W. W. Norton, 1982), 130.

116. For a discussion of Truman's literalizing rhetoric, see Robert L. Ivie, "Literalizing the Metaphor of Soviet Savagery: President Truman's Plain Style," *Southern Speech Communication Journal* 51 (1986): 91-105.

117. S. Hoffman, "Détente," in *The Making of America's Soviet Policy*, ed. J. S. Nye, Jr. (New Haven, Conn.:   Yale University Press, 1984), 231-263.

118. S. P. Huntington, "Renewed Hostility," in Nye, *Making of America's Soviet Policy*, 268, 289.

119. See Ground Zero, *What About the Russians*, for an overview of established perceptions of the Soviets, both negative and positive.

120. For example, Caldicott, *Missile Envy*, 350-367.

121. George F. Kennan, *The Nuclear Delusion: Soviet-American Relations in the Atomic Age* (New York: Pantheon, 1982), 197.

122. Turbayne, *Myth of Metaphor*, 65.

123. Lifton and Falk, *Indefensible Weapons*, 242.

124. Ibid., 242.

125. D. P. Barash and J. E. Lipton, *Stop Nuclear War! A Handbook* (New York: Grove Press, 1982), 9, 44.

126. J. L. Gaddis, *Strategies of Containment: A Critical Appraisal of Postwar American National Security Policy* (New York: Oxford University Press, 1982).

PART III
IDEOLOGY

8

Critical and Classical Theory: An Introduction to Ideology Criticism

Philip Wander

Rhetoric and ideology limit choices and guide the decisions of men [and women]. For [they] are influenced in their use of the powers they possess, by the rhetoric they feel they must employ, and by the ideological coin in which they transact affairs with one another. The leaders as well as the led, even the hired mythmakers and hack apologists, are influenced by their own rhetoric of justification and the ideological consolidation that prevails.[1]

C. Wright Mills

Ideology criticism does not represent another technique, a new approach to criticism embedded in some mysterious European intellectual tradition. First introduced by French revolutionaries, the term "ideology" referred to the critical study of ideas. Napoleon, annoyed by attacks on his policies and the myths used to justify them, contrasted ideology with knowledge of the heart and the lessons of history. Ideologues, in his view, were mere intellectuals, impractical thinkers with subversive impulses. Marx appropriated the term and used it to mean the ruling ideas of the ruling class. He stressed the connection between established economic interests and the spiritual formulations in law, religion, and philosophy growing out of them and working in their favor. In the twentieth century, critical theorists, those associated with the Frankfurt school of sociology, noting that even the term "Marxism" can be exploited in defense of an established order, used it to designate the lack of totality or completeness in any attempt to generalize. Ideology, in this view, encompasses not only the partiality or party interest in any formulation, but also the connection between what is embraced or concealed and the interests served by a particular formulation.

While one may intone a phrase like "ideology criticism" with a solemn and mysterious look, it lives on in the world of affairs as robust common sense—skepticism not as a well of life, but as a leavening making its way among high-sounding ideals, innocence, and hype.   No credo, however lyrical, authentically expressed, or truly believed, should escape cross-examination.

Criticism takes an ideological turn when it recognizes the existence of powerful vested interests benefiting from and consistently urging policies and technology that threaten life on this planet, when it realizes that we search for alternatives.   The situation is being constructed; it will not be averted either by ignoring it or placing it beyond our province.   An ideological turn in modern criticism reflects the existence of crisis, acknowledges the influence of established interests and the reality of alternative world views, and commends rhetorical analyses not only of the actions implied but also of the interests represented.   More than informed talk about matters of importance, criticism carries us to the point of recognizing good reasons and engaging in right action.   What an ideological view does is to situate "good" and "right" in historical context, the efforts of real people to create a better world.[2]

IDEOLOGY CRITICISM: CRITICAL AND CLASSICAL THEORY

Experience shows us
Wealth unchaperoned
by Virtue is never
an innocuous neighbor[3]

(Sappho)

Although I have something against the Aristotelian virtue of moderation and of the mean, I do feel myself drawn to the middle in questions like this (between theorists of continuity and theorists of total discontinuity).   In any case one has to look at it as an empirical question: in which historical situations could and should fairly strong continuities be preserved with a declining social formation, and in which situations would almost anything have to be rejected to achieve even the smallest step toward emancipation?[4]

(Jürgen Habermas)

The theory underlying ideology criticism—Critical Theory[5]—is not confined to a modern world.   There are two related lines of argument here, one embedded in the debate between the modernists and post-modernists, and the other in the debate between the ancients and the moderns.   With regard to postmodernism, Critical Theory inquires into the social and political conditions for constructing even a postmodernist future. If the possibility for a future exists, if it represents an alternative, and if a collective effort is required to create it, if in other words postmodernism is able to get beyond witnessing the unpresentable to conceive of the possibility for acting, it too will entertain the effort to draw together the displaced, decentered, deconstructed, and the marginal. In this moment, archaeological sites, carnivals, and rock concerts give way to more functional staging areas. In this moment, public deliberation once again becomes important and a rhetoric of difference will yield to a rhetoric of similarity or sameness.[6]

With regard to the debate between the ancients and the moderns and, if they are momentarily reconciled, postmoderns, Critical Theory rehabilitates what I shall call Classical Theory in two ways. One fixes on the moment, referred to above, in which the problem of concerted activity presents itself. In our time, this problem includes the limited access to political action (praxis) allowed publics in a world dominated by *techne* and a science based not on dialogue but on the monologues of order and control. Jürgen Habermas contrasts this modern condition with the meaning of praxis in classical and renaissance rhetorical theory:

Unlike the mere technical application of scientific results, the translation of theory into praxis is faced with the task of entering into the consciousness and convictions of citizens prepared to act: theoretical solutions must be interpreted in concrete situations as the practically necessary solutions for the satisfaction of objective needs—indeed, they must be conceived from the very outset with this perspective of active human beings. It is in this sense that Vico recommends the art of rhetoric, which "throughout deals with the audience to which it is addressed." This art knows that truths which are to have consequences require a consensus prudentially attained: this is the "semblance" of truth in the *sensus communis* of citizens participating in public discussion.[7]

Critical Theory recovers a classical (i.e., ancient Greek) notion of praxis grounded in an effort to achieve a consensus required for cooperation within and among politically active audiences or publics.

A second way Critical Theory recovers Classical Theory is through its Marxist orientation. The Frankfurt school of critical theorists—Max Horkheimer, Theodore Adorno, Walter Benjamin, Herbert Marcuse, and more recently Jürgen Habermas, among others—are variously referred to as Marxists, Marxist-Hegalians, or neo-Marxists. It is, in our world, important to acknowledge this, but it is also important to break the silence this often evokes or the satisfaction it sometimes inspires. Joining Critical Theory with Marxism may, because of political fears and prejudices, obscure its connection with the ancient world.

That there is a connection should not be all that surprising. As a German doctoral student, Marx studied Greek and read the ancients. In a letter to his father, November 10, 1837, Marx mentions, as part of his studies, translating part of Aristotle's *Rhetoric*.[8] Marx's interest in Aristotle, however, was more than merely academic. Three years later, in 1840, he planned a work on the subject of dialectic, took extensive notes on Aristotle, and proposed to write a critique of a contemporary author demonstrating that whereas Aristotle was dialectical the German

philosopher was merely formal.[9]   Seventeen years later, in a letter to
Ferdinand Lassale (December 21, 1857), Marx thanked him for sending
him a copy of his book on Heraclitus: "I have always had a tenderness
for that philosopher, whom, among the classics, I prefer to all others
except Aristotle."[10]

Greek philosophy, Aristotle's work in particular, was an important
influence on Marx's political theory. Alan Gilbert, a Marxist scholar,
comments on this influence: "Marx characterized Aristotle as that 'giant
thinker' who 'first analyzed so many forms of thought, society and
nature.' His [Marx's] broad judgments about human goods resemble
Aristotle's eudaimonism; his novel social theory reveals the appropriate
social and political arrangements for furthering a good life."[11] The link is
important. It means, among other things, that Critical Theory in general
and ideology criticism in particular cannot and should not be confined
either to modern or radical treatments of society and politics.

The links between Critical and Classical Theory call for a rereading of
Aristotle, one which goes beyond studying his lectures in isolation.
Christopher Lyle Johnstone, a rhetorical theorist, argues that Aristotle's
discussion of rhetoric, no matter how carefully done or how steeped in
contemporary scholarship, cannot be understood, unless it is read in
relation to his work on ethics and politics.[12] Once we read more of
Aristotle than what our specialized fields of study either demand or justify,
we confront the primacy of political science in his system, though as we
shall see his view of political science differs markedly from the statistically
based studies making up the study in our time. For Aristotle, sciences
dealing with subjects for which change is possible are subordinated to
politics. As Sir Ernest Barker, a translator and interpreter of Aristotle,
wrote at the turn of the twentieth century:

Science differs from science in the dignity of the end it serves: political science is the
greatest and most dignified of all practical [as opposed to theoretical sciences which
study phenomena which cannot be altered by humankind] sciences, because its end is
the ultimate end to which all others are subservient, the end of man's life. . . .
Political science is a master-science, 'architectonic' in its character, from which all
other practical sciences take their cue.

The primacy of politics among the practical sciences and the subordination
of other practical sciences to it, is quite clear; so is the audience for and
the agents of this science. Barker continues:

By political science they [the legislator and statesman] have learned to know both the
end and the means; by political science they impart their knowledge to others.
Political science, therefore, must needs be the master science, declaring what other
sciences are to be studied, and by whom, and to what extent: it must needs have
subject to itself the science which men most value, like economics, strategy, and
rhetoric.[13]

When the *Rhetoric* is related to the *Ethics* on the one hand, and the *Poetics* on the other, and these three works are subordinated to the *Politics*, what we discover are not arbitrary prescriptions or tedious and dated descriptions, but a meditation on individual and collective action, the production of culture (speeches and plays), and the nature of the polis.

Politics, in Classical Theory, concerns the struggle for power in Greek city-states. Aristotle tells us that, in each city-state, there were those who favored rule by one in the interests of stability (monarchy); those who wanted rule by one in order to enjoy the fruits of power (tyranny); those who favored rule by the few in the interests of wealth (oligarchy); those who favored rule by the few in the interests of the polity (aristocracy); those who favored rule by the many in the interests of the poor (democracy); and those who favored rule by the many in the interests of power (anarchy).

Politics, in Classical Theory, also includes a critical component and commitment to act. Aristotle did not simply describe or identify groups struggling for power, he favored one group over the others—the aristocracy. But by this he did not mean a monied aristocracy, as we now think of it, but a philosophical one, roughly equivalent to what we now call the technocracy. Quite clearly, Classical Theory is not democratic. It is, from a democratic point of view, offensive to suggest that a few citizens have superior sensibilities, training, or breadth of vision, and should therefore rule. Plato is no more inspiring on this issue, as Socrates, in the *Republic*, makes a case for a monarchy. Add to this Aristotle's celebration of slavery (widely quoted in the South prior to the Civil War), domination of women, and acquiescence in, if not enthusiasm, for wars against barbarians (i.e., non-Greeks) as part of the "natural" scheme of things, and it becomes tempting to dismiss Aristotle and with him all of Classical Theory as a bastion of elitism, sexism, and racism.

Before throwing up our hands, we need to follow the argument in Classical Theory beyond the limits imposed by our sense of indignation. I do not believe that reading Aristotle or Plato will cause us to stray in these matters. What we stand to gain by going on is not only an understanding, but also an appreciation for the relevance of other arguments advanced in Classical Theory. What we stand to gain is: (1) an appreciation for what democracy means coupled with its possibilities, its limitations, and its dangers, and (2) a sense of historical context which not only gives meaning to theory, but also enables us to move analogically back and forth between ancient and contemporary in a way that illuminates both.

With regard to democratic government, for example, Aristotle, despite his preference for aristocratic rule, rejects the notion that a philosopher-king or a group of philosophers or "experts" should enjoy absolute power. While any individual citizen may be a worse judge than an expert, he observes, ordinary people, when allowed to deliberate, are in no way inferior, and they often prove superior. Aristotle also reminds us that there are areas in which the philosopher-expert, no matter how intelligent or well-trained, is not as good a judge as those unskilled or ignorant of the art in question. Who, for example, is in the best position to judge a feast? Not the chef, answers Aristotle, but the person who sits down to the feast, the diner. Who is in the best position to judge a house? Not the builder, but the person who must live in it, the dweller. Who then is in the best position to judge the adequacy of the laws? This is the important question. Not the legislator, concludes Aristotle, but the citizen who must live under them.

There are also various temptations facing real people which may be concealed when treating experts or philosophers as ideal types, social roles, or professional abstractions. Living, breathing, desiring, suffering people in the here-and-now find wealth, power, and special privilege alluring. Personal profit is too often and too easily equated with the public good. When they are confused by an aristocrat, he or she no longer works in the interests of the polis and the good life, but has instead become one more member of the party favoring rule by the few in the interests of wealth.[14]

Aristotle's aristocracy refers to a group of citizens that works for the good of all citizens. They belong to no one party or faction. They are not, however, merely dreamers or isolated theorists. They actively seek out a constituency. The constituency they court consists of other citizens who do not endorse the workings of any one party or faction. This constituency is not an aggregate of apathetic, quiescent citizens—a silent majority; on the contrary, this group (it is a group because the members actually meet and deliberate the issues), situated between the oligarchs on the one hand and the democrats on the other, is decidedly active. Not only Aristotle, but Classical Theory in general looked on apolitical citizens as a contradiction. Such people were not regarded as prudent or neutral. They were thought to be addled.

In concert with a nonaligned, but no less active in-between or "middle" class, the aristocrats were to protect the polis from factional abuse, a problem that becomes especially acute during periods of crisis, when one side or the other, unable to tolerate the chaos, begins to organize around a powerful leader (i.e., a demagogue). Demagogues offer rule by one inside a party and, therefore, if the party is successful in its struggle for power it threatens the polis with Caesarism, the man-on-the-white-horse (Napoleonism), Hitlerism, Stalinism; in brief, tyrannical rule.

There are differences within Classical Theory, not only between Plato and Aristotle, but also among Plato, Aristotle, and the sophists.[15] The differences within Classical Theory and between Classical and Critical Theory, however, must be situated historically if we are to relate them to one another and to politics in our time. Critical Theory encounters a modern world dominated by entrenched oligarchic interests—*corporate* in the case of capitalism, *bureaucratic* in the case of centralized socialism. During periods of crisis in Germany and the Soviet Union, when the established order fell, the move was not toward democracy but toward tyranny—fascism, military dictatorship, personality cults. Consequently, Critical Theory therefore takes up the problem of democracy—how to protect and create an effective coalition of the many, including workers, the poor, women, minorities, gays, senior citizens, and the handicapped. It studies ways of reducing oligarchic and tyrannical power—the ideology and structures encouraging concentrations of wealth and power in a world largely dominated by such interests.

Classical Theory, especially that part of it represented by Socrates, Thucydides, Plato, and Aristotle, takes up not the collapse of democracy but the problem of civil war. During the Peloponnesian War (B.C. 431-404), oligarchic factions in the Greek city-states aligned with Sparta, while democratic factions aligned with Athens. First one side, and then the other would capture the city, using its power to hunt down and destroy the enemy. Thucydides describes the personal, cultural, and political impact of these wars:

Revolutions broke out in city after city, and in places where the revolutions occurred late the knowledge of what had happened previously in other places caused still new extravagances of revolutionary zeal, expressed by an elaboration in the methods of seizing power and by unheard-of atrocities in revenge.

Language itself was destroyed, and with it the public space and public speech, the instruments necessary for creating and recreating a commons (i.e., "communicating"):

To fit in with the change of events, words, too, had to change their usual meanings. What used to be described as a thoughtless act of aggression was now regarded as the courage one would expect to find in a party member; to think of the future and wait was merely another way of saying one was a coward; any idea of moderation was just an attempt to disguise one's unmanly character; ability to understand a question from all sides meant that one was totally unfitted for action. Fanatical enthusiasm was the mark of a real man, and to plot against an enemy behind his back was perfectly legitimate self-defense. Anyone who held violent opinions could always be trusted, and anyone who objected to them became a suspect. To plot successfully was a sign of intelligence, but it was still more clever to see that a plot was hatching.

The dangers lay not in speech or program, often these sounded innocent enough, but in motive and means:

Love of power, operating through greed and through personal ambition, was the cause of all these evils. To this must be added the violent fanaticism which came into play once the struggle had broken out.   Leaders of parties in the cities had programmes which appeared admirable—on one side political equality for the masses, on the other the safe and sound government of the aristocracy—but in professing to serve the public interest they were seeking to win the prizes for themselves.   In their struggles for ascendancy nothing was barred; terrible indeed were the actions to which they committed themselves, and in taking revenge they went farther still.   Here they were deterred neither by the claims of justice nor by the interests of the state; their one standard was the pleasure of their own party at that particular moment.[16]

The result was that the moderates, or, in Aristotle's system, the middle classes, were destroyed. The struggle became polarized, bringing with it the warlike logic of either/or: friend or foe, good or evil, victory or defeat. The diplomatic logic of both/and collapsed, and politics came to mean the commingling of opportunism and deceit, the good life becoming little more than a dream.

In this context, Classical Theory asks how ordinary citizens can lead a good life free of the fear of civil war. When violent conflict is the rule and neither side can win, but can only achieve power long enough to terrify the other, theory seeks to understand how it is possible to avoid carnage on the one hand, and tyranny on the other. At least this was the course taken by Classical Theory. Plato, in his famous seventh letter, writes that anyone with some small measure of right opinion "must be aware that those who have engaged in civil war can never rest from their troubles until those who are victorious cease to keep feuds alive by contention and by sentencing men to exile or death, and cease to execute vengeance on the opposing party."[17] He recommends self-control and equitable laws. Aristotle, responding to the same problem, calls for an aristocracy that rises above party and faction, whose vision of the good is grounded in an ideal, law, or Nature, and a polis dedicated to making the good life possible.   In Aristotle's view, the agents for change are statesmen and legislators who seek a middle way—a political golden mean—by balancing opposing forces.

This difference in historical context, between the crisis occasioned by oligarchic control and that occasioned by ongoing civil war, explains why Critical Theory can advance policies, heightening class conflict and goals such as sharing wealth and power (i.e., socialism), which Classical Theory, following Aristotle, is obliged to oppose. As Aristotle remarks:

We must admit that a system which gives equal properties to all the citizens has a certain advantage, in that it helps to prevent mutual discord; but the advantage, on the whole, is inconsiderable. Men of education would be aggrieved by the system, feeling that they deserved something more than mere equality; indeed, as a matter of actual observation, they often rise in revolt and cause civic discord for this very reason.[18]

Such programs would exacerbate the crisis Classical Theory would resolve. They threaten and would be seen as a threat by the oligarchy.

Faced with a loss of power or with expropriation, the oligarchy would fight; faced with the inability to enjoy inequality, they would rebel. This conclusion followed decades of bloody, enervating, and disastrous wars in Greek city-states all over the ancient world.

This does not mean that Classical Theory is oblivious to the dangers of great wealth. Aristotle warns against accumulating more than is necessary to run the household, because it diverts one from the good life. He urges a system of moral training to educate citizens in the right attitude toward wealth and property. Ultimately, Aristotle rejects oligarchic rule, because the pursuit of wealth—one citizen accumulating at the expense of another—destroys the bonds of community. It leads to class conflict and increases the likelihood of war.

We have noted differences between Classical and Critical Theory over politics and economics and situated them in their respective historical contexts. We may now consider their similarities. Both Classical and Critical theory oppose the acquisitive impulse and stress the political dangers posed by economic elites. In a footnote to his translation of Aristotle's *Politics*, Barker compares the ancient Greeks, including Plato, Thucydides, and Aristotle, with Marx. There is, he writes, "a steady theme of Greek political theory that political power tends to be used, and should not be used, to secure economic advantages. That theme was not the invention of Marx—though he varied and amplified it."[19] Accordingly, Critical and Classical Theory employ some form of class analysis—the struggle between rich and poor, capitalist and proletariat—to explain conflict.

There is another difference between Classical and Critical Theory, apart from their approaches to politics and economics, having to do with wars between city-states. Aristotle thought such wars natural. The superior—the more powerful or more civilized—will and should dominate the less powerful and uncivilized. This appeal of natural domination applies not only to peoples inside the polis, as between masters and slaves and men and women, but also between city-states. Where there is conflict among citizens or equals, they may, inside the polis, seek justice. Outside the polis, in conflicts between city-states, there is no such thing as justice, for no power or authority exists outside the polis able to adjudicate disputes or enforce agreements between city or nation-states.

While holding war between city-states natural (in contrast to wars inside a city-state), Classical Theory is critical of imperialism. Aristotle adopts a cynical attitude, declaring that those who believe in the cause of empire do so "on the ground that empire leads to a large accession of material prosperity."[20] Plato is also quite critical of Pericles's foreign policy. Socrates, in the *Phaedrus*, denies that Pericles was a statesman, and in the *Menexenus*, ridicules Pericles's funeral oration, claiming that it was written by someone else, Aspasia, who taught both Pericles and himself how to speak, and warning against the tendency of such speeches to enchant and inspire in Athenians a false and troubling sense of what we would now call national superiority.

But among the Greeks, it was Thucydides who systematically explores the issue of empire. Thucydides studied oratory under Antiphon, and his history of the Peloponnesian War may usefully be thought of as a speech, especially since he approaches his subject not as a recorder of events but as a critic trying to warn future generations. Thucydides inveighs against a policy of empire for two reasons: It leads to defeat, and it destroys the moral resources of the imperialist state.

Why does the path of imperialism lead to defeat? Not because of the intervention of the gods, but because the fear of an expanding power will cause its weaker neighbors to form alliances against a common threat. The greater the threat the stronger the alliance, until finally the expanding state reaches its limits and, pressed by its enemies, begins to collapse back on itself.

But even in moments of success, an imperial power will encounter failure, or rather risks such a transformation in traditional values that, culturally speaking, it begins to be dominated by all that it opposes. With the defeat of Athens's expansionist policies, Thucydides also explores the impact such policies had on the values of justice and democracy at home and abroad. The speech embedded in Thucydides's history that justifies a policy of domination is Pericles's funeral oration (B.C. 431). Pericles, in this speech, celebrates Athenian culture:

Our Constitution is called a democracy because power is in the hands not of a minority but of the whole people. When it is a question of settling private disputes, everyone is equal before the law; when it is a question of putting one person before another in positions of public responsibility, what counts is not membership of a particular class, but the actual ability which the man possesses. No one, so long as he has it in him to be of service to the state, is kept in political obscurity because of poverty.

Athenian democracy emphasized free and open deliberation:

We Athenians, in our own persons, take our decision on policy or submit them to proper discussions: for we do not think that there is an incompatibility between words and deeds; the worst thing is to rush into action before the consequences have been properly debated.

Because of these and other virtues, concludes Pericles, no enemy who invades is ashamed of being defeated, and no subject can complain of being governed by a people unfit for their responsibilities. Mighty indeed are the marks and monuments of our empire, he boasts. In the future people will marvel at us, just as people in the present age wonder at us now.[21]

But there is a second speech by Pericles included in Thucydides's history. This speech, not nearly so famous, was given in the year following the funeral oration (B.C. 430), when Athens's military fortunes had turned and the city was suffering a plague. In this speech, Pericles admits that, in contrast to his earlier speech, his policies have little to do with democratic values. In relation to other city-states, they are tyrannical. Inside Athens itself, they could not easily be called democratic. Regarding those citizens who criticized his policies, who would debate them and spell out their consequences, he declared that such people are fit only to be citizens of city-states dominated by Athens.

This retreat from democratic values in Thucydides's narrative becomes a rout in the Mytelinian debate, when Cleon, Pericles's successor and leader of the democratic party in Athens, calls for the massacre of all adult males in a city-state rebelling against Athens. Cleon questions the appropriateness of a democratic form of government carrying out such policies:

Personally I have had occasion already to observe that a democracy is incapable of governing others. . . . What you do not realize is that your empire is a tyranny exercised over subjects who do not like it and who are always plotting against you; you will not make them obey you by injuring your own interests in order to do them a favour; your leadership depends on superior strength and not on any goodwill of theirs.

Not only is rule by the many a hinderance, but so also are many of the virtues associated with it and the discursive practices it implicitly commends:

To feel pity, to be carried away by the pleasure of hearing a clever argument, to listen to the claims of decency are three things that are entirely against the interests of an imperial power. Do not be guilty of them.[22]

Cleon loses the vote. In the Milian dialogue, however, Athenian ambassadors demand the surrender of a Spartan colony that had remained neutral in the war between Athens and Sparta. The Athenians threaten them with destruction if they do not comply. The Milians object to this injustice. The ambassadors respond that justice is not that which pleases the gods or which enables those in power to act in a fair and equitable manner; rather, justice has become what the strong can compel of the weak. The Milians deliberate and decide to fight. They are willing to risk destruction to avoid being enslaved. In the end they are overcome, and the victorious Athenians execute every adult male and sell the women and children into slavery.[23]

Breaking off Thucydides's argument against Athenian imperialism, let us fold it back into Classical Theory and its relationship to Critical Theory. If there is any utility to exploring the similarities within and between Classical and Critical Theory, it lies in what they together have to say about wealth, war, realpolitik, imperialism, and community values. Their differences should not be overlooked—as with naturalness of war and the social structure, the dangers of economic reform, and the threat of criticism in the polis. But these differences must be placed in historical context. As M. I. Finley, comparing ancient and modern utopias, has said:

Utopian ideas and fantasies, like all ideas and fantasies, grow out of the society to which they are a response. Neither the ancient world nor the modern world is an unchanging entity, and any analysis of Utopian thinking which neglects social changes in the course of the history of either antiquity or modern times is likely at some point to go badly wrong.[24]

Regarding political theory differences in the agency for change, the nature and purpose of the actions being commended, the place and role of the agent (critic or legislator) become more an argument for respecting the here-and-now of purpose and historical struggle than an argument for the incompatibility of two sets of abstract or abstracted ideas.

IDEOLOGY CRITICISM IN THE MODERN WORLD

Democracy was not merely patriotic in its origins: it could become imperialistic too. The French made this discovery after 1870, the Americans somewhat later. Both took pains to hide the truth from themselves.[25]

(George Lichtheim, *Imperialism*)

The war that goes on is our war
for our own land. To take it,
to hold it
to form it again new
out of nightmare splitting
open into dream:
half collage of cannibalized machines,
half wailing child.[26]

(Marge Piercy, "War, long war")

In the area of American foreign policy, Classical and Critical Theory address a similar rhetorical problem: democratic ideals used to justify domination of weaker countries. The United States has had a crisis over imperialism from the beginning. The march westward proceeded over the bodies of native Americans and Mexican nationals. A history of broken treaties signals a truth at odds with the story of the march of civilization, the truth of an expansionist war and the expropriation of other peoples' land. The crisis expanded in the nineteenth century with repeated invasions by U.S. troops into Central and South America, the "creation" of Panama, and the "acquisition" of the Philippines. It further expanded, after World War II, with the decision to consolidate the remnants of the old European empires and the ruins of the short-lived Japanese empire into that transnational entity known as the "free world." Those in power justified this vast increase of American responsibility through the threat represented by the Soviet Union. The efforts made by these two great empires, after World War II, to dominate various parts of the world and the conflicts this occasioned between them came to be known as the Cold War.

It is here, over the issue of war between city- or nation-states, however, that we discover another major difference between the concerns of Classical and Critical Theory. For Classical Theory, civil war was unthinkable; it destroyed the polis; without the polis political activity and philosophical contemplation, civilization itself is no longer possible. For us, however, the unthinkable, the unspeakable, the horrifying has to do not with civil war, but in Olga Cabral's words, with megadeath, megawars, megadust, megakill.[27]

Whatever their differences, Critical and Classical Theory agree that in political matters the end does not lie in understanding. Both reject amoral, apolitical, ahistorical criticism. Both are interventionist, leading the critic and his or her audience, in light of what is, to ask what ought to be done. Plato writes, explaining his motives for advising the Tyrant of Syracuse, that his chief concern was his own self-respect: "I feared to see myself at last altogether nothing but words, so to speak—a man who would never willingly lay hand to any concrete task."[28] Aristotle is also clear on this matter. How is it possible for a person to become just, he asks. One becomes just, he says, by performing just actions. There is no other way, though this is not, he admits, a popular line to take:

. . . men [and women] preferring theory to practice under the impression that arguing about morals proves them to be philosophers, and that in this way they will turn out to be fine characters. Herein they resemble invalids, who listen carefully to all the doctor says but do not carry out a single one of his orders. The bodies of such people will never respond to treatment—nor will the souls of such "philosophers."[29]

Habermas, in addressing the question of practice (praxis), similarly argues that criticism ("critique") is moved by practical interests in resolving a crisis favorably, in light of the good. Echoing Aristotle, Habermas uses the metaphor of a physician, but with a subtle and important difference. Whereas Aristotle likens the philosopher to a physician and his or her audience to patients, Habermas likens the critic along with his or her audience (i.e., Man) to a physician. In this way, he reminds a democratically inclusive us—speakers and hearers—of our involvement in the object of criticism:

All efforts are equally condemned to remain without consequences, if they do not go beyond critique and intervene in the crisis, employing the means of the crisis itself, namely practically. . . . Because the crisis, become world-historical, overpowers every merely subjective critique, the decision is shifted over into praxis, so that only by the success of this praxis can the critique itself become valid.[30]

Why are things not other than as they are?   What are the practical alternatives?   What ought to be done?

It should have become clear by now, as Michael Calvin McGee has argued, that ideology criticism, informed by either Critical or Classical Theory, is not simply one perspective among many open to the critic. This grudging inclusion into the guild of academic critics illustrates what Herbert Marcuse called repressive tolerance.[31]   Ideology criticism is not a lens held up to the eye through which to see things differently.   It is more than seeing and thinking.   It is both a deliberating and a doing.   The questions animating ideology criticism are asked, not in the abstract, but in the here-and-now of historical struggle where the future is being constructed in the same way that the present, as an alternative future, was constructed in the past.

C. Wright Mills, writing simultaneously inside of, outside of, and about the limits and potential of an academic context, produced a body of ideology criticism in the 1950s and 1960s, a period in the United States when, for many academics, the threat of being called a Communist, fellow traveler, leftist, or subversive transformed silence on the great issues of the time into a prudent, if not a patriotic, act.

Mills taught sociology at Columbia University, but he refused to accept the fact that his professional standing obliged him either as a sociologist or a citizen to ignore the threat of nuclear war.   What, asked Mills, ought we as intellectuals, scientists, ministers, rabbis, and priests do in the face of this crisis?[32]   Mills probed the contradictions between what must be done, the limits set by gild ideology, and the values and principles underlying that ideology.   What scientist, asks Mills, can lay claim to the legacy of science and remain a hired technician of the military machine? What man or woman of God can claim to partake of the Holy Spirit and the community of man and woman and yet uphold the spiritual irresponsibility of the Caesars of our time?   What Western scholar can claim to be part of the discourse on reason and yet retreat into formal trivialities and exact nonsense in a world in which reason and freedom are being destroyed?   Here is, writes Mills, what we must do:

We must release the human imagination in order to open up a new exploration of the alternatives now possible for the human community; we must set forth general and detailed plans, ideas, vision; in brief, programs.   We must transcend the mere exhortation of general principle and opportunist reactions.   What are needed are commanding views of the future, and it is our opportunity to provide them.   We must develop and debate among ourselves—and then among larger publics—genuine programs; we must make of these programs *divisive* and *partisan* political issues within the U.S.A.

We must be willing to be polemical, to take on the great issues of our time. We find the ground for this response in *democratic* political theory:

We should take democracy seriously and literally. Insofar as we accept the democratic heritage—as not only our heritage but as of use and of value to the world tomorrow—we must realize that it has been a historically specific formation, brought about by a set of factors, a union of procedural devices and ideological claims quite specific to Western civilization; and that it is now in a perilous condition not only in the world but in the West itself, and especially in the United States of America.

Mills further urges intellectuals to engage in controversy, proceed in a way informed by democratic political theory, and explore channels of communication outside academic conventions and scholarly journals:

What we, as intellectual, ought to do with the formal means of communication—in which so many now commit their cultural default—is to use them as we think they ought to be used, or not to use them at all. We should assume that these means are among our means of production and work; that they have been arbitrarily expropriated from us, privately and illegitimately incorporated; and that they are now being used for stupid and corrupting purposes, which disgrace us before the world and before ourselves. We should claim these means as important parts of our means of cultural endeavor, and we should attack those among us who prostitute their talents and disgrace us as an intellectual community. We should write and speak for the mass media on our own terms or not at all. We should attack those who allow themselves to be used by them merely for money or merely for prestige. We should make the mass media the means of liberal—which is to say, liberating—education.

Take on the controversial issues, revitalize democratic values, reach out to larger audiences in the name of humanity, urges Mills; he also emphasizes the importance of being an intellectual in America:

As intellectuals, and so as public men [and women], ought we not to act and work as if this peace, and the interchange of values, programs and ideas of which it consists, is everybody's peace, or surely ought to be? As Americans, we might realize the place in the world of the power of this nation, and we might take upon ourselves the responsibility of stating how it is being used and how we believe it ought to be used. As intellectuals of the world we should awake and unite with intellectuals everywhere.[33]

Such are the alternatives and obligations for intellectual work, grounded in Critical and Classical Theory, communicated through ideology criticism, and exemplified by Mills for whom the nuclear crisis called (and still calls) for open and honest debate over alternatives to annihilation.

CONCLUSION

I do not scream, it makes me proud.
I take to dying like a man.
I do it to impress the crowd.
My sin lies in not screaming loud.[34]

(Maya Angelou, "My Guilt")

For Socrates, Thucydides, Plato, and Aristotle the unimaginable lay in civil war and the destruction of the polis. For us the unspeakable lies in the destruction of all life on the planet, whether through a nuclear calamity or through the gradual collapse of the environment. This is why, in our time, democratic political theory cannot stop with improving the lot of the masses, but must also examine the means undertaken to achieve that end in light of their systemic impact. What is the agency for change in opposing imperialism, war, the production of nuclear weapons, nuclear and chemical wastes, the destruction of the ozone layer? What are the strengths and weaknesses of rule by the many in these tasks? What are the realities of political power now in relation to these issues, and what is the potential for change? There has never been a greater need to deliberate such practical matters.

NOTES

1. C. Wright Mills, *The Marxists* (New York: Dell Publishing Co., Inc., 1962), 27.

2. This introduction originally appeared in my essay, "The Ideological Turn in Modern Criticism," *Central States Speech Journal* 34 (Spring 1983): 1-18. For larger explorations of the issues involved, see the responses appearing in the next two issues of the journal and my rejoinder, "The Third Persona: An Ideological Turn in Rhetorical Theory," *Central States Speech Journal* 35 (Winter 1984): 197-216.

3. Sappho, "To an army wife, in Sardis," *Sappho*, trans. Mary Barnard (Berkeley: University of California Press, 1958), 86.

4. Cited in *Habermas: Autonomy and Solidarity*, ed. Peter Dews (London: Verso, 1986), 102-103.

5. See Max Horkheimer, "Traditional and Critical Theory," *Critical Theory: Selected Essays*, trans. Matthew J. O'Connell (New York: Seabury Press, 1972), 186-234.

6. That the distinction between a rhetoric of similarity and difference is politically important may be traced to Aristotle's *Topics* and his debates with the sophists during a period when Greek city-states were riven by political factions. Aristotle, interestingly enough, did not hold that

sophists could be identified according to the ways they argued, but by their motive or goals. Notes Habermas:

Forms of life are totalities which always emerge in the plural. Their coexistence may cause friction, but this difference does not automatically result in their incompatibility. Something similar is the case for the pluralism of values and belief systems. The closer the proximity in which competing 'gods and demons' have to live with each other in political communities, the more tolerance they demand; but they are not incompatible. Convictions can contradict one another only when those who are concerned with problems define them in a similar way, believe them to need resolution, and want to decide issues on the basis of good reasons" ("Questions and Counterquestions," *Habermas and Modernity*, ed. Richard J. Bernstein (Cambridge, Mass.: The MIT Press, 1985), 194.

On the debate over modernity, Richard Rorty seeks a reconciliation between postmodernism and Critical Theory over the possibility for social change ("Habermas and Lyotard on Modernity," *Habermas*, 161-175), while Russel Burman sees in the inability of postmodernism to envision an alternative to a postbureaucratic society or a place for culture in local communities or civil society as a failure to escape the categories of bureaucratic culture ("The Routinization of Charismatic Modernism and the Problem of Post-Modernity," *Cultural Critique* 5 [Winter 1986-87]: 49-65). For another effort to explore these issues, see my introduction to Henri Lefebre's *Everyday Life in the Modern World* (New Brunswick, N.J.: Rutgers University Press, 1983); and "The Politics of Despair," *Communication* (in press).

7. Jürgen Habermas, "The Classical Doctrine of Politics in Relation to Social Philosophy," *Theory and Practice*, trans. John Viertel (Boston: Beacon Press, 1973), 74-75.

Julia Kristeva also makes use of the classical tradition, in spite of its obvious limits for feminist theory:

Classical humanism helped dissolve the epic monologism that speech welded together so well, and that orators, rhetoricians and politicians on the one hand, tragedy and epic, on the other, implemented so effectively. . . . Socratic truth ("meaning") is the product of a dialogical relationship among speakers; it is correlational and its relativism appears by virtue of the observers' autonomous points of view (*The Kristeva Reader*, ed. Toril Moil [New York: Columbia University Press, 1986], 50-51).

This points to an important distinction in Classical Theory between Socrates and Aristotle, one that would be amended had Aristotle's reportedly graceful dialogues and Plato's technical works survived antiquity. It also recalls the debate between Sartre and Foucault over the critic as spokesperson for the universal and those silenced on the margins of society and life. The monological, consensual style of rhetoric, when deployed by those in power, can also efface difference, silence criticism, and marginalize the powerless.

It is not quite clear what the implications would be if the marginalized, the day after the carnival, if they were able to attend, were to engage in an oppositional, consensual, oppositional, and progressive style of discourse. Is this impossible? Would they be incorrect? Should we ignore them or the possibilities for such discourse in ourselves? These questions point, on the one hand, to a different moment in political analysis, a moment that may have passed, but the memory of which must be saved from nostalgia on one side and cynicism on the other as a living possibility and, on the other hand, to a different locus of concern (i.e., the problems of groups compared with those of individuals, and, where incompatibility threatens all life, international as well as domestic conflicts).

8. David McLellan, ed., *Karl Marx: Selected Writings* (New York: Oxford University Press, 1977), 8.

9. Saul K. Padover, trans., *The Letters of Karl Marx* (Englewood Cliffs, N.J.: Prentice-Hall, Inc., 1979), 419.

10. David McLellan, *Karl Marx: His Life and Thought* (New York: Harper & Row, 1973), 39.

11. Alan Gilbert, "Marx's Moral Realism: Eudaimonism and Moral Progress," in *After Marx*, ed. Terence Ball and James Farr (Cambridge: Cambridge University Press, 1984), 155.

12. Christopher Lyle Johnstone, "An Aristotelian Trilogy: Ethics, Rhetoric, Politics, and the Search for Moral Truth," *Philosophy and Rhetoric* 13 (1980): 1-24.

13. Sir Ernest Barker, *The Political Thought of Plato and Aristotle* (New York: Dover, 1959; originally published in 1906, rev. 1918), 239-244.

14. According to Gadamer, Plato's philosopher-king, when understood dialectically, argues not for installing such a ruler—this would be impossible on the face of it—but rather for appreciating the questionable ways in which leaders were in fact being selected in Athens. The call for the total elimination of the family, argues Gadamer, calls attention to the "ruinous role of family politics, nepotism, and the idea of dynastic power in the so-called democracy of Athens at that time (and not only there)" (Hans-Georg Gadamer, *The Idea of the Good in Platonic-Aristotelian Philosophy*, trans. P. Christopher Smith [New Haven, Conn.: Yale University Press, 1986], 71).

15. The term "Classical Theory," while useful in some ways, is misleading. Confined to Aristotle, the sophists are not included among classical theorists. The sophists introduce difference (both as a strategy and as a group of philosophers and rhetoricians). They question absolute ideas, Nature, and the rule of law as ways of justifying oppression and ordering society. Windelband comments on their politics:

Lycophron desired to do away with the nobility. Alcidamas and others combated slavery from this point of view. Phaleas demanded equality of property as well as of education for all citizens, and Hippodamus was the first to project the outlines of an ideal state, constituted according to reason. Even the thought of a political equality of women with men came to the surface in this connection (Wilhelm Windelband, *A History of Philosophy*, trans. James Tufts, vol. 1 [1901; reprint, New York: Harper Torchback, 1958], 74-75).

They are dissident voices, often preserved by Plato and Aristotle. They transform Classical Theory into a debate.

Donald Kagan takes the traditional view of this debate, pitting Socrates against the sophists ("Politics and Morality: The Sophists and Socrates," in *The Great Dialogue: History of Greek Political Thought from Homer to Polybius* [New York: The Free Press, 1965], 113-132), while Hans Meyerhoff, struck by Aristophanes' stinking, garrulous Socrates who teaches students how to produce arguments to avoid paying their debts, contrasts Socrates, the sophist who questions certainty, with Plato, the philosopher who needs to know ("From Socrates to Plato," in *The Critical Spirit: Essays in Honor of Herbert Marcuse*, ed. Kurt H. Wolff and Barrington Moore, Jr. [Boston: Beacon Press, 1967], 187-210).

16. Thucydides, *The Peloponnesian War*, trans. Rex Warner (New York: Penguin, 1958), 242-244.

17. Edith Hamilton and Huntington Cairns, ed., "Letter: VII (328, C-D)," trans. L.A. Post, *Plato* (Princeton: Princeton University Press, 1982), 1585.

18. Aristotle, *Politics*, trans. Ernest Barker (New York: Oxford University Press, 1969), 67.

19. Ibid., 230n.

20. Aristotle, *Ethics*, trans. J. A. K. Thomson (Baltimore: Penguin Books, 1966), 318.

21. Thucydides, *Peloponnesion War*, 145-148.

22. Ibid., 213-216.

23. M. I. Finley argues, on the basis of evidence internal to the dialogue, that it "represent Thucydides' own reflections, fairly late in the war (at least later than the Sicilian disaster . . .), about the moral problems of empire and power" (*Thucydides, Peloponnesian War*, 616).

24. M. I. Finley, "Utopianism Ancient and Modern," *The Critical Spirit*, 6.

25. George Lichtheim, *Imperialism* (New York: Praeger Publishers, 1971), 87.

26. Marge Piercy, "War, long war," in *The Twelve-Spoked Wheel Flashing* (New York: Alfred Knopf, 1978), 14.

27. Olga Cabral, *In the Empire of Ice* (Cambridge, Mass.: West End Press, 1980), 75.

28. Post, trans., "Letter: VII," 1,578.

29. Aristotle, *Ethics*, 62. Classical and Critical Theory are not alone in enjoining praxis. Secular and religious humanism join forces in rejecting acquiescence. Thomas Merton, for example, writes:

It is one thing to form one's conscience and another to adopt a specific policy or course of action. It is highly regrettable that this important distinction is overlooked and indeed deliberately obfuscated. To decide, in the forum of conscience, that one is obligated in every way, as a Christian, to avoid actions that would contribute to a world-wide disaster, does not mean that one is necessarily committed to absolute and unqualified pacifism. One may start from this moral principle, which is repeatedly set before us by the Popes and which cannot be seriously challenged, and one may then go on to seek various means to preserve peace. About these different means, there may be considerable debate. . . . It is no longer reasonable or right to leave all decision to a largely anonymous power elite that is driving us all, in our passivity, towards ruin. We have to make ourselves heard ("Peace: A Religious Responsibility," *The Nonviolent Alternative*, ed. Gordon Zahn [New York: Farrar, Straus, Giroux, 1980], 125-127).

The link among classical philosophy, contemporary social criticism, and theology makes itself known through an obligation to go beyond the merely academic, the boundaries erected between professionals and reason, compassion, and profound spiritual insight. Hans Küng notes the affinities between Critical Theory and Christian theology and quotes Max Horkheimer approvingly when he writes: "Politics that does not contain theology within itself, however little considered, may often be shrewd but remains in the end no more than a business" (*Does God Exist?* [New York: Vintage Books, 1981], 490).

30. Habermas, "Classical Doctrine of Politics," 214. Habermas makes a distinction between *techne* and *praxis*. Following Hannah Arendt and Hans-Georg Gadamer, he refuses to reduce politics to technical administration or power to force. Instead, according to Martin Jay, Habermas embraces "Aristotle's concept of *phronesis* as the proper model for the political realm, where a prudent consideration of alternatives should be carried out through an uncoerced process of discursive reasoning" (Martin Jay, *Marxism and Totality* [Berkeley: University of California Press, 1984], 476-477).

31. Michael Calvin McGee, "Another Phillipic: Notes on the Ideological Turn in Criticism," *Central States Speech Journal* 35 (Spring 1984): 43-50.

32. Here Mills adumbrates a potential coalition. For an attempt to identify this coalition as a class and an agent for socio-political change, see Alvin Gouldner's three-volume work on the "dark side of the dialectic" (*The Dialectic of Ideology and Technology* [New York: Seabury Press, 1976]; *The Future of Intellectuals and the Rise of the New Class* [New York: Seabury Press, 1979]; *The Two Marxisms* [New York: Seabury Press, 1980]).

33. C. Wright Mills, *The Causes of World War Three* (New York: Simon and Schuster, 1958), 139-145.

34. Maya Angelou, "My Guilt," *Just Give Me a Cool Drink of Water 'fore I Die* (New York: Random House, 1971), 42.

9

The Rhetoric of American Foreign Policy

Philip Wander

It is noble to avenge oneself on one's enemies and not to come to terms with them; for requital is just, and the just is noble; and not to surrender is a sign of courage. . . . We must also (with ceremonial oratory) take into account the nature of the particular audience . . . it is not difficult to praise the Athenians to an Athenian audience.

Aristotle

Like any other body of stock phrases or standardized code of expression, the rhetoric of American foreign policy protects us against reality, that is, against the claim on our attention that any event or fact makes by virtue of its existence. If one were always responsive to such claims, writes Hannah Arendt, one would soon be exhausted, and yet such claims must be kept firmly in mind if one is to remain alert to matters too important to be obscured by language.[1] "Defending the Free World," "protecting our National Security," "weighing our National Interest," "countering the Communist Menace," the language is familiar. It has, over the last half century, set aside whole worlds of fact and contained, when it did not encourage, some of the most disturbing events in American history.

In one sense, the commonplaces of such rhetoric are dictated by the occasions. They are part of a ritual wherein government officials represent foreign policy to the people. If talk about foreign policy is understood as a government's definition of the state's international objectives combined with a plan for reaching them and if policy expresses the needs and wants of the state whose fulfillment the government conceives of as beneficial, then the public justification of policy may or may not have any relation to the deliberation of policy. Ideology, according to one former State Department official in the early 1970s, plays little or no part in actual decisions which are garbed in moral terms to satisfy onlookers.[2]

In another sense, however, it will not do in politics to make too sharp a distinction between the contexts of justification and deliberation. Another student of international relations, Grant Hugo, worries about the tendency in foreign affairs to create a discrepancy between the natural meaning of words and their practical significance. He finds this tendency troubling because the speaker often ends up as misled as the audience, a problem which becomes apparent when a speaker or a government ends up publicly committed to a view of foreign affairs embracing impractical or dangerous policies.[3]

Apart from whether or not government officials try to mislead the public is the larger concern about how their words work. Whatever answer one gives to this question will greatly influence what one decides is an appropriate critical response. If it is assumed, for example, that official statements about foreign policy are supposed to express the thoughts of the speaker or reflect accurately the facts of the situation, criticism will proceed along lines of moral fault. Such criticism favors maxims about distortion and lying. An analysis of the speaking situation which includes institutional arrangements, sanctioned roles, and the existence of vested interests, however, will press beyond the claims of individual morality to understand the political system and its limitations. What I am suggesting is that a full understanding of the rhetoric of American foreign policy must take into account: (1) the ceremonial nature of that rhetoric; (2) its function in domestic politics; and (3) its relation to facts and events beyond the language employed, matters on which the lives of tens of millions, if not the whole of humanity, now depend.

DOMESTIC POLITICS AND FOREIGN POLICY RHETORIC

Placing rhetoric in relation to real people whose passivity, assent, or action has a bearing on a speaker enables us to get at the pragmatics of political communication. The pivotal term in communication theory is "audience," in political theory "group" or "party." The domestic audience for foreign policy address is in a position to determine whether or not an administrative advocate and his or her party will remain in power. Organized elements within that audience—economic interests, ethnic groups, popular socio-political movements—are in a position directly to influence the outcome of an election. Because America's relations with other governments may be of consequence, for economic, ethnic, or ideological reasons, to such groups, because national elections are determined on the basis of a given party's ability to link such groups into loose coalitions and to appeal to the mass electorate, foreign policy rhetoric takes on meaning in the context of domestic politics which would be lost in an exclusive focus on international relations.

This is not peculiar to the United States. In societies where relatively autonomous and conflicting groups struggle for power, observes Marcel Merel, a French scholar, the facts of international affairs tend to take on the coloring—light or dark—of the society envisioned by those seeking office.   Trapped in the contradiction between the demands of their representative function and those of their ambition to acquire power, he writes, the parties often have no choice but to camouflage the facts of international politics under the colors of domestic politics.[4] The "facts" not only reflect the world view of a particular party and the coalition it represents, but also, if only through negation, the world view and the "facts" promoted by rival parties and coalitions. It is this dynamic, I think, which explains why the rhetoric of American foreign policy seems, on the face of it, so empty, vague, and misleading.

Whatever attitude one takes toward foreign policy rhetoric, that it is meaningless, misleading, dangerously provocative, or following Merel, an important buffer between governments and excitable mass electorates; whatever special interests, political groups or institution one believes, on any given moment, to be most influential in shaping mass opinion, this much is clear.[5] A systematic examination of the rhetoric of American foreign policy will take into consideration a variety of audiences, the relative importance of any given audience within the context of domestic politics, and the ways in which official statements are or are not adapted to them. While the meaning of such rhetoric will not be exhausted in audience analysis—government action does have real and sometimes terrible consequences—any effort to understand or, for that matter, to change policy must take such audiences into account.

While the definition of audience in relation to statements about foreign policy is fairly clear, both in terms of historically identifiable groups and through survey opinion research, what constitutes an "argument" in debates over foreign policy presents a problem. It is tempting to leave the definition of argument operational—it is what we say it is. But argument in the world of affairs is not arbitrary. Foreign policy refers to actions undertaken by a government in relation to other nations. We do not, in this context, talk about propositions in the logical sense of statements about which something is affirmed or denied. And while we may define an argument as that which offers good grounds for supporting a proposal, stressing the facts of the situation, "facts" in foreign affairs even when knowable are so changeable, so responsive to political calculation, so shaped by differing points of view that one is soon driven from precise philosophical or scientific formulations.

The study of argument need not be abandoned because neither logic nor science provides an adequate body of rules for either definition or evaluation. If we are prepared to admit that there are times when formal definitions and technical solutions are not very useful, and assuming that

this is one of them, then we may proceed to study argument in context—the historical context in which real people were in fact debating what
for them were important issues. We can, therefore, approach debates over
foreign policy searching for arguments, grounding the meaning of those
arguments in a context of groups or parties engaged in a struggle for
political power, articulating that struggle through the ways such groups
spell out their interests in an effort to inspire their partisans, attract other
groups with whom coalitions might be formed, and recruit from that vast,
unorganized aggregate known as the "mass audience." Our definitions of
both audience and argument, therefore, are rooted in historical struggle
and the ideological conflicts in which they appear.

I have discussed the assumptions underlying ideological criticism for
political communication, mass media, and rhetorical theory and criticism
elsewhere;[6] I have also explored the world views or ideologies of
particular movements.[7] What follows is not another theoretical statement
or historical study, but a critique of the rhetoric of American foreign
policy. It begins with an attempt to isolate a mode of argument employed
during the early stages of American involvement in Vietnam, a mode I call
"prophetic dualism." The questions here concern the precise form this
argument takes, its function in and relation to political coalitions arrayed
under, represented, or sought out by the Democratic and Republican
parties at the time, and its implications for the formulation and conduct of
foreign policy.

The essay then turns to another mode of argument employed in
Vietnam, this during a period when decisions were being justified over the
number of advisors to be stationed there, and later, whether or not more
combat troops were needed, a mode I call "technocratic realism." This
argument will also be considered in light of Democratic and Republican
political coalitions and the implications it holds for the conduct of foreign
policy.

Finally, this essay examines the ground of foreign policy rhetoric, what
"prophetic dualism" and "technocratic realism" agree upon, an agreement
so fundamental that it has become tacit public knowledge. We will
consider this agreement in relation to interests working to influence
government policy, whoever is in power, over the expenditure of public
funds on the military and the making and enforcing of economic, political,
and military commitments.

The debate over American foreign policy, with the pressures of
overpopulation, environmental destruction, the development of weapons of
terrifying potential, and the depletion of natural resources, will grow more
intense. Apart from the arms race, which receives most of the attention,
and rightfully so, are problems associated with a projected decline of raw
materials—manganese, cobalt, chromium, aluminum, tin, nickel, petro-
leum, iron, titanium, etc.—necessary for the operation of modern

technological societies. With this decline, we can expect more energetic competition between nations over both markets and raw materials. Surveying this prospect, Paul Varg warns against the attractions of "gut nationalism." Domestic politics in the United States and other liberal democracies are not divorced from questions of foreign relations. Foreign policy issues, he notes, have traditionally been used to secure party advantage. But we can no longer afford political partisanship that exploits popular ignorance for the sake of taking office.[8] The dangers are real; the need for debate over our "national interest" obvious.[9] This essay is a preface to such a debate.

"PROPHETIC DUALISM": THE EISENHOWER-DULLES ADMINISTRATION

On April 6, 1984 at the Georgetown Center for Strategic and International Studies, President Reagan denounced second-guessing in Congress about keeping American forces in Lebanon. "Unfortunately," he complained, "many in Congress seem to believe they are still in the troubled Vietnam era . . . clearly Congress is less than wholly comfortable with both the need for a military element in foreign policy and its own responsibility to deal with that element."[10] He ended his speech with a discussion of the "lessons" to be learned from Vietnam. He was right; there are lessons to be learned, but not necessarily those he would teach. In the early 1950s, during the Eisenhower-Dulles administration, a prominent and recurring argument supporting American policy in Vietnam concerned America's moral or spiritual superiority. Religious faith, moral insight, a respect for the laws of God formed a set of virtues attributed to the nation which, as we shall see, could be called upon not only to explain why those in power deserved to be there, but also why the United States should engage in certain kinds of action abroad. The argument, as it appears in statements about foreign policy, I shall call "prophetic dualism."

In its perfected form prophetic dualism divides the world into two camps. Between them there is conflict. One side acts in accord with all that is good, decent, and at one with God's will. The other acts in direct opposition. Conflict between them is resolved only through the total victory of one side over the other. Since no guarantee exists that good-will triumphs, there is no middle ground. Hence neutrality may be treated as a delusion, compromise appeasement, and negotiation a call for surrender. [11]

To appreciate this argument and how it works requires one to go beyond denunciations of moralism to meditate not only on American history and the political situation in which the argument was actually employed, but also on the composition of the group employing it. It is perhaps obvious, but there is, in American history, a religious cast to public discourse.[12] Piety becomes especially thick about the "nation." Only in the United States, writes Sacvan Bercovitch, tracing the metamorphosis of the Puritan "jeremiad" into rhetoric, ideology, and ritual in American culture, has nationalism joined with the Christian meaning of the sacred.[13] However much influenced by Puritanism, the nation underwent an apotheosis during two World Wars. America's "mission," her moral and spiritual superiority, became an official part of the war effort, themes absorbed in and recapitulated in a thousand different ways through popular culture.   During these periods of national crisis, patriotism virtually became law, criticism of government policies grounds for censorship, public protest evidence if not of treason then some lesser form of un-Americanism.

With Dwight Eisenhower, commander of the allied armies in Europe, running for the office of president, patriotism, high moral purpose, and the religious tone that went with it became associated with the political coalition supporting the Republican party. The fact that the party was dominated by what E. D. Baltzell calls the "Protestant Establishment,"[14] which has traditionally adopted a posture of moral and social and economic superiority, further encouraged a patriotic and high moral tone. It was, moreover, a tone contrasting the Republican with the Democratic party which, during the late 1940s and early '50s, the "McCarthy period," was being attacked for being soft on Communism, losing China, and harboring traitors.

The attack on the Democratic camp by Senator Joseph McCarthy, with the support of the "old stock" wing of the Republican party led by Senator Robert Taft, made inroads into traditionally Democratic constituencies—Irish Catholics in particular, Catholics and labor in general.[15] Again, a religious, though non-denominational, tone was indicated. Thus, the pro-American, anti-Communist movement McCarthy came to symbolize broadened the Republican coalition, bringing with it a style of discourse—patriotic, moral, and religious—for which Americans had been prepared during the Second World War; it was a style appropriate to a Protestant establishment with fundamentalist followers, since it included, through McCarthy, an attack on the Truman-Hiss-Acheson side of the establishment which excluded poor Protestants as single-mindedly as it did poor Catholics;[16] and it was a style highlighting the "disloyalty" and "un-Americanism" attributed to the recent Democratic administration. In this larger context, "prophetic dualism" constituted a sophisticated ideological apparatus for coping with a "Communist menace" at home and abroad. A domestic division between "fellow travelers" and "loyal Americans" resonated with an international division between the "Free World" and "Atheistic Communism."

To see how this argument worked in the context of foreign policy, one has to turn to concrete examples. Those who sought to justify foreign policy along moral lines include Democrats like Truman and Acheson, but it is principally associated with John Foster Dulles, Secretary of State under Eisenhower. "We have our principles," Dulles declared in a speech before the American Legion, October 10, 1955:

Our productivity and our power do not rattle haphazardly about the world. They are harnessed to basic moral principles. There is a school of thought that claims that morality and foreign policy do not mix. That never has been, is not, and I pray never will be the American ideal.

With the spiritual, there was a pragmatic reason for framing arguments about moral principles:

Our people can understand, and will support policies which can be explained and understood in moral terms. But policies merely based on carefully calculated expediency could never be explained and would never be understood.[17]

Beyond the domestic audience (the "American people"), however, lay a world of international affairs and the specter of evil.

In an address made before the American Bar Association, August 24, 1955, President Eisenhower fused government and religion in American foreign policy, drawing the contrast between Good and Evil that is the hallmark of prophetic dualism:

The central fact of today's life is the existence in the world of two great philosophies of man and government. They are in contest for the friendship, loyalty, and support of the world's peoples. On the one side, our Nation is ranged with those who seek attainment of human goals through a government of laws administered by men. Those laws are rooted in moral law reflecting a religious faith that man is created in the image of God and that the energy of the free individual is the most dynamic force in human affairs.

The contrast is balanced:

On the other side are those who believe—and many of them with evident sincerity—that human goals can be most surely reached by a government of men who rule by decree. Their decrees are rooted in an ideology which ignores the faith that man is a spiritual being, which establishes the all-powerful state as the principal source of advancement and progress.[18]

As it was articulated during the Eisenhower-Dulles administration, prophetic dualism involved religious faith, the faith of our fathers, the ideals of freedom, individuality, a militant God, and the existence of evil in the world.

The God officially invoked was the God who presided over the founding of America, the God who abhorred atheists and loathed communist slavery. It was the God who had been America's "co-pilot" during World War Two. For the Eisenhower administration, God was not dead. He, and it was most definitely a "He," was a living God, a God to whom government officials, in moments of national crisis, might turn for support. It is also the God of Bible-Belt Protestantism and working-class Catholicism; the God, not surprisingly, of the more authoritarian elements in the body politic and certain personality profiles.[19] But while this God might be located in a particular constituency or in a psychological type, He may, in moments of confusion, terror, or terrible disappointment, be summoned. It is in such moments that a figure, which for the unbeliever counts as a rhetorical convention, may become a source of political influence, a Presence above and beyond what the Enlightenment or "secular humanism" celebrates as the Rule of Reason.

In the context of domestic politics, there are advantages for state managers to be gained from the use of prophetic dualism. Put quite simply: God dampens public debate. How can one argue with God's will when it is clearly expressed? How does one argue over obvious, absolute principles? While a "crisis" may argue for an end to debate, spiritual imperatives close it down. "The government and every leader of a business or profession," Eisenhower declared on May 20, 1954, "must band together to show that the United States is a great organism of free men who put freedom above all other values." Sometimes he thought Patrick Henry might have overstated the case—"Give me liberty or give me death!"—but still, Eisenhower concluded, the statement was true for "our race."[20] There is a synthesis here of nationalism and spiritualism, a way of thinking. Eisenhower does not so much urge a point of view as call on absolute support for an absolute.

I find it difficult, since the great divisions opened up by Vietnam, not to marvel at the serenity with which Eisenhower and Dulles could count on the support of every American. Dulles thought it was a matter of policy following from principle:

The reality of the matter is that the United States, by every standard of measurement, is the world's greatest power not only materially but spiritually. We have national policies which are clear and sound. They fit a civilization based on religious faith. They are strongly implemented but at a cost we can afford to live with. They have evolved on a nonpartisan basis, and, in broad outlines, they are overwhelmingly backed by our people.[21]

As a form of argument, prophetic dualism calls for overwhelming support—a response appropriate to the world's greatest spiritual power. In the context in which Dulles spoke during the 1950s, there were real obstacles facing those who might have been willing to dissent. These obstacles, now known as "McCarthyism," also favored "nonpartisan" support.[22]

One advantage of prophetic dualism, for those in office, is that it stifles debate; another is that, because it posits a life-and-death struggle, it encourages a heightened dependence on the established order. Conflict is inevitable between Good and Evil. Serious enough in the face of two World Wars, such conflict becomes positively chilling in a nuclear age. Dulles, however, did not draw back from the abyss. There were, he declared in a news conference in 1956, "basic moral values and vital interests for which we stand, and the surest way to avoid war is to let it be known in advance that we are prepared to defend these principles if need be by life itself."[23] Without the will to defend basic principles, thought Dulles, civilization declines; the good, through compromise, intimidation, and weakness, may cease to exist. Writing in *Foreign Affairs*, in 1957, Dulles observed that the United States was not content to rely upon a peace which could be preserved only by a capacity to "destroy vast segments of the human race." Though horrifying, and both Eisenhower and Dulles repeatedly expressed their longings for peace, nuclear war nevertheless remained a "last alternative." The good news, according to Dulles, was that American scientists had developed nuclear weapons that did not involve such widespread harm to humanity.[24]

While it restricts debate and encourages dependence on existing authority, prophetic dualism has serious drawbacks for those in power. Prophetic dualism leaves little room for adaptation or compromise, as was demonstrated following the French defeat in Vietnam. On July 15, 1955, President Eisenhower, on the eve of his departure for the Heads of Government meeting to be held in Geneva to negotiate French withdrawal, addressed the nation over radio and television. The problem facing Eisenhower was not only the political and military realities surrounding the defeat and the need to explain the failure of the "Free World" in its struggle with the "Communist menace," but also, and more importantly, how to explain negotiations with the forces of Evil. How could an American audience, for whom the perfidy of Communist leaders promised deception and lies, accommodate itself to the reality of a Communist victory and a negotiated settlement?

The precedent offered by Korea did not apply. Korea was not a war but a "police action" designed to uphold the law. The conflict had been assigned to a Democratic administration's failure to take a hard-line against Communism. The line in Korea was drawn at the 38th parallel. The line held. The French (i.e., "Free World") defeat in Vietnam, however, represented a complete collapse and withdrawal. Eisenhower, therefore, had to justify what, in the brutal dualities of right-wing American politics, was unjustifiable.

Eisenhower recognized the problem. America's purpose in attending the conference was not a sign of weakness; on the contrary, the willingness of the Free World to participate in negotiation set it apart from the Communist bloc.

We (the Free World) are not held together by force, but we are held together by this great factor, and it is this: The free world believes, under one religion or another, in a Divine Power. It believes in a Supreme Being. Now this, my friends, is a very great factor for the conciliation and peace at this time because each of these religions—each one of them—has as one of its basic commandments the words—the terminology—that is similar to our Golden Rule. . . . This means that the thinking of those people is based upon ideas of right and justice and mutual self-respect, consideration for the other man. And this means peace, because only in peace can such conceptions as these prevail. This means that the free people of the world hate war, and they want peace and are dedicated to it.

But how does one negotiate with forces not committed to the Golden Rule, committed in fact to its opposite? How can the forces of Light make agreements with the forces of Darkness and hope to survive? Eisenhower's answer is instructive. He transcends, yet does not abandon, the great spiritual struggle.

Now, it is natural for a people, steeped in a religious civilization, when they come to moments of great importance—maybe even crisis—such as we now face, to turn to the Divine Power that each has in his own heart, believes in his own heart, for guidance, for wisdom, for some help in doing the thing that is honorable and is right. I have no doubt that tonight, throughout this country, and indeed, throughout the free world, such prayers are ascending.

In a spiritual struggle, communing with one's God not only strengthens the supplicant, but it can also, in the case of an interventionist God, affect the outcome. Thus it was not deliberation, debate, or discussion of the great national issues which became appropriate. It was, instead, the isolating act of prayer, an act which, nevertheless, took on political significance: "Prayer is a mighty force. And this brings me to the thought that through prayer we could also achieve a very definite and practical result at this very moment." The United States could be conciliatory, because it did not seek conquest, tolerant, because it had no wish to impose its way of life on others, and, secure, because its representatives were firm in the consciousness of its citizens' "spiritual and material strength and . . . defense of the right."[25]

The dualities embedded in the rhetoric of American foreign policy did not originate with Eisenhower or Dulles, nor can they be explained adequately through a kind of residual Puritanism in American society. And while it is true that such dualities resonate with the millennial beliefs of Fundamentalist Christians and that the Communist Menace has come to stand for the anti-Christ, Fundamentalism prior to the Great War was committed to Pacifism. The militant anti-Communism associated with the Bible Belt does not appear in Fundamentalist literature until 1924-25.[26] What is more, the dualities now so common in talk about foreign policy appear in the rhetoric of many European societies in the first quarter of the twentieth century.

Through modern literature, Paul Fussell traces a vision of a bifurcated and hostile world back to the Great War with its hundreds of miles of parallel trenches, orange belts of barbed wire, the stench of decaying flesh, and massive efforts to justify the catastrophe to civilian populations on both sides of the struggle.[27] What we have called prophetic dualism in the rhetoric of American foreign policy during the 1950s neither originated with the Republican party nor with Fundamentalism in this country. While it forms an important element in the world view of the right-wing in American politics, it must also be understood as part of the cluster of images, themes, grammatical forms, and emotions making up the culture of war in the twentieth century.

"TECHNOCRATIC REALISM": THE KENNEDY-JOHNSON ADMINISTRATIONS

For all the charm of Camelot, the poignancy of its fall and the eloquence of its court historians, the change from a conservative Republican to a liberal Democratic administration not only failed to lead America away from the abyss, it also seemed, in the early days of the Kennedy administration, to lead even closer to it.[28] This was the period of the Cuban invasion, Berlin crisis, the decision to send troops into Thailand and Vietnam, resumption of atmospheric nuclear tests in response to a Russian breach of an unofficial agreement to halt such testing, and the "Cuban Missile Crisis," which at the time felt like the moment before the final conflagration. Yet there is some basis for associating the end, or perhaps, a beginning of the end of the Cold War with the Kennedy administration.

However the election victory in 1960 is explained—the want of a shave, the return of the Irish, Catholics, and unions to the Democratic party, Chicago theft, etc.—the fact remains that a coalition dominated by labor, racial and ethnic minorities, middle-class professionals, and the intelligentsia, scornful of an America shaped along lines laid down by a Republican God and Protestant fundamentalists, calling for a variety of liberal reforms, took on a much more secular, humanistic, scientific, and negotiable tone than the previous administration.[29] The Faith of our Fathers, though still ritually invoked, gave way to the prospect of a managerial-technocratic revolution and a greater horizon for irony, wit, and compromise.

A measure of the difference in style this coalition allowed, encouraged, and found beneficial may be gleaned from one of the most eloquent speeches ever made by an American official on foreign policy—Kennedy's address on June 10, 1963, at the American University in Washington, D.C. Three months before the signing of the Nuclear Test Ban Treaty, Kennedy announced a major shift in American foreign policy through a frontal assault on Manichean dualities in the articulation of foreign affairs. The way in which he confronted the orthodox patriotism and religiosity associated with the Bible Belt, veterans groups, and the business community in the United States is, in itself, a work of political art. He attacked the dualities associated with the right wing by showing that they were shared by the leaders in the Soviet Union. In doing so, he expressed the hope that what the Russians said did not express what they believed.

It is discouraging to read a recent authoritative Soviet text on military strategy and find, on page after page, wholly baseless and incredible claims—such as the allegation that "American imperialist circles are preparing to unleash different types of wars . . . that there is a very real threat of preventive war being unleashed by American imperialists against the Soviet Union . . . and that the political aims of the American imperialists are to enslave economically and politically the European and other capitalist countries . . . and to achieve world domination . . . by means of aggressive wars."

Such views were inaccurate, untrue, propagandistic. They were also dangerous, though possibly revealing: "Truly as it was written long ago, 'the wicked flee when no man pursueth.'" The Biblical allusion speaks to those who would frame foreign policy in apocalyptic terms, linking together Soviet propagandists and their American counterparts. The Soviets become less a symbol of evil and more a "warning to the American people not to fall into the same trap as the Soviets, not to see only a distorted and desperate view of the other side, not to see conflict as inevitable, accommodation as impossible, and communication as nothing more than an exchange of threats."

And yet, how are international affairs to be understood, if not through conflict between the Soviet Union and the United States? Answering this question, Kennedy approached the sublime. In order to appreciate this move, however, one must grasp the problem of cold-war dualities here and now. What Kennedy did was to confront the dualism implicit in right-wing rhetoric in the United States and the Soviet Union and deny the implication that either side has to be destroyed:

Let us not be blind to our differences but let us also direct attention to our common interest and to the means by which these differences can be resolved. And if we cannot end now our differences, at least we can make the world safe for diversity.

What is the basis for a willingness to tolerate Evil or, in Kennedy's words, a "profoundly repugnant" system? Here he offers not merely a rejoinder to traditional dualities, but also a way to transcend them. "In the final analysis," a phrase taking on new life in a nuclear age, "our most basic common link is that all inhabit this planet. We all breathe the same air. We all cherish our children's future. And we are all mortal."[30]

Thus Kennedy offered a rhetorical alternative to the "natural" divisions underlying the Cold War, a critique of a right-wing coalition opposed to any negotiations with the "enemy," and an alternative to the culture of war which had, as a result of two world wars, wormed its way into the deepest recesses of modern consciousness.

A liberal administration might reject the notion that any system can be so evil that its people must be considered as lacking in virtue; yet it must, in the world of affairs, be able to respond to real threats. How can an administration dedicated to tolerance and accommodation protect American interests in international affairs? The answer lies in the mode of argument I call "technocratic realism." In technocratic realism, negotiation becomes possible over areas of mutual interest—a retreat from the horrors of nuclear war, for example. But while negotiation and compromise become possible, competition between the United States and the Soviet Union over economic, military, and scientific matters would remain keen.

Instead of a Holy War, therefore, technocratic realism looked to peaceful, though vigorous, competition. How does one win such a contest? Not through harsh religious sentiments, but through hard-headed calculation. Addressing a conference on Cold War Education at Tampa, Florida in July, 1963, Roger Hilsman, Assistant Secretary for Far Eastern Affairs, discussed the "Challenge to Freedom" in Southeast Asia. He denounced the traditional dualities underlying foreign policy rhetoric. They were, he thought, oversimplified. He detailed a more complex, more "realistic" approach:

Precision, wisdom, realism: These require the utmost in cool and unemotional judgment and what I called earlier cool, deliberate analysis. Tough minds, analytical minds, are required to carry this nation through the dangerous era in which we live. Our minds must be keen enough to recognize that no situation is simple: that untidiness is characteristic of most problems; that there are no shortcuts to success, no neat, swift solutions anywhere. Today the critical issues we face demand of all of us the capacity to live in a complex world of untidy situations and yet do what is required of us with steady nerves and unflinching will.[31]

Technocratic realism finds the modern world much too complex for old-time religion. Not the prophet, but rather a skilled, tough expert is what is needed, one whose mind is unclouded by violent and dangerous emotions; one who is wise, analytical, precise.

The persona of the technocrat emerged out of the university intellectuals, government bureaucrats, and skilled professionals who formed part of the coalition which brought the Kennedy administration into power. If problems in foreign affairs were simple, direct, mere matters of holding to sure principles, such an expert would not be needed, but the problems were, in what has become a familiar term, "complex." It is rare, observed U. Alexis Johnson, in an address delivered at the University of Nebraska in 1963, that "there are just two sides to a problem or that the issues are black and white in good Western movie fashion—and the business of carrying out foreign policy can be complex indeed in this complex world."[32]

Where prophetic dualism took its stand on principle, technocratic realism (Dulles called it "calculated expediency") began with a hard-headed look at American interests. Such interests, it concluded, were ill-served by military conflict. Economic competition was infinitely more desirable. Thus it stressed "efficiency" over "morality," and argued that the affluence of the Free World evidenced not only its greater humanity, but also its superior economic and social systems. Dean Rusk, Secretary of State under both Kennedy and Johnson, characterized the role of the United States in world affairs as competitive but in economic rather than in military terms:

The performance of our economic system under the conditions of liberty is itself one of the most powerful supports of the simple notions of liberty to which we as a nation are dedicated. We need not dwell on our military power; it is so vast that the effects of its use are beyond the comprehension of the mind of man. It is so vast that we dare not allow ourselves to become infuriated.[33]

An economic contest between the Free World and the Communist Bloc transformed a Holy War into an international game of profit and loss, a game which, during the boom years of the early 1960s, government officials could realistically and happily argue that the United States was winning. Within this view of the world, the United States was to encourage prosperity at home and "nation building" abroad, for Communism, so the argument went, held no fascination for prosperous, well-fed peoples. Growth in gross national products did not depend on a belief in God or adherence to the Golden Rule. In place of war and the threat of war, America offered the world technical assistance.

One of the advantages of technocratic realism was that it could be adapted to explain hostile actions in international affairs and justify a more moderate course of action than would otherwise be the case when confronting Evil. Scientifically conducted cost-benefit analyses provided by "experts" could be counted on to reveal the advantages not only to the United States, but more importantly to the native populations in "underdeveloped" countries falling within America's "sphere of influence" (terms

Era and domestic reforms that inspired and commended American liberalism up to and beyond the New Deal.[36]

Exponents of this tradition in the Kennedy-Johnson administrations articulated America's managerial role in the early stages of Vietnam, a role confined to advisory, logistic, and technical assistance. This approach had considerable appeal in domestic politics. President Johnson, in his Johns Hopkins speech, April 7, 1965, offered a team of "experts" to design a food program for South Vietnam and a plan to develop the Mekong River region as an inducement to end the war. What he did was to extend his domestic programs, called the "War on Poverty," from the home front to the Third World. This portion of the speech was meant to placate domestic liberals, while the portion responding to an appeal from seventeen nonaligned "bellwether" nations to begin immediate negotiations was intended to influence correspondents like Walter Lippman.[37]

There were references to atrocities committed by the "enemy," but in the early stages of Vietnam the technocratic ethos predominated. The unwillingness of the "men of the North" to help in fulfilling the unsatisfied wants of the people of the region was, thought Humphrey, unfortunate.[38] "I long for the day," declared President Johnson in July, 1966, "when we and others—whatever their political creed—will turn our joint resources to battle against poverty, ignorance, and disease." This day had not arrived; American expertise and know-how had been thwarted in its attempt to assist others, because, Johnson went on, "some men, in some places, still insist on trying to force their way of life on other peoples."[39]

The ends were given. Like the War on Poverty, the War in Vietnam was being undertaken by those better trained and educated and therefore better able to minister to the needs of the people. There was no need for debate. The only problem lay in eliminating obstacles to enlightened management.

The failure of the Johnson administration to negotiate with the "men from the North" (the official line was that conflict was taking place between two nations, a North and a South Vietnam, and that the North had invaded the South), military reversals, a growing need to mobilize public opinion in the United States for what could no longer be characterized as advisory, logistical, or merely technical assistance, but had become or was about to become an even larger military effort on the part of the United States, led to a change in the rhetoric of American foreign policy. What one sees is the inclusion of another, not unfamiliar, mode of argument. It was displayed as early as August, 1964 in a speech President Johnson made dedicating the Samuel I. Newhouse Communications Center at Syracuse University. His reason for having American troops in Vietnam was the same, he said, as that of Presidents Eisenhower and Kennedy before him—to make certain that the governments of Southeast Asia leave each other alone, resolve their differences peacefully, and devote their

like "underdeveloped" and "developed" countries, "sphere of in
and "power vacuum" are part of the vocabulary of "realism" ii
affairs).[34] American technical assistance in military matters, as
quence, could be justified through the improved management and
organization it provided.

Technocratic realism has, from an official point of view, the ad
of doing away with the need to consult those affected by specific
about their social, political, or economic preferences. Natives ar
the position to make informed judgments. They do not possess th
They have no experience in the potential of modern techniques for
building. The problem, then, for a more advanced society is hov
efficiently and effectively to diffuse modern innovations into undei
oped countries. The appeal to expertise implicit in computer-as
statistically based calculations of the facts of the situation also raises
beyond people living in "advanced" societies. Ordinary people,
assumed, are not equipped to grasp the demands made on Ame
foreign policy, to deliberate issues about which most of the inform;
for reasons of national security, cannot be made available, or to u
stand the technical instruments used to select, process, and interpre
data relevant in the formation of government policy.[35]

The rhetoric of technocratic realism, with its commitment to dis
sionate, informed, and pragmatic expertise, did not originate with
Kennedy administration any more than prophetic dualism originated
Eisenhower and Dulles. The most immediate and pertinent source for
technocratic intelligentsia—the scholars, intellectuals, and skilled pro
sionals making up part of the Kennedy coalition and who were represen
in his administration—grew out of the Progressive Era in the Uni
States. The shift away from public participation in important politi
matters toward reliance on "expertise" was an explicit part of t
Progressive movement. Between 1916 and 1922, during the "Red Scare
academics and business leaders began to lose faith in public debate in th
country as a way of solving political problems. They thought it exacerba
ed class conflict, divided labor and management, and was beset b
pressure groups.

The Brookings Institute, the New School for Social Research, th
Twentieth Century Fund, and the *New Republic* magazine were originall
part of efforts made by corporate liberals to initiate social, political, and
economic reforms through increased governmental efficiency and control,
through research and recommendations for new policies, and through
educating those who would implement these reforms. Thus faith in
efficient management, avoiding public controversy and debate, and in
developing a more scientific approach to decision making and policy
implementation underlying foreign affairs has its origins in the Progressive

talents to bettering the lives of their peoples by working against poverty, disease, and ignorance. But then, shifting to another mode, Johnson referred to the Gulf of Tonkin and an attack on American warships:

None can be detached about what has happened there. Aggression—deliberate, willful, and systematic aggression—has unmasked its face to the entire world. The world remembers—the world must never forget—that aggression unchallenged is aggression unleashed. We of the United States have not forgotten. That is why we have answered this aggression with action.[40]

American action in Vietnam was helping the world remember a lesson, a lesson it should have learned during the Second World War about the terrors of systematic and unchecked aggression.

The tendency to treat the other side as the "enemy," the conflict as irreconcilable, and the struggle as a Holy War was fully developed in a nationally televised speech the Commander of American forces in Vietnam, General William Westmoreland, gave to a joint session of Congress, April 26, 1967. Within his capabilities, said Westmoreland, the "enemy in Viet Nam is waging total war all day, everyday, everywhere. He believes in force, and his intensification of violence is limited only by his resources and not by any moral inhibitions." Endeavoring to show the support American policy enjoyed in other parts of the world, he listed a number of countries—Korea, Australia, New Zealand, Thailand, and the Philippines who had sent detachments to Vietnam. These countries become rhetorically significant, in Westmoreland's words, a "symbolic reminder that the whole of free Asia opposes Communist expansion."[41]

Despite their logical and seemingly political incompatibility, prophetic dualism and technocratic realism not only can co-exist, elements of each may appear in the same speech.[42] This does not mean that these modes of argument do not speak to different audiences. A prophetic persona coupled with Manichean dualities resonates with the world view of Christian Fundamentalism, an important constituency in American politics, while a technocratic persona and the secular calculations associated with science and technology relate to the world view of a managerial-humanist elite, the "new class" described by Alvin Gouldner.[43] A useful theoretical distinction, however, may obscure what is in fact occurring. Was the emergence of these two forms of argument during the Johnson administration a logical error, a blurring of categories? Does it approach something like mixing metaphors? Not, I think, in politics. If an administration seeks, in the face of a crisis in foreign affairs, to broaden its constituency, then one may expect arguments relating to the world views of various groups to be employed. Thus the emergence of prophetic dualism and its growing importance in the rhetoric of the Johnson administration may be understood as an effort to appease, neutralize, or enlist the same political constituency appealed to during the Dulles-Eisenhower years. Once one

penetrates the logic of coalition formation, one moves beyond philosophical and literary notions of argument into the practical demands of political struggle.

This, then, leads to a deeper level wherein foreign policy rhetoric, apparently trapped in a means-ends dilemma and the vicissitudes of domestic politics, achieves cohesion. To reach this level, however, one must ask what binds together prophetic dualism and technocratic realism, what renders attacks on them unrealistic, idealistic, an academic exercise. Beneath isolated and abstracted forms of argument and the demands of political pluralism is the realization that arguments over foreign policy share a view of the world, literally "the world," so deep and fundamental as to be called the "ground" on which foreign policy is debated in this country. It is ground shared by various administrations, Republican and Democratic. It is ground so pervasive, so obvious, so free of challenge that, once articulated, one can but say that such is the nature of foreign policy rhetoric. And yet what we may be prepared to call "nature" in this matter contains the potential for destruction.

PROPHETIC DUALISM, TECHNOCRATIC REALISM, AND NATIONALISM

The rhetoric of American foreign policy has to do with nations. Nations, in official statements, are personified. They act morally and immorally. They use force. They violate one another's rights. The "United States," in the debate over Vietnam was "obliged," just as any individual is obliged, to help those whose rights are being threatened by brute force, to help the man who is being forced to defend himself.[44] Both prophetic dualism and technocratic realism agree that nations are the irreducible units in foreign affairs, that nations are to be understood as people, that they are, literally, actors in international affairs, and that nations live in a world where, if the freedom of one nation is threatened, other nations are obliged to help.

Both modes of argument agree that the international community embraces a hierarchial order—there are superior and inferior nations. Moreover they agree that one nation is clearly superior to all the rest, and that is the United States. The "United States," in the rhetoric of American foreign policy, is much more than a geographical designation, an administrative unit, or a large number of people sharing language, culture, and a history. The United States is the manifestation of Truth, Justice, and Freedom placed on this earth by a God whose purpose it is to make of it an instrument for extending His spiritual and material blessings to the rest of humanity. The ground on which the rhetoric of American foreign policy is situated is the Nation. Its personification as an Actor with a sense of purpose, an important mission in a world of nations, and a moral and spiritual center raising it above all other nations forms the essential story out of which reasons are given in support of foreign policy.

A language which takes nations as its irreducible unit, like any other that trades in vast numbers of people, differs from and will, under certain circumstances, conflict with ways of talking about the world that centers on human beings as individuals. These conflicts become acute when the subject is an action having human suffering as its inevitable consequence. This becomes obvious when what is called "common language" has embedded in it some sense of individual worth, the precepts of "common law," the universalizing inclination of Human, Natural, or Inalienable Rights. Such language will prove inadequate precisely at the point at which pain and death come to people who have committed no crimes, whose guilt has not been established, or whose punishment is out of all proportion to the alleged offense (i.e., having the wrong beliefs, being in the wrong "zone," refusing to obey orders). This is why, in order to avoid getting bogged down in moral concerns, government officials develop a special language to explain policies having to do with people outside the society in whose name policy is being planned and executed.

This situation is not peculiar to American foreign policy, George Orwell pointed to the abstract and facile euphemisms British officials called upon while trying to justify the use of force in Burma in the 1920s and '30s:

Defenseless villages are bombarded from the air, the inhabitants driven out into the countryside, the cattle machine-gunned, the huts on fire with incendiary bullets, this is called "pacification." Millions of peasants are robbed of their farms and sent trudging along the roads with no more than they can carry: this is called "transfer of the population" or "pacification of the frontiers."[45]

Language dealing with vast numbers of people typed according to race, religion, or nationality obscures the relationship between official policy and human experience. What "national interest" dictates in the Third World may enable one to calculate the effects of a given course of action, but it automatically dehumanizes the people most immediately and profoundly affected.

A similar result occurs when conceiving of national interest in relation to industrialized countries. "Force," for example, as Aldous Huxley noted in 1937, is a dangerously abstract word when applied to the affairs of nations. He demonstrates this point by translating the phrase, "You cannot have international justice, unless you are prepared to impose it by force," into common language.

You cannot have international justice, unless you are prepared, with a view to imposing a just settlement, to drop thermite, high explosives and vesicants upon the inhabitants of foreign cities and to have thermite, high explosives and vesicants dropped in return upon the inhabitants of your cities.[46]

To contemporary ears, the phrase "thermite high explosives" does not have the impact it did for Huxley and his audience, but the development of nuclear weapons has not had any appreciable effect on the language of foreign policy by virtue of the fact that millions more lives now hang in the balance.

Nuclear weapons are profoundly unsuited for distinguishing between the guilty and the innocent, or for taking into account the distinction between the guilt of individuals and that of peoples. They are, as Robert Oppenheimer noted in 1946, the supreme expression of Total War.[47] And yet when talking about foreign policy, their darkness is often passed over or minimized. In a debate over what America's response should have been in support of the French in Indochina, the moderator, Arthur Krock, asked then Senate minority leader, Mike Mansfield, whether or not he agreed with Senate majority leader William Knowland's solution, which was the use of "massive retaliation." Mansfield demurred. He did not see how it could be applied there with any effect.

I believe that there is a tremendous deficiency in this massive retaliatory striking arm of ours. It is all right to have these things on paper but . . . where would you drop bombs in Indo-China? There are few places you could drop them in China except at Mukden or Harbin.

"Massive retaliation" was inappropriate because of the absence of metropolitan areas. Atomic bombs are designed to destroy cities. They would have minimal effect in the jungle area around Dienbienphu. Mansfield offered another reason for not using atomic weapons:

I think that many of these people are looking to China today as the champion of the colored races. And they are going to say, "Why, these white folks are taking it out on us. They don't drop atom bombs on white people but they drop them on the Japanese, the Chinese." And I think the revulsion against us would be great.[48]

Nowhere in the debate did either Mansfield or Knowland consider the vast and indiscriminate slaughter of men, women, and children, the charred villages, the human consequences of the use of atomic weapons. Theirs was an analysis of what was in the "national" interest. Even so, their exchange has a kind of clarity, almost innocence, when compared with how policy planners now talk about such matters.

It is in the context of the continued development of nuclear weapons and multibillion dollar weapons systems and the knowledge that the United States is not secure from attack that more sophisticated ways of talking about the use of "force" have evolved. Dr. Fred Charles Ikle, an official in both the Nixon and Reagan administrations and an authority on nuclear disarmament, claims that arms experts and military planners "insulate themselves from the potential implications of their labors by layers of dehumanizing abstractions and bland metaphors." The term "assured destruction," for example, does not really indicate what is to be destroyed. But then, he goes on in language uncharacteristic of government officials, the term "'assured genocide' would reveal the truth too starkly."[49]

Even if one chooses to deliberate foreign policy under the aegis of the national interest, and nations will continue to be the building blocks of the international order for some time, the debate over what constitutes America's interests in Third World countries as well as in nuclear armaments remains muddled.[50] The debate is distorted in pluralistic societies by the advantages foreign affairs offer in domestic political struggles. It is further distorted by a willingness on the part of the electorate to allow state managers, aspirants for office, along with their scientific and military "experts" to set the agenda, determine the issues, and select the vocabulary. As a consequence, the debate over foreign policy rarely gets to fundamental issues, such as what will, in the long run, serve our "national interests."

With regard to the Third World, the countries not only in Southeast Asia and Africa, but also in countries like Panama, Chile, Nicaragua, El Salvador, Guatemala, Grenada making up Central and South America, terms like "military aid," "sphere of influence," "power vacuum," "Communist infiltration," and "counterinsurgency" mystify both the policies being advocated and their human consequence. Moreover, they obscure changes which have taken place over the last few decades in how such terms have been officially employed. The phrase "helping free world nations defend themselves from armed aggression" implies assisting countries to defend themselves from threats posed by other, more powerful, hostile countries. Yet American "aid" has changed, according to Asbjorn Eide, from arms designed to protect countries from external aggression to arms designed to suppress internal uprisings, designed to strengthen the "capacity of the police and the military of the Third World for local control by their own forces, but with equipment and training from the outside."[51] Thus the term "counterinsurgency" refers to the ability of those in power rapidly to deploy troops on a guerilla battlefield at the first sign of native unrest. More than military assistance on the part of the United States, this involves an extended network of military bases, the acquisition of giant transport aircraft, fast supply ships, along with the political resolve to send supplies, "advisors," even combat troops into areas where "freedom" is threatened.

The rhetoric of American foreign policy does not become any less opaque over the issue of nuclear weapons. Alexander Haig, as Secretary of State under Reagan, observed:

Restraint of the Soviets, reinvigoration of our alliances, a new approach to the Third World, a healthier U.S. economy and a stronger military—these are the signals of our determination to restore leadership in the world.[52]

But what did this mean? "Restraint of the Soviets"—how does this phrase relate to the development, threat of development, or use of nuclear weapons? The issue is not clear; nowhere is it more vague than over the conception, development, and use of modern weapon systems, presumably a part of the "stronger military" to which Haig refers.

Public debate over such matters is, when it is not deemed inappropriate, certainly confusing. There is a tendency to assume that the highly technical aspects of a weapons system are beyond the capacity of the ordinary citizen to understand and that, in the interests of "national security," such information ought to be kept secret. And yet, because of the complexity of modern weapon systems, it takes several years before a system can contribute to national security. This means that debates over "defense" will, at certain points, transcend engineering and enter the world of science fiction. Here the hypothetical example becomes pivotal. Frank Barnaby put it precisely: "Since the range of conceivable developments in the opponent's weaponry is more or less unlimited, a case can be made for initiating programs to protect oneself against as many conceivable developments as possible."[53] The rhetorical morass *this* creates he calls the "worst case syndrome"; this is where the development of new weapons systems depends on the degree to which one is animated by fear.

The problem, however, is neither purely psychological nor semantic. The debate over the need for new weapon systems does not begin with a dispassionate, scientific weighing of "data" by certified "experts." It begins in the context, in both the Soviet Union and the United States, of a military-industrial-bureaucratic-professional-political coalition of interests reaping enormous benefits from each new commitment to spend hundreds of billions of dollars on each new system. A "military-industrial complex" is what President Eisenhower called it. In his final address to the nation, on January 17, 1961, he characterized the problem in this way:

The U.S. has been compelled to create a permanent armament industry of vast proportion and to maintain a defense establishment employing 3.5 million persons and spending huge sums. This conjunction of an immense military establishment and a large industry is new in the American experience. The total influence—economic, political, even spiritual—is felt in every city, every state house, every office of the federal government. We must recognize the imperative need for this development. Yet we must not fail to comprehend its grave implications.[54]

The unfortunate effect of Eisenhower's warning has been to provide a noun, "military-industrial complex," for a political process. What the "complex" refers to is the existence of a powerful coalition of interests in this society that seeks to influence political decisions in disturbingly predictable ways.   At the time Eisenhower spoke, the economies of twenty-two states depended heavily on military spending.   In fourteen states military industries made up a significant percentage of total manufacturing employment.   Defense assets during this period were greater than the combined wealth of the 100 largest corporations in America.   The annual purchases of the Air Force alone were larger in volume than the output of General Motors.[55]   The ongoing interests of this coalition are not irrelevant to the forty-four Senators and over two hundred Representatives from such areas.

Translating this into public debate as it now exists, arguments over "defense," the desirability of weapon systems, arms sales to the Third World, the stance taken by the United States in world affairs are, in various ways, shaped by an enormously wealthy and powerful coalition of vested interests.   For this coalition, increases in military spending and the continued production and sale of armaments becomes less a matter of disinterested judgment about the nature of nuclear war or the need for social programs than an article of faith, an ideological commitment.[56]

Public debate over strategy tends to be grounded in the assumption that ever more powerful weapons systems (anti-ballistic missiles, B-1 bombers, MX missile system, laser satellites, etc.) *will* be produced and that the real issue has to do with technical feasibility and cost effectiveness.   Instead of debate over "first-strike capability," "counter-value" versus "counter-strike force," and "genocide" along with their economic, social, political, and moral implications, observes Barnaby, arguments in this country tend to dissolve into a "mass of detail on specific new weapon systems or particular improvements to existing weapons and in equally narrow comparisons with Soviet capabilities."[57]   Even as the ethos of "technocratic realism," with its claims on objectivity and expertise, has, for scientists themselves, lost much of its allure,[58] the debate over armaments gets lost in "scientific" shorthand and in accounting mentality invited by the context in which most of these debates take place—the piecemeal review of military spending that occurs when the federal budget is up for consideration.[59]

SUMMARY

The rhetoric of American foreign policy lends itself to cynical and bitter commentaries on lies, half-truths, and macabre scenarios.   Because of this, foreign policy rhetoric's connection with real issues having to do with human suffering may be overlooked.   Even when such issues are identified, critics rarely get beyond denouncing the devil-theory underlying "prophetic dualism," the cult of expertise in "technocratic realism," or the humanistic void in "nationalism."   Foreign policy, however, reaches beyond what is officially said about it. The task of criticism in our time is to raise real issues and to assist in the creation of publics able to and, in the interests of human survival, willing to rise above parochial concerns. Criticism confronting technique with purpose, euphemism with reality, and silence—the threatened silence of future generations—with speech will not alter the predicament in which we find ourselves; but it will keep the task clearly before us.

NOTES

1. Hannah Arendt, *The Life of the Mind*, vol. 1 (New York: Harcourt Brace Jovanovich, 1978), 4.

2. Werner Levi, "Ideology, Interests, and Foreign Policy," *International Studies Quarterly* 14 (1970): 28. Robert P. Newman's review of the deliberations which took place during the Cuban Missile Crisis also supports this view: "Foreign Policy: Decision and Argument," *Advances in Argumentation Theory and Research*, ed. J. Robert Cox and Charles Arthur Willard (Carbondale: Southern Illinois University Press, 1982), 318-42.

3. Grant Hugo, *Appearance and Reality in International Relations* (New York: Columbia University Press, 1970), 19.

4. Marcel Merel, "Political Parties and Foreign Policy in Pluralist Regimes," *International Social Science Journal* 30 (1978): 84. He wrote: "[Political parties] promise happiness and security if they eventually reach office or if they remain there a little longer . . . they offer foreign policy to their electors as a 'bonus'" (85). Pluralism is a political term describing a society in which no one group rules; rather, various groups work together to form coalitions. There is serious debate over: (1) the degree to which vested interests (the corporate state, military-industrial complex, power elite) have consolidated their hold on the state and (2) the desirability of greater public participation in government.

5. Over the last twenty years, there has been a major shift in thinking on this issue in the United States. Seymour Martin Lipset wrote in 1966 that "polls do not make policy so much as follow policy in international affairs . . . the president makes opinion, he does not follow it" ("The President, the Polls and Vietnam," *Trans-Action* 3 [1966]: 20). The gradual but steady decline in support for government policy in Vietnam, despite all official efforts to the contrary, see Hazel Erskin, "The Polls, Is War a Mistake?" *Public Opinion Quarterly* 34 (1970): 134-50, requires a revision of what used to be conventional wisdom if not in politics then among social scientists. This is the conclusion of William Lunch and Peter Sperlich in "American Public Opinion and the War in Vietnam," *Western Political Quarterly* 31 (1979): 21-44. Stressing the relationship

between foreign policy and domestic issues like energy, employment, and defense, the Brookings Institute recommends new instruments for carrying out foreign policy that will be more effective and responsive to "public" and congressional concerns; Graham Allison and Peter Szanton, "Organizing for the Decade Ahead," *Setting National Priorities: The Next Ten Years* (Washington, D.C.: The Brookings Institution, 1976), 227-70.

6. See my chapter "Cultural Criticism" in *The Handbook of Political Communication*, ed. Dan Nimmo and Keith R. Sanders (Beverly Hills: Sage, 1982), 497-528; "The Ideological Turn in Modern Criticism," *Central States Speech Journal* 34 (1983): 1-18; "The Aesthetic Dimension: A Note on Ideology, Criticism, and Reality," *Argument in Transition: Proceedings of the Third Summer Conference on Argumentation*, ed. David Zarefsky, Malcolm O. Sillars, and Jack Rhodes (Annandale, VA: Speech Communication Association, 1983), 159-69; "An Ideological Turn in Rhetorical Theory: The Third Persona," *Central States Speech Journal* 35 (1984): 197-216.

7. See my "The John Birch and Martin Luther King Symbols in the Radical Right," *Western Speech* 35 (1971): 4-14; "Salvation Through Separation: The Image of the Negro in the American Colonization Society," *Quarterly Journal of Speech* 57 (1971): 57-67; "The Savage Child: The Image of the Negro in the Pro-Slavery Movement," *Southern Speech Journal* 37 (1972): 335-60.

8. Paul Varg, "Foreign Policy: Past and Future," *Centennial Review* 21 (1977): 261-72. The dangers associated with industrialized societies trying to secure markets and raw materials have become apparent over the past century. Sartre noted the efforts by "developed" nations to divide the world into "spheres of influence" and subjugate smaller, less-developed countries through colonial rule, native chiefs or heads of state. He placed Vietnam in the context of French, German, English, and Italian colonial history: *Between Existentialism and Marxism*, trans. John Mathews (New York: William Morrow and Company, 1974), 67-83. Whatever the differences, there are remarkable similarities between colonial and modern techniques for controlling native populations. See Asbjorn Eide, "The Transfer of Arms to Third World Countries and their International Uses," *International Social Science Journal* 28 (1976): 307-25.

9. The need for such a debate and a larger sense of "argument" required is addressed in Walter R. Fisher, "Narration as a Human Communication Paradigm: The Case of Public Moral Argument," *Communication Monographs* 51 (1984): 1-22.

10. *The New York Times* (April 7, 1984): 5.

11. This mode of argument has, by one name or another, attracted the attention of rhetorical theorists. For a history of the ways in which the "enemy" has been characterized, see Robert L. Ivie, "Images of Savagery in American Justifications for War," *Quarterly Journal of Speech* 47

(1980): 279-94.   F. Michael Smith ("Rhetorical Implications of the 'Aggression' Thesis in the Johnson Administration's Vietnam Argumentation," *Central States Speech Journal* 22 [1972]: 217-24) and Richard Cherwitz ("Lyndon Johnson and the 'Crisis' of Tonkin Gulf: A President's Justification of War," *Western Journal of Speech Communication* 42 [1978]: 93-104) stress its use in the context of Vietnam. John Cragan and Donald C. Shields summarize this mode under the term "Cold War Drama" and evidence its continuing appeal in "Foreign Policy Communication Dramas: How Mediated Rhetoric Played in Peoria in Campaign '76," *Quarterly Journal of Speech* 63 (1977): 281-89.

12. On the connection between religion and politics, see Roderick Hart, *The Political Pulpit* (West Lafayette, Ind.: Purdue University Press, 1977).

13. Sacvan Bercovitch, *The American Jeremiad* (Madison: University of Wisconsin Press, 1978), 176. The classic statement on this issue is Robert N. Bellah's essay, "Civil Religion in America," *Daedalus* 96 (1967): 1-21. See also John F. Berens, "The Sanctification of American Nationalism, 1789-1812," *Canadian Review of Studies in Nationalism* 3 (1976): 172-91; and "'Like A Prophetic Spirit': Samuel Davies, American Eulogists and the Deification of George Washington," *Quarterly Journal of Speech* 63 (1977): 290-97.

14. Digby Baltzell, *The Protestant Establishment: Aristocracy and Caste in America* (New York: Random House, 1966). See also Christopher Lasch, "The Foreign Policy Elite and the War in Vietnam," *The World of Nations* (New York: Vintage Books, 1974), 232-49.

15. Baltzell, *Protestant Establishment*, 277-93.   For a statistical breakdown of what Joseph McCarthy meant for Republican votes in 1952 and 1956, see Kevin Phillips, *The Emerging Republican Majority* (New York: Anchor Books, 1970), 156-62.

16. On the appeal of "McCarthyism" to people alienated from the political establishment, growing economic centralization, and impersonal bureaucracies, and how this has been overlooked in the alarm over McCarthy's attacks on personal freedoms, see Martin Trow, "Small Businessmen, Political Tolerance, and support for McCarthy," *American Journal of Sociology* 64 (1959): 270-81.

17. John Foster Dulles, *Department of State Bulletin* (hereafter *DSB*), 22 (1955): 640-41.

18. "The Peace We Want," *DSB* 33 (1955): 375-76.

19. See F. D. Herzon, J. Kincaid, and V. Dalton, "Personality and Public Opinion: The Case of Authoritarianism, Prejudice and Support for the Korean and Vietnam Wars," *Polity* 11 (1978): 92-113.

20. Dwight D. Eisenhower, "The Influence of Business on American Freedom," *DSB* 30 (1954): 837-38.

21. John Foster Dulles, "The Goal of Foreign Policy," *DSB* 30 (1954): 894.

22. The limits "McCarthyism" placed on critical activity in a number of spheres—religion, labor, politics, culture, scholarship, and intellectual activity—are explored in *The Specter: Original Essays on the Cold War and the Origins of McCarthyism*, ed. Robert Griffith and Athan Theoharis (New York: New Viewpoints, 1974). See especially Norman Markowitz's essay, "A View from the Left: From the Popular Front to Cold War Liberalism," 90-115. Robert P. Newman, in a brilliant essay, anchors McCarthyism in domestic politics through Protestant fundamentalism and the "loss of China" and reveals its ideological utility in the struggle for power between the Republicans and Democrats. See "Lethal Rhetoric: The Selling of the China Myths," *Quarterly Journal of Speech* 61 (1975): 113-28. Failure in Vietnam, explained President Johnson in private, would make the "loss of China" and "McCarthyism" look like "chicken-shit" by comparison; cited in Henry De Weerd, "Strategic Decision Making: Vietnam, 1965-68," *The Yale Review* 67 (1978): 482.

23. John Foster Dulles, "News Conference," *DSB* 34 (1956): 155.

24. John Foster Dulles, "Challenge and Response in United States Policy," reprinted in *DSB* 37 (1957): 572.

25. Dwight D. Eisenhower, "To See the Road to Peace," *DSB* 33 (1955): 133.

26. See George Marsden, *Fundamentalism in American Culture: The Shaping of Twentieth-Century Evangelicalism* (New York: Oxford University Press, 1980), 206-11.

27. Paul Fussell, *The Great War and Modern Memory* (New York: Oxford University Press, 1975), 75-113. Robert Ivie notes the use of "binary opposition" in justifying war throughout American history in his "Images of Savagery" and Ronald Reid examines it in his study, "New England Rhetoric and the French War, 1754-1760: A Case Study in the Rhetoric of War," *Communication Monographs* 43 (1976): 259-86. But the "paranoid melodrama" to which Fussell refers is peculiarly modern in its psychological depth and global reach. The "absolutistic" and "totalizing" style characterizing it resonates with two World Wars and the "total" annihilation promised by a Third; it was also, during the Great War, a conscious part of the propaganda campaigns conducted by the parties involved; see Harold Lasswell's chapter on "Satanism" in *Propaganda Technique in World War I* (Cambridge: MIT Press, 1971), 77-101.

It may be, however, that the term "savage" provides the nineteenth-century analogue, for while government officials did not press anything like the modern dualities on France, England, or Mexico in the eighteenth and nineteenth centuries, certainly not after the initial conflict, "savage" (unless preceded by the word "noble") connotes ferocity and unspeakable cruelty. Used as a noun, as in "Indian savage," it could be and was in fact called upon to justify policies of extermination or what we now call "genocide." See Robert L. Ivie, "The Metaphor of Force in Prowar

Discourse: The Case of 1812," *Quarterly Journal of Speech* 68 (1982): 240-53.

28. Between 1961 and mid-1962, the "Kennedy Administration could not lessen Cold War tensions but only intensify them. These policies differed in no important essential from the Eisenhower policies after 1954. The New Administration was only more efficient and determined in carrying them out" (Walter LeFeber, *America, Russia, and the Cold War 1945-1971* [New York: John Wiley and Sons, Inc., 1972], 227).

29. See Kevin Phillips, 160-65. In 1960 the Union vote was nearly two to one for Kennedy (it had been equally divided between Republicans and Democrats in 1956); 3-1 for Kennedy among Catholics (it had gone Republican in 1956); professional and managerial support was up 12 percent in 1960 over 1956. See Fred I. Greenstein, *The American Party System and the American People* (Englewood Cliffs, N.J.: Prentice Hall, Inc., 1963), 24.

30. John F. Kennedy, "Towards a Strategy of Peace," *DSB* 49 (1963): 3-4. Khrushchev's visit four years earlier and his call for "peaceful coexistence" anticipated many of the themes in Kennedy's speech. See Khrushchev's article, "On Peaceful Coexistence," *Foreign Affairs* 38 (1959): 1-18. For an insightful analysis of this speech and its domestic and international significance, see Theodore Windt's essay, "Seeking Detente with Superpowers: John F. Kennedy at American University," in *Essays in Presidential Rhetoric*, ed. Theodore Windt with Beth Ingold (Dubuque, Ia.: Kendall/Hunt, 1983), 71-84.

31. Roger Hilsman, "The Challenge to Freedom in Asia," *DSB* 49 (1963): 49.

32. U. Alexis Johnson, "Address," *DSB* 49 (1963): 78

33. Dean Rusk, "The Role of the United States in World Affairs," *DSB* 56 (1967): 770.

34. Technocratic realism refers to "official" explanations of foreign policy. "Realism" as an alternative to the murderous dualities of the Cold War grew out of the work of professional diplomats, academic experts, and intellectuals. In its critical phase, before the liberals took power, the position taken by George Kennan, a career diplomat and the major intellectual influence on the articulation of American foreign policy during the late 1940s and early '50s, and liberal academics sounded much the same. But the tension was manifest even then. David Riesman and Michael Maccoby called for more realism in foreign affairs, but criticized foreign policy "experts" and the assumption that their "style of rationality" does not suppress important concerns. They questioned the requirement of "technical knowledge" and a "polished" vocabulary for entering into the debate over disarmament. At the same time, they commended the Rand Corporation and the CIA. See "The American Crisis, *The Liberal Papers*, ed. James Roosevelt (New York: Doubleday Anchor, 1962), 13-47. By

1970, humanist critics included those who embraced technocratic realism, those who saw government officials falling away from realism, and those who saw liberalism's reliance on experts and belief in the "system" as fatal. See Grant Hugo, "Cant and Foreign Policy," *Appearance and Reality* (New York: Columbia University Press, 1970), 17-32; Ralph K. White, "Black and White Thinking," *Nobody Wanted War: Misperception in Vietnam and Other Wars* (New York: Doubleday Anchor, 1970), 241-319; and *Power and Consciousness*, ed. C. O'Brien and W. Vanech (New York: New York University Press, 1969); especially Peter Nettl, "Power and the Intellectuals," 15-32, and Noam Chomsky, "Objectivity and Liberal Scholarship," 43-136.

35. See Walter R. Fisher, "Narration," and also my "The Rhetoric of Science," *Western Journal of Speech Communication*, 40 (1976): 226-35.

36. See David Eakins, "The Origins of Corporate Liberal Policy Research, 1916-1922: The Political-Economic Expert and the Decline of Public Debate," *Building the Organizational Society*, ed. Jerry Israel (New York: The Free Press, 1972), 163-80.

37. See Kathleen J. Turner, "Press Influence on Presidential Rhetoric: Lyndon Johnson at Johns Hopkins University, April 7, 1965," *Central States Speech Journal* 33 (1982): 425-36.

38. Hubert H. Humphrey, "Perspective on Asia," *DSB* 55 (1966): 6.

39. Lyndon B. Johnson, "Two Threats to Peace: Hunger and Aggression," *DSB* 55 (1966): 115.

40. Lyndon B. Johnson, "Address," *DSB* 51 (1964): 260-61.

41. William Westmoreland, "Report to Congress," *DSB* 56 (1967): 739-40. The rhetorical escalation represented by a shift to prophetic dualism alarmed some liberals who were prepared to take a "realistic" approach to foreign policy. Thus Reinhold Niebuhr urged that Vietnam be understood as a practical matter of imperial politics and not a holy war between two powerful ideologies. In the tradition of technocratic realism, Niebuhr blamed the problem on the "public":

The average voter knows little and cares less about these imperial responsibilities, such as assuring the safety of the non-Communist nations on the fringes of Asia, but is moved only by appeals to our democratic idealism, which usually is formed by static anti-Communism. Our engagement in Vietnam has consequently forced the administration to create a series of obvious fictions or myths calculated to obscure the hiatus between our idealism and our hegemonical responsibilities. See "The Social Myths of the 'Cold War,'" *Journal of International Relations* 21 (1967): 55.

42. These two modes do not exhaust the possibilities. Prophetic dualism, for example, is but one way of drawing moral principle into foreign policy. The Bill of Rights, the basis of the Civil Rights and Anti-War movements claiming the right to disobey immoral laws, translated, in the Carter administration, into an international commitment to "Human

Rights." Again, though, the move from principle to action clarifying a domestic coalition's world view proved confusing in international affairs and ill-suited in justifying compromise. "The mindset of those whose experience in foreign affairs was shaped by Vietnam and the civil rights struggle," writes Linda Miller, "has proved inadequate to the task of forming a new consensus. Charges of crisis-coping are leveled at those who plead devotion to 'world order'." See "Morality in Foreign Policy: A Failed Consensus?" *Daedalus* 109 (1981): 46. Miller offers a psychological, a formal, and a "complex world" explanation for the failure of the Carter "mindset"; she ignores a Cold War coalition including powerful economic and political interest groups whose appeal expands when official policy eschews the use of force or places limits on our "hegemonical responsibilities." The resurgence of a nationalist-militarist-fundamentalist coalition over the Panama Canal Treaty is a case in point. See Ronald A. Sudol, "The Rhetoric of Strategic Retreat: Carter and the Panama Canal Debate," *Quarterly Journal of Speech* 65 (1979): 371-91.

43. Alvin Gouldner, *The Future of Intellectuals and the Rise of the New Class* (New York: Seabury Press, 1979).

44. Johnson, "Two Threats to Peace," 115-16.

45. George Orwell, "Politics and the English Language," *The Orwell Reader*, intro. Richard Rovere (New York: Harcourt, Brace & World, 1956), 363.

46. Aldous Huxley, "Words and Behavior," *Collected Essays* (New York: Harper & Brothers Publishers, 1958), 249.

47. "The Atom Bomb as a Great Force for Peace," *American Foreign Policy Since 1945*, ed. Robert Divine (Chicago: Quadrangle Books, 1969), 33.

48. William F. Knowland and Mike Mansfield, "Our Policy in the Far East: A Debate," *American Foreign Policy Since 1945*, 107-8. It is, in our time, difficult to fathom the seriousness with which the French defeat was viewed in light of a Communist Monolith; as Knowland declared:

The loss of Southeast Asia would lead to the loss of the balance of Asia. That might mean the ultimate destruction of Europe based on Lenin's theory that the road to Paris is through Peking. And if we had the entire world pass into the Communist orbit, it would make, in effect, a continental Dienbienphu out of the United States (106).

49. Fred Charles Ikle, "Can Nuclear Weapons Last Out the Century," *Foreign Affairs* 51 (1973): 280-81. Ikle was not arguing for abandoning nuclear weapons, but for directing them not at major population centers but at crucial links in the economic and industrial structure located in less populated areas.

50. This is the view of Harlan Cleveland, a former diplomat, in his essay, "The Future of International Relations," in *Knowledge and the*

Future of Man, ed. W. J. Ong, S. J. (New York: Simon and Schuster, 1968), 73-4.

51. Eide, 310.

52. Alexander Haig, *Santa Cruz Sentinel*, May 10, 1981.

53. Frank Barnaby, "The Dynamics of World Armaments: An Overview," *International Social Science Journal* 28, (1976): 253.

54. Quoted in R. Joseph Monsen, Jr. and Mark W. Cannon's excellent chapter, "The Military Bureaucracy," in *The Makers of Public Policy: American Power Groups and Their Ideologies* (New York: McGraw-Hill Book Company, 1965), 262-63.   For an interesting debate over the "military-industrial complex," see the exchange between Seymour Melman and Jacques S. Ganster in the *Defense Management Journal* 15 (1979): 2-13.

55. Monsen and Cannon, "Military Bureaucracy," 264-69.

56. Barnaby, "Dynamics of World Armaments," 264.   The same mechanism, it must be emphasized, exists in the Soviet Union. They feed off one another, each new technological breakthrough, each new idea providing the basis for a "worst case" scenario on the other side.

57. Barnaby, 255.

58. See Dixon T. Long, "The Changing Role of Science in the Foreign Policy Process," *The Policy Sciences Journal* 5 (1976): 193-98. It was not simply that scientific experts came to be associated with American failures in Vietnam, as Irving Louis Horowitz points out. When social scientists developed misgivings about continued escalation, they lacked a constituency with which to resist military and political advisors who were able consistently to isolate and suppress the opposition of scientifically trained experts within the government. This lack of constituency, coupled with the enthusiastic support of other "experts" for the war, for new weapons systems, nuclear arms, etc. has led to a disillusionment with science and scientists as the answer to America's problems. See Horowitz's chapter, "The Pentagon Papers and the Tragedy of American Research," in *Ideology and Utopia in the United States* (New York: Oxford University Press, 1977), 275-91.

59. Barnaby, "Dynamics of World Armaments," 255.

10

Political Rhetoric and the Un-American Tradition
Philip Wander

Some say a cavalry corps,
some infantry, some, again,
will maintain that the swift oars

of our fleet are the finest
sight on dark earth; but I say
that whatever one loves, is.[1]

Sappho

Sometimes I feel ashamed that I've written so few poems on political themes, on causes that agitate me. Then I remind myself that to be a poet at all in twentieth-century America is to commit a political act.[2]

Stanley Kunitz

In the foundation myth of this nation, there is a story about the rights of humanity or, as it was then known, the rights of "Man." It tells of freedom from domination, individual joy, life itself. These rights were to be secured by a nation to come, but they did not depend, for their existence, on a new state. Rather they lived in the human breast. When government interfered with these rights, people had a God-given obligation to revolt and to fashion a new state, one ruled not by an elite few or by a monarch, but by the people. The purpose of this state would be to make government more responsive to human rights. Such is the meaning of phrases like "all men are created equal," and the claim that they are endowed, not by the state, but by their "Creator" with certain "unalienable rights," and that these rights included "life, liberty, and the pursuit of happiness."

The foundation myth, however, concealed a conflict. It had to do with "human" rights. Human rights in contrast to the rights of colonial rebels in America conveys a generous and expansive vision. This is part of its rhetorical force, its inclusiveness. But at the moment of utterance, in the here-and-now of its being spoken, heard, and acted upon in the late eighteenth century, it also served as an ideological tool. It provided an umbrella under which a coalition of disenchanted colonists could cooperate to, in their words, throw off the chains of British imperialism.

After the Revolution, and with the writing of the Constitution, the conflict between agitational ideals and established authority became apparent. Slaves, women, and unpropertied men discovered that they were not as equal as others in the newly founded republic. The contradictions between American ideals and actual, political inequality left the privacy of individual suffering to become a public, nationwide political struggle toward the middle of the nineteenth century. A "war between the states," a "civil war," struck at the myth of a unified nation-state, along with its commitment to freedom, equality, and human rights. This myth could not be sustained, as President Abraham Lincoln argued at the time, in a nation that was half-slave and half-free.

With the end of the war, the victors reaffirmed a national commitment to human rights—the right, for example, not to be whipped, or maimed, or held as property; the right of black men to run for office and vote in elections. This commitment, limited as it was, did not last long. Less than twenty years after the war, a counterrevolution arose that opposed political equality and "human" rights. The turning point came after the Tilden-Hays election in 1876, when federal troops left the South as part of a political agreement which allowed the Republican party to remain in office.

The effect was catastrophic. A resurgent white power structure removed black politicians from office, took the right to vote away from black citizens, and divided the working class into black and white, leaving it unable to organize and therefore to protect itself. Between 1870 and 1920, upwards of 20,000 black people were lynched—shot, hanged, beaten, burned to death—in the United States. The terror this spread throughout the population, the wild and guilty fantasies about race that this promoted, the terrible suffering that this caused cannot be measured.

As the promise of political progress faded in the United States, a new engine for progress took its place. It appeared to transcend race, religion, and national borders, and did not depend for its success on armed struggle. This new mechanism had its origins in Europe and in a reunited United States where, because of the need to gear up for war, the northern states had rapidly industrialized. It was known by different names: "Yankee ingenuity," "free enterprise," "industrialism." But what it promised was a "modern" world. Walt Whitman wrote about this world and its political potential in his poem "Years of the Modern":

> Years of the modern! years of the unperform'd!
> Your horizon rises, I see it parting away for more august dramas,

I see not America only, not only Liberty's nation but other
    nations preparing,
I see tremendous entrances and exits, new combinations, the
    solidarity of races,
I see that force advancing with irresistible power on the world's
    stage, (Have the old forces, the old wars, played their
    parts? are the acts suitable to them closed?)
I see Freedom, completely arm'd and victorious and very haughty,
    with Law on one side and Peace on the other,
A stupendous trio all issuing forth against the idea of caste;
What historic denouements are these we so rapidly approach?
I see men marching and countermarching by swift millions,
I see the frontiers and boundaries of the old aristocracies
    broken,
I see the landmarks of European kings removed,
I see this day the People beginning their landmarks, (all others
    give way;)
Never were such sharp questions ask'd as this day,
Never was average man, his soul, more energetic, more like a God,
Lo, how he urges and urges, leaving the masses no rest!

The old political ideals—still inspiring for Whitman—found a new source
of energy in modern technology and economic progress:

His daring foot is on land and sea everywhere, he colonizes the
    Pacific, the archipelagoes,
With the steamship, the electric telegraphy, the newspaper, the
    wholesale engines of war,
With these and the world-spreading factories he interlinks all
    geography, all lands . . .
Years prophetical! the space ahead as I walk, as I vainly try to
    pierce it, is full of phantoms,
Unborn deeds, things soon to be, project their shapes around me,
This incredible rush and heat, this strange ecstatic fever of
    dreams O years!
Your dreams O years, how they penetrate through me! (I know not
    whether I sleep or wake;)
The perform'd America and Europe grow dim, retiring in shadow
    behind me,
The unperform'd, more gigantic than ever, advance, advance upon
    me.[3]

The modern world, however, did not eliminate the conflict between
governments and human rights. This was a conflict that Whitman himself
did not immediately grasp. But while he, at one time, celebrated
America's "Manifest Destiny"—the inevitability of her ruling a large part
of the world—and invoked divine support for our imperial ambition,
Kunitz eventually concluded:

In vain have we annex'd Texas, California, Alaska, and reach north for Canada and south for Cuba. It is as if we were somehow being endow'd with a vast and more thoroughly-appointed body, and then left with little or no Soul.[4]

Whitman turned his democratic sympathies back on America and her relations with other nations. He noted the conflict between a spirit of liberation, freedom from arbitrary power, even that exercised in the name of political ideals and national interest in his poem, "Thick-Sprinkled Bunting:"

> Thick-sprinkled bunting! flag of stars!
> Long yet your road, fateful flag—long yet your road, and lined
>   with bloody death,
> For the prize I see at issue at last is the world,
> All its ships and shores I see interwoven with your threads greedy
>   banner;
> Dream'd again the flags of kings, highest borne, to flaunt
>   unrival'd?
> O hasten flag of man—O with sure and steady step, passing highest
>   flags of kings,
> Walk supreme to the heavens mighty symbol—run up above them all,
> Flag of stars! thick-sprinkled bunting![5]

Whitman contrasts a cloth flag, with stars stitched on it, with the star-spangled heavens. He contrasts imperial ambition and the desire for profit (the "flags of kings") with policies grounded in human rights (the "flag of man").

How much we can draw out of Whitman's poetry, I am not sure. For many, his poems are difficult, even embarrassing to read aloud. Does the problem have to do with style, Whitman's expansive and redolent romanticism? Is this what makes it difficult to sing his songs of America? Or is it, moving to a political context, his naiveté, and our superior, more up-to-date knowledge of a more complicated world? Or is it perhaps something darker, deeds now performed, cloth flags unfurled by the CIA in the dead of night? Regardless of the explanation, one thing is sure, the meaning of America has changed, and this change makes Whitman's songs difficult to sing, if not painful to hear.

There are, I think, some historical changes affecting our response that are worth exploring. One change has to do with the rise of the Soviet Union. The Bolshevik revolution, in the early part of the twentieth century, produced another universalizing ideology. It stressed equality, the rights of the working classes, a withering away of the state, and an economic structure eliminating concentration of great wealth. Its anti-wealth, anti-elitist, anti-state, pro-humanity ideology was called "social-ism" or "communism," but this foundation myth and the economic realities on which it turned was not unique to the Russian revolution. It had been a force in European politics since before the French revolution. Rousseau, in 1743, wrote that the ideal of moral and lawful equality is an illusion under a bad government: "It serves only to keep the poor in their wretchedness and sustain the rich in their usurpation." He carried this observation beyond particular governments to consider the conflict between the ideal of political equality and the realities of great wealth. "In truth," he concludes, "laws are always useful to those with possessions and harmful to those who have nothing; from which it follows that the social state is advantageous only when all possess something and none has too much."[6] Although a number of socialistic revolutions failed in the century after Rousseau spelled out the social contract—1848 was the high-water mark in efforts to create democratic, socialistic societies all over Europe—economic equality remained a powerful ideal up to and beyond the Russian revolution.

Socialism was not, however, the only major ideological formation at the turn of the twentieth century. In response to the "threat" of socialism and the sudden disillusionment with traditional religion, democracy, free enterprise or capitalism, and the Great War, another transnational ideology emerged, celebrating the state, sacrificing individual rights, demanding absolute loyalty to those in power in the interests of law, order, and the future. Fascism, with its base in the army, the state, and widespread feelings of nationalism, was a worldwide movement. Fascists took power in Italy in the 1920s. Fascists took control in Germany, Spain, and Japan in the 1930s. Strong Fascist movements existed in Austria, France, and other European countries. During this period, thousands of Fascists clad in brown, quasi-military uniforms marched down Pennsylvania Avenue.

It is difficult to fathom, but there were, early in the twentieth century, two powerful ideologies that encountered "America" or "Americanism." One was on the left, and the other was on the right. This was no mere conflict of ideas. After the Great War and in the midst of the Great Depression, private armies fought for control, for the future in several countries. The struggle was over the control of a nation. The cultural sphere, within which the struggle took place, concerned the meaning of the nation—what it stood for, who it included, what it promised. The meaning of "America" was not then and is not now the product of free and open debate. The issue is not only how the nation is defined, but also who gets to do the defining. In the 1930s, Congress set up a committee to preside over this matter. It was authorized to investigate citizens to determine whether or not they were "pro-American." Martin Dies, chair of the House Un-American Activities Committee of the U.S. Congress, declared on August 12, 1938:

In investigating unAmerican activities, it must be born in mind that because we do not agree with opinions, or philosophies of others, does not make such opinions, or philosophies unAmerican. The most common practice engaged in by some people is to brand their opponents with names when they are unable to refute their arguments with facts and logic. Therefore, we find a few people of conservative thought who are inclined to brand every Liberal's viewpoint as communistic. Likewise, we find some so-called Liberals who stigmatize every conservative idea fascistic. The utmost care therefore must be observed to distinguish clearly between what is obviously unAmerican, and what is more or less an honest difference of opinion with respect to some economic, political or social question.[7]

This balancing of Communism and Fascism, regardless of historic validity, made political sense in the United States during this period.

The fascist states (the axis powers) formed an alliance, and war broke out in Europe and Asia in the late 1930s. Ten years later, this alliance was defeated in a second great war, World War II. This was the war to make the world safe from fascism. But with the destruction of the axis powers, a shift occurred in this country, in the ideological balance observed by the House Un-American Activities Committee. Suddenly there was no longer any transnational fascist menace. The right wing no longer had to explain a threatening fascistic movement. The left wing, however, faced a vastly expanded centralized government and a security industry, built up during the war, including: (1) a surveillance component—the FBI, military intelligence services; (2) a production component—defense industries, national laboratories; (3) a skills component—the educational system, including defense education acts, defense contracts, military academies; (4) an action component—the military services, the CIA; and (5) a public relations component—the Defense Department, Joint Chiefs of Staff, Veterans of Foreign Wars, National Space Administration with their recruitment spots, news announcements, interviews, background briefings, support for television shows and movies, newsletters, magazines, and the like. For this loosely related but cooperatively run system, Communism now served as its reason for being, an unimpeachable justification for increased funding, power, and influence. The security industry pointed to an international threat—a Communist nation (the Soviet Union) as a world power, challenging the United States hegemony in Europe, Africa, and Asia. It pointed to a domestic threat inspired by the same ideas, guided by foreign agents, and the threat of internal subversion. Communism, after the defeat of international fascism, was the sole remaining menace facing America.

And the menace grew. After the war, the Soviet Union took in Eastern Europe. But even more dramatic and more terrifying to the American public, Soviet scientists broke the American monopoly on nuclear weapons, detonated a hydrogen bomb, and developed long-range bombers and intercontinental ballistic missiles capable of reaching the United States. The challenge to national security presented by a rival nuclear colossus was real. The question then, in this country, was officially framed: How can we most effectively protect our national interest?

There were two responses offered by officials in the Truman and Eisenhower administrations: (1) in foreign affairs, oppose the Soviet Union wherever possible; (2) in domestic affairs, root out any and all Communists and their friends and allies and suppress Communistic, socialistic, Un-American ways of thinking and acting. These responses were at times brutal and misguided. Lies were told in the national interest or to cover up official error. Millions of lives were lost in an effort to protect the "free world." However misguided or unfortunate we may now view these events, the seriousness of this crisis, as it was perceived by both public officials and the masses at the time, cannot be overestimated.

There were those in government who believed that the Soviet Union had achieved its nuclear capability because of traitors in the United States. Robert Oppenheimer lost his security clearance after a lengthy investigation by the Atomic Energy Commission. Ethel and Julius Rosenberg were tried, found guilty, and executed for having given "atomic secrets" to the Soviet Union. The government initiated the Marshall Plan in Europe and entered the Korean War to "stem the Communist tide." The military budget swelled, dispersing hundreds of billions to develop new weapons systems—long-range bombers, missiles, advanced atomic, chemical, and biological weapons—and the corporate monoliths (Lockheed, Boeing, General Electric) necessary to design and build such systems. The several states and congressional districts vied for federal monies. Population shifts during World War II into areas built up by the military and its support systems continued after the war, as people migrated to where the federal jobs were located—Arizona, Texas, California, Washington.

All these policies, programs, and changes were justified as a response to the "Communist Menace." But beyond the several components of the security industry justifying their yearly budgetary requests by appealing to this threat, a mass-based cultural and political movement arose in the late 1940s and early 1950s committed to rooting out the Communist menace at home and abroad.   The anti-Communist, or McCarthy, movement (McCarthyism) empowered the right wing in this country. It marked the careers of anti-Communist, Cold War conservative and liberal politicians, labor organizers, scholars, and entertainment figures including Harry Truman, John Foster Dulles, Richard Nixon, Hubert Humphrey, George Meany, Henry Luce, John Wayne, Jimmy Stewart, Ronald Reagan, Sidney Hook, Richard Hofstadter, and Seymour Martin Lipset.

The larger cultural-political agreement focused not on the leadership of one senator (Joseph McCarthy), but on the threat of the Soviet Union and Un-Americanism. What is often overlooked in the focus on Senator McCarthy is that the movement communicated a view of "America" that had been officially endorsed and propagated during two world wars.

"American" became "Americanism."   Nationalism and loyalty to the state—to those in power—became the overriding test of true Americanism, while Un-Americanism became synonymous with Communism, socialism, internationalism.   Being Un-American during this period became a criminal offense, having Un-American sympathies grounds for dismissal from government, the entertainment industry, education, and labor unions.

In this new formulation, with its emphasis on loyalty and patriotism, the conflict between the founding myth and the power state disappeared. Americanism, calling for loyalty to those temporarily in power regardless of the policies they pursued or the God-given rights they abused, inspired a popular slogan in the 1950s: My country right or wrong.

"America," the founding myth embracing human rights, committed to equality, freedom, liberty, life, and happiness for all peoples, abandoned the political center and entered the cultural margins in the United States. Lawrence Ferlinghetti, in the late 1950s, probed the meaning of "America." In San Francisco coffee houses, backed by jazz musicians, he sang:

> I am waiting for my case to come up
> and I am waiting
> for a rebirth of wonder
> and I am waiting for someone
> to really discover America
> and wail
> and I am waiting
> for the discovery
> of a new symbolic western frontier
> and I am waiting
> for the American Eagle
> to really spread its wings
> and straighten up and fly right
> and I am waiting
> for the Age of Anxiety
> to drop dead
> and I am waiting
> for the war to be fought
> which will make the world safe
> for anarchy
> and I am waiting
> for the final withering away
> of all governments
> and I am perpetually awaiting
> a rebirth of wonder.

He then questioned the connection of "Americanism" with God or, in a political context, with organized, right-wing religion:

> I am waiting for the Second Coming
> and I am waiting

for a religious revival
to sweep thru the state of Arizona
and I am waiting
for the Grapes of Wrath to be stored
and I am waiting
for them to prove
that God is really American.[8]

Opposition to "Americanism" and the political party benefiting from the great anti-Communist movement of the 1940s and 1950s, the Republican party, grew into a mass-based socio-political movement. The ideology of this movement decried the abuse of human rights inside the United States and invoked the dream of political equality and democracy located in the foundation myth. This was the civil rights movement of the 1950s and 1960s.

The civil rights movement attracted all sorts of outsiders—black radicals, white and black Christians, socialists, Communists, bohemians, beatniks, Jewish intellectuals, pacifists, anarchists, artists, educators, young college students—all those marginalized by government, Republican and Democratic, and a social order committed to centralized control, racial hierarchies, and political oppression. The vehicle for this motley band of dissenters was the party then out of power, the Democratic party. In 1960 the Democratic candidate for president, John F. Kennedy, barely won. Four years later, Lyndon Johnson and the Democrats, with their intellectual, Catholic, pro-civil rights martyr, overcame the Republicans and Barry Goldwater. They swept into office. Once in, they introduced new social programs providing housing, food, and better education for the lower classes and expanded rights at home—the right to vote for minorities, the right to go to a "public" school, play in "public" parks, drink at "public" water fountains, and enjoy all the facilities subsidized by "public" tax dollars.

At the same time, however, the Johnson administration also promoted policies, begun in the Truman and continued during the Eisenhower and Kennedy administrations, destroying the human rights of millions abroad. Known variously as a "no-win war," a "tragedy," "failure," "folly," "atrocity," and "imperialist" war, or simply the war in Vietnam.

As the war in Vietnam expanded into a national commitment, it engulfed the civil rights movement, blunting the movement's claims on America through a racist draft that exempted college students, most of whom were white. Resistance to the war and the draft grew. Hundreds of thousands marched in opposition. This resistance, inspired by "outside agitators" and a "Communist menace" according to some in government, J. Edgar Hoover included, called for an official response—Tac Squads, agent provocateurs, and FBI subversion. Thus, a political party that came to power, in part, on the basis of its commitment to civil rights ended up trying to "defend freedom" by drafting poor white, brown, and, above all, black young men and shipping them off to Southeast Asia to risk their lives for "America."

Martin Luther King, Jr., was assassinated. Cities burned. Bobby Kennedy was assassinated. Dissenters marched, shouted obscenities, challenged state authority. Some were shot, others beaten in the Chicago police riot. Thousands were jailed. Black ministers were replaced by black-power advocates and arguments crafted by W. E. B. DuBois and Malcolm X.

At the 1968 Democratic convention in Chicago, Vice President Hubert Humphrey's nomination attracted thousands of war protesters and a police riot. Amid war and repression, concerns about human rights and a commitment to nonviolent social and political change seemed remote, no longer feasible, not up to the challenge of officially sanctioned violence at home and abroad.

The growing disillusionment with an America in which the promise of civil rights had vanished informs Maya Angelou's poem "America," published in 1975:

> The gold of her promise
>   has never been mined
> Her borders of justice
>   not clearly defined
> Her crops of abundance
>   the fruit and the grain
> Have not fed the hungry
>   nor eased that deep pain
> Her proud declarations
>   are leaves on the wind

Rejecting the exposed claims of 1960s liberalism to be able to solve the problems of poverty, hunger, and disease at home and abroad, Angelou recalls the historic failure of the United States in relation to black people:

> Her southern exposure
>   black death did befriend

This tragedy pierces the official myth of "America." What it reveals cannot and must not be ignored:

> Discover this country
>   dead centuries cry
> Erect noble tablets
>   where none can decry
> "She kills her bright future
>   and rapes for a sou
> Then entraps her children

        with legends untrue"
    I beg you
    Discover this country.[9]

About the cultural and political margins, various groups advanced issues that would affect the struggle for power: fear of a nuclear catastrophe; a resurgence of civil rights concerns including the old and the young, women, black, brown, and red people, and poor whites; opposition to the use of violence against other nations (Nicaragua); workers' fears about jobs and foreign competition; and oppression in South Africa. Issues rose and fell in the opinion polls.   There were marches, sit-ins, demonstrations.   They entered the evening news, informed TV programs, movies, and popular novels.   These issues and their constituencies waited, with Jesse Jackson and his Rainbow Coalition, in the outer offices of the Democratic party.

But these issues and the "America" Maya Angelou discovered did not find official endorsement in the 1980s.   Ronald Reagan, an informer for the House Un-American Activities Committee when head of the Screen Actors' Guild in the 1950s, was elected president.   During his eight years in office, government became more responsive to and enjoyed the support of a well-to-do white constituency.   Nixon's term had been cut short, but with the Reagan years, right-wing anti-Communists with their coalition of military, fundamentalist Christians, and nationalists captured the government.   In 1988, this same coalition accepted the candidacy of George Bush, shaped his campaign rhetoric, and continued the push for continued high levels of military spending, along with other projects and policies favored by the security industry.

It is in this historical context that campaign rhetoric over the last fifty years in general, and the rhetoric of presidential campaigns in particular, manipulative, banal, and forgettable as it may be, takes on significance. In the 1988 presidential campaign, for example, Vice President Bush attacked the patriotism of Democratic candidate Governor Michael Dukakis because he vetoed a bill requiring Massachusetts's teachers to say the Pledge of Allegiance before each class, because of his membership in the American Civil Liberties Union (ACLU), and because of his "liberalism." The response from some newspaper columnists and most Democrats was that this was a smear tactic, an echo of McCarthyism.

Whether or not the attack was accurate or fair, it proved effective. When Bush visited flag factories and boasted that his campaign had increased their sales, he entered far enough into the parodic to be considered a postmodernist politician.   Whether serious, droll, or a conscious parody, Bush's campaign managed, in subtle, sophisticated, and even amusing ways, to recuperate right-wing ideology.   What his campaign did was re-cast 1950s Republican campaign themes in more modern terms, terms acceptable to a middle class more alarmed about drugs in the schools, disrespect for authority, and the cost of social programs than the specter of an American Communist party.

In response, Bush's campaign managed to equate tax increases for social programs with liberalism, a commitment to the poor with socialism, membership in the ACLU with fellow traveling, opposition to the death penalty with pro-criminality, reluctance to endorse invasions of other countries or support "freedom fighters" with Communist or defeatist sympathies. These paradigmatic links produced an almost secret language.

Politically speaking, it was a code temporally linking together real people and groups into a successful political coalition. It joined together, on the one hand, those who opposed tax increases, those who feared minority violence (the black man furloughed from prison who killed again becoming an exemplar), those who believed in the need for more force to defend law and order at home and abroad, and those who feared a subversion of American values by foreigners, with, on the other hand, those who profited from the sale of weapons for the domestic market (the National Rifle Association and its corporate supporters), those who profited from a greatly expanded military and the production of high-tech military weapons for the international market, and the U.S. military.

In this enriched ideological context, the conflict surrounding the Pledge of Allegiance and Dukakis's veto of a bill requiring school teachers to begin each class with it takes on meaning. The Pledge celebrates the national religion, which is nationalism itself, and recalls the historic effort of the right wing to stem the tide of Un-American or non-nationalistic religions opposed to capitalism and undermining the "free world." In this way, those who would oppose profiteering at home, who favor a better life for the poor here and in the Third World, though they may not be criminals, remain the enemy, the group to be kept from power.

The Pledge, rhetorically speaking, calls for allegiance to the nation as an abstract entity. In more concrete terms, it now calls for an allegiance with those who run the nation (Colonel Oliver North's defense was that he was pledged, not to the Constitution, but to the president of the United States), take the white middle-class family as an ideal, endorse "Christian" values, and favor a strong national defense. What this project depends on, apart from patriotic (pro-American) government officials, are loyal, patriotic judges, news commentators, teachers, and students who are loyal to "Americanism." This is how the system reproduces itself, promotes stability, and educates another generation of children in the responsibilities of citizenship and the need to defend this great country of ours and the rest of the "free world" against whatever menace should present itself.

But, what happens when politicians or educators do not grasp this vision, or actually take an Un-American view of the world? The answer is that they encourage subversion and agitation. The problem here has to do with transformations. When disobedience is equated with disloyalty, when dissent is equated with agitation, and when agitation is equated with subversion, the issues underlying civil disobedience and dissent are irrelevant. The issue becomes the need for greater vigilance and control in the defense of freedom, a situation calling for increased surveillance and stricter discipline.

What are the institutions responsible for surveillance and discipline in this country? They are the police in domestic matters, and our armed forces in foreign affairs. The point here, with regard to the meaning of Americanism, is that the issues underlying political dissent may be ignored when dissenters are associated with Un-Americanism. The turn here occurs when the act of dissent becomes, if not in itself an Un-American act, then evidence of Un-American sympathies. With this attitude toward history, those who dissented from U.S. foreign policy in the 1960s, students and teachers in particular, constitute a group that must be kept under surveillance. It follows, then, that they should be required to affirm their loyalty and to obey the laws.

Within this world view, a refusal on the part of a government official to require, when the opportunity offered itself, the Pledge of Allegiance to the United States of America indicates not a respect for the Constitution or an individual citizen's civil rights, but something quite ominous: a secret affinity for subversion and a reluctance to get tough on crime at home and uphold America's national security. This impression was strengthened, during the election, when Bush brought up Dukakis's ironic declaration that he was a "card-carrying member of the ACLU," an organization protecting individual liberties against the state, whether the individuals are on the right (Ku Klux Klan, General Edwin Walker, Col. Oliver North), or on the left (Communist party), or engage in cultural dissent or profiteering (merchants of sex images). It was not the irony that emerged, the play on the HUAC investigations of the 1940s and the McCarthy hearings of the 1950s, but the echo of "card-carrying member of the Communist party," and with it the hint of secret subversive impulses which was a staple of the right-wing rhetoric of the 1950s.

This brief attempt to explicate the campaign rhetoric of the 1988 presidential campaign highlights a link between right-wing rhetoric in the 1950s and 1980s. What anti-Communist conservatives accomplished during the 1980s, rhetorically speaking, is the recuperation of anti-Communist ideology. It has changed, to be sure. In this new incarnation, liberal means fellow traveler, and fellow traveling is linked with child-pornographers, welfare breeders, rapists, abortionists, homosexuals, along with those who want to redistribute the wealth of hard-working Americans.

In this way, the definition of Un-American, which, immediately after World War II, focused on subversive ideas and left-wing intellectuals, has expanded, reaching an audience concerned about not only left-wing subversives, but also groups wanting to raise taxes, subvert middle-class morality, and cut defense spending (weaken "our" national security). Un-Americanism, by implication, comes to mean socialistic, hedonistic, and permissive on the one side, greedy, perverse, and enjoying the profits derived from child sex, pornography, and drugs on the other. Thus, the specter of Communism with a cadre of carefully trained and dedicated agitators and saboteurs, the staple of the old rhetoric, has given way to an anarchy of addicts, perverts, con, porn, and rad-lovers bent on aborting unborn children or weaning them away from their families and exploiting them in the big cities. Instead of a dark conspiracy of identifiable people such as Communist party members and their dupes, the new enemy takes on the aspect of an ink blot, a personification of widespread fears and irritations. To put it in terms of popular culture, the right-wing continues to cast the world into a contest between good and evil. If this contest were understood to be a wrestling match, the announcer at Caesar's Palace would step up to the microphone to bring us the main event: "Ladies and gentlemen, in the far corner, dressed in red tights, the challengers for the tag-team championship of the world—Boris Badinof and Chester the Molester. In the near corner, dressed in the red, white, and blue tights, Captain America and the Moral Majority." The match is filled with grunts and groans, plastic packets of red liquid are slapped against the forehead, the wrestlers thrash about in this way for several months. Then it is over. The campaign is filled with heroes and villains. The struggle has been carefully scripted.[10]

A similar lack of inspiration informed left-wing rhetoric during the campaign. What the 1988 election revealed is that the institutionalized Left has not yet gathered together an ideology for the 1980s and 1990s. On being accused of masking its identity—refusing to speak the "L" word (liberal)—Dukakis and the Democrats fell silent. They represented a cause that could not speak its name. What the professional liberals offered was a kind of managerial ethos, a reprise of the Johnson-Goldwater campaign of 1964—the kindly technocrat versus the dangerous ideologue. This was much less dramatic, but no less an attempt to publicize a cartoon contest between good and evil or, at least, between competence and incompetence, efficiency and inefficiency, capability and incapability.

It would be a serious error, however, to allow moral outrage to conceal the theoretical brilliance of transforming "America" into "Americanism" in the United States, privileging the flag, patriotism, and an "American" way. There is no question but that it has proved politically useful and financially profitable for powerful interest groups in this country. At the same time, a critique denouncing right-wing scoundrels, a military-industrial-educational complex, or cynical voters and uninformed masses abandons the political struggle. Moreover, such denunciations ignore the bankruptcy of a liberalism unable to speak its name or advance its programs, no matter how desperately needed, without worrying over questions of cost and efficiency, and reluctant to attack the defense budget—the federal budget's Fort Knox, that bastion of true "American-ism," the protector of our national faith, the institution in whom, during moments of national crisis, our fortunes must be, have been, and are now being placed. Liberalism, wedded to the corporate state on one side and mindless nationalism on the other, has abandoned both principle and theory. It is the exhausted remnant of the old anti-Communist, corporate liberalism of the 1960s. It has not proved up to the task of addressing human issues. Meanwhile, the right wing and its coalition of interest groups continue to thrive on a mass-based sense of perpetual crisis. National and international crises do not merely call for, they demand a stronger, more powerful fortress-America.

It will not do to leave all this as some kind of spiritual conflict. The political struggle in this country is anchored in a material world and conflicting economic interests. Military expenditure, during the Reagan years, became an engine of Keynesian economics, an instrument for "heating up" the economy. It was used, during the 1980s, by a conserva-tive administration calling for a balanced budget, as a means for disman-tling liberal welfare programs, the Keynesian engine on the left during the 1960s. Liberalism managed, in the 1930s and the 1960s, to transform human rights into a profitable investment. The billions that went into food stamps, public works, job training, housing, and the like had an impact on the national growth rate and the gross national product. Liberal econo-mists happily calculated a "multiplier effect," the amount of investment generated by the expenditure of each federal dollar. Conservative economists, following the model of two world wars (through military contracts at home and arms sales abroad), made "national security" profitable in the 1980s. Along with this, they celebrated a top-down as opposed to a bottom-up method of distribution of federal tax-dollars known as "trickle-down economics."

An economy is not simply a matter of statistical increases and decreases. What expenditures are for—the stuff they buy and build, and the services they render, the lives people live inside and outside the econo-my—cannot be set aside. In the short run, military investment gives the illusion of prosperity. It is a prosperity of armaments and war. And the result, in the absence of any actual threat to a nation—tiny Nicaragua marching behind an enormous red arrow through Mexico into Galveston, Texas, does not and will not, except for the feeble-minded, constitute such a threat—is a poverty of spirit and fellow feeling. In the long run, if we can still entertain something like a future in this country, more generous dreams will have to confront wealthy and entrenched realities.

This struggle may inspire us. It will give rise to impassioned and artistic critiques, but their very eloquence will be a symptom both of crisis and powerlessness. The rediscovery of an American dream will not be accomplished by fine words and searching films and docu-dramas and films. An American dream, and I contrast this to the prevailing American fear, awaits a principled and resourceful Un-American movement dedicated to the propositions that other peoples should not be dominated and that the future of the United States is not captured in a portrait of a shining garrison on the hill.

NOTES

1. Sappho, "To an army wife, in Sardis," *Sappho*, trans. Mary Barnard (Berkeley: University of California Press, 1958), 41.

2. Stanley Kunitz, *Next-to-Last-Things* (Boston: Atlantic Monthly Press, 1985), 126.

3. Walt Whitman, *Leaves of Grass*, intro. Christopher Morley (New York: Doubleday, Doran & Co., 1940), 209-210.

4. Kunitz, *Next-to-Lost-Things*, 64.

5. Whitman, *Leaves of Grass*, 175.

6. John Jacques Rousseau, *The Social Contract*, trans. Maurice Cranston (New York: Penguin, 1968), 68.

7. Quoted in Eric Bently, *Thirty Years of Treason* (New York: Viking Press, 1971), xvii-xviii.

8. Lawrence Ferlinghetti, "I Am Waiting," *A Coney Island of the Mind* (New York: New Directions, 1958), 51-52.

9. Maya Angelou, "America," in *Oh Pray My Wings Are Gonna Fit Me Well* (New York: Random House, 1975), 29-30.

10. For those who do not find the wrestling arena culturally satisfying and who crave a less comic, more ambiguous cultural analogue, the film *Taxi Driver* with its wet neon-lit streets, psychotic moralist, empty politicians, teenage prostitute, and a society given over to the adulation of violence may serve.

PART IV

CONCLUSION

11

The Prospects of Cold War Criticism

Robert L. Ivie

After more than four decades, the Cold War remains a rhetorical reality that demands a critical response, for there are better and worse ways of talking about a world endangered by instruments of its own making—even when chronic tensions between the superpowers appear to subside. Accordingly, each of the perspectives discussed in this volume evaluates a different facet of the rhetorical choices comprising the Cold War—past, present, and future. Observations from all three perspectives reveal the relevance of past choices to present perceptions and suggest possibilities for modifying the conventional wisdom that has sustained East-West tensions at a level too near the threshold of confrontation. United by a common goal of constructing a less dangerous future, these otherwise distinct points of view comprise a relatively comprehensive framework of criticism.

The strategic approach seeks to understand how discourse is designed intentionally to achieve particular goals with specific audiences within the constraints of given situations. Understanding these relationships enables the critic to judge whether the possibilities of rhetorical modification have been fully exploited at designated points in time. Cold War, from this perspective, is primarily a matter of symbolic action serving certain strategic ends, including the efforts of both superpowers to fulfill their national aspirations short of triggering a nuclear war. Thus, attention is focused on the opportunities for influence afforded by choices related to timing, place, medium, speaker, audience, content, style, and purpose. Just as effective rhetoric is adapted to realistic readings of existing situations, situational realities are rhetorically modified over time by a series of strategic adaptations.

While the strategic approach emphasizes contextual constraints and opportunities for rhetorical adaptation, the metaphorical approach focuses attention on conceptual resources for constructing rhetorical strategies. It enables the critic to expose the sources of rhetorical invention that sustain

Cold War motives, thereby facilitating the search for practical alternatives. A metaphorical perspective fosters critical inquiries aimed at liberating the vehicles of political imagination by exposing the conceptual conventions of Cold War discourse. It adds to the general framework of criticism an approach that monitors rhetoric's restraints on its own reality-constructing potential and thus prepares the way for an ideological critique of political culture.

With its focus on culture and politics, an ideological critique seeks to enhance human potential by intervening rhetorically on the side of democratic political theory. It attempts to preserve the prerogatives of the many by rescuing misappropriated symbols of democracy from the grip of imperialistic foreign policies. Ideological analysis, which culminates in political action through the agency of its own rhetoric, cannot hope to succeed without also undertaking a critique of strategic constraints and metaphorical resources. Likewise, the strategic and the metaphorical perspectives are rendered serviceable through their identification with ideology—whether conservative, liberal, or radical.[1]

The pluralism endemic to a comprehensive framework of rhetorical criticism insures a diversity of perspectives without sacrificing the potential for arriving at general observations. Moreover, a pluralism of perspectives enhances the confidence conferred upon any generalization derived from separate examinations of Cold War discourse. One such generalization, supported by the various studies in this volume, pertains to a pervasive form of rhetorical inertia that delimits the prospect of sustaining any momentary reduction of superpower hostilities.

The central tendencies of Cold War rhetoric remain intact despite Mikhail Gorbachev's celebrated policies of *glasnost* and *perestroika*—both of which became associated with the achievement of an Intermediate-Range Nuclear Forces (INF) agreement, which eliminated an entire class of nuclear missiles and renewed hopes for negotiating substantial reductions in conventional force structures. Instead of interpreting *glasnost* and *perestroika* as policies designed to further Soviet national interests, Ronald Reagan construed them as "signs of change, steps toward greater freedom in the Soviet Union."[2] Addressing students at Moscow State University one day before exchanging the INF treaty's instruments of ratification, Reagan spoke in glowing terms of Russian reforms that might eventually bring about an end to the Cold War:

> Your generation is living in one of the most exciting, hopeful times in Soviet history. It is a time when the first breath of freedom stirs the air and the heart beats to the accelerated rhythm of hope, when the accumulated spiritual energies of a long silence yearn to break free.
>
> . . . .
>
> We do not know what the conclusion will be of this journey, but we're hopeful that the promise of reform will be fulfilled. In this Moscow spring, this May 1988,

we may be allowed that hope: that freedom, like the fresh green sapling planted over Tolstoi's grave, will blossom forth at last in the rich fertile soil of your people and culture. We may be allowed to hope that the marvelous sound of a new openness will keep . . . ringing through, leading to a new world of reconciliation, friendship, and peace.[3]

Four months later, while addressing the United Nations, Reagan repeated his vision of eventual world peace. Once more, it was a hope premised on the emergence of Western-style freedoms in the Soviet Union:

For the first time, the differences between East and West—fundamental differences over important moral questions dealing with the worth of the individual and whether governments shall control people or people control governments—for the first time these differences have shown signs of easing, easing to the point where there are not just troop withdrawals from places like Afghanistan but also talk in the East of reform and greater freedom of press, of assembly, and of religion. Yes, fundamental differences remain. But should talk of reform become more than that, should it become reality, there is the prospect of not only a new era in Soviet-American relations but a new age of world peace.[4]

Clearly, the president had not altered his standard criteria for assessing Soviet-American relations; he had only entertained the possibility of converting Russia into a Western democracy and thereby realizing the Wilsonian dream of eternal peace among free and civilized nations. Accordingly, anything short of a complete ideological conversion by the Soviets will produce only disappointment and deepen disillusionment among Reagan's, and now President Bush's, followers, further undermining prospects of peaceful coexistence with the "Evil Empire."

The terms of Reagan's tenuous bargain with Gorbachev's Russia should come as no surprise to those familiar with the legacy of Cold War rhetoric in America.

From an ideological perspective, the foundation myth of freedom has become associated with an Americanism that preaches absolute loyalty to the state. Patriotism has surpassed all other considerations regardless of whether the policies pursued undermine the rights of other nations to determine their own course of action. Such blind devotion to nationalism has been grounded throughout the Cold War era in powerful appeals to prophetic dualism and technocratic realism.

From a metaphorical perspective, the arguments in support of America's absolute superiority over its Cold War adversary have depended upon a fundamental distinction between civilization and savagery—an image advanced by Reagan and his predecessors through various categories of decivilizing vehicles, from darkness to demons.[5] Even when the pursuit of Communist subversives has led to domestic excesses in the name of freedom and civilization, as in the case of Joseph McCarthy, the situation has been rectified rhetorically by associating demagoguery with the dark forces of tyranny. Ironically, the rhetoric of the leading critics of American Cold War policies, from Henry Wallace to William Fulbright and Helen Caldicott, has been darkened as well by the vehicles of savagery.

From a strategic perspective, we have seen how the Eisenhower administration conducted an anti-Soviet propaganda campaign under the guise of sponsoring the peaceful use of atomic energy, even though it harbored no intention of turning weapons into plowshares in the foreseeable future. The goal instead was to win a psychological victory over the Soviets by advancing a proposal that would isolate them as a foe of the entire free world. The Kennedy administration as well legitimized its resumption of atmospheric testing of nuclear weapons by contrasting a rhetorical portraiture of the President as a man of good will and moral purpose with a portrayal of the Soviets as secretive and deceptive.

Regardless of one's specific perspective, the general pattern of America's reluctance to coexist with the Soviet Union and the rest of the world on equal terms is readily apparent. America's peace is premised strictly on the demise of Communism. Thus, the eventual failure of *glasnost* and *perestroika* to democratize the Soviet system consistent with Western standards can only intensify American insecurities and reinforce the call for "peace through strength" on the grounds that a barbaric enemy is responsive solely to superior force.

What, then, are the opportunities to intervene rhetorically on behalf of a less Manichean vision of Soviet-American relations? While there is no immediate or easy answer to such a question, various starting points can be identified within the current framework of criticism.

Strategically, we have John F. Kennedy's example on March 2, 1962, of creating a rhetorical space that enabled him a year and a half later to conclude the first nuclear test ban treaty with the Soviets. Careful analysis of similar episodes may begin to reveal the most efficacious uses of rhetorical timing, sources, and arguments in the continuing pursuit of nuclear disarmament.

Metaphorically, the task is twofold. First, critics can continue to track down the network of literalized vehicles guiding overly confrontational attitudes toward Cold War adversaries. Identification of such vehicles is the initial step toward their eventual modification where circumstances would seem to warrant a revised understanding of international realities. Second, critics can engage their linguistic imaginations in a search for revised or substitute concepts of Soviet-American relations, concepts to replace the unrealistic expectation of achieving eternal peace by civilizing and converting one's enemy. We have yet to discover the metaphorical resources for conceiving a realistic world of ideologically diverse but mutually secure polities.

Ideologically, the challenge amounts to a cultural performance: a rhetorical enactment of ideological commitments that subsumes the products of strategic analysis and metaphorical invention. Ideologically engaged critics aspire to realize the full potential of culturally powerful, but often misappropriated, symbols such as life, liberty, justice, peace, and happiness. They compete rhetorically with others who allocate the same symbols differently and who utilize them to legitimize a continuation of Cold War hostilities.

Whichever route critics take to intervene in the discourse of the Cold War, they are likely to cross the path of others who started the journey elsewhere. By comparing impressions of what each critic experiences along the way, they can enrich one another's knowledge of the terrain that lies ahead, the obstacles to be encountered, and the opportunities that exist for completing the journey successfully. The pluralism of their perspectives is indeed a virtue to be celebrated, for the more they learn from one another about each facet of Cold War rhetoric, the better equipped they will become to construct alternative realities.

NOTES

1.   For an example of the link between conservative ideology and strategic criticism, see Glenn E. Thurow and Jeffrey D. Wallin, eds., *Rhetoric and American Statesmanship* (Durham, N.C.: Carolina Academic Press, 1984).

2.   Ronald Reagan, "Remarks and a Question-and-Answer Session with the Students and Faculty at Moscow State University," 31 May 1988, *Weekly Compilation of Presidential Documents* (Washington, D.C.: U.S. Government Printing Office), 706.

3.   Ibid., 708.

4.   "Excerpts from President's Speech" *New York Times*, 27 September 1988, 6.

5.   For a list of these decivilizing vehicles, see Robert L. Ivie, "Speaking 'Common Sense' About the Soviet Threat: Reagan's Rhetorical Stance," *Western Journal of Speech Communication* 48 (1984): 42.

Selected Bibliography

Altenberg, Les, and Cathcart, Robert. "Jimmy Carter on Human Rights: A Thematic Analysis." *Central States Speech Journal* 33 (1982): 446-457.

Arnn, L. P. "Principles and Phrases: The Place of Rhetoric in the Statesmanship of Winston Churchill." In *Rhetoric and American Statemanship*, ed. Glen Thurow and Jeffrey D. Wallin. Durham, N.C.: Carolina Academic Press, 1984.

Baskerville, Barnet. "The Illusion of Proof." *Western Speech* 25 (1961): 236-242.

Bass, Jeff D. "The Rhetorical Opposition to Controversial Wars: Rhetorical Timing as a Generic Consideration." *Western Journal of Speech Communication* 43 (1979): 180-191.

Bass, Jeff D. "The Appeal to Efficiency as Narrative Closure: Lyndon Johnson and the Dominican Crisis, 1965." *Southern Speech Communication Journal* 50 (1985): 103-120.

Bass, Jeff D. and Cherwitz, Richard. "Imperial Mission and Manifest Destiny: A Case Study of Political Myth in Rhetorical Discourse." *Southern Speech Communication Journal* 43 (1978): 213-232.

Bennett, William. "Conflict Rhetoric and Game Theory: An Extrapolation and Example." *Southern Speech Communication Journal* 37 (1971): 34-46.

Birdsell, David S. "Ronald Reagan on Lebanon and Grenada: Flexibility and Interpretation in the Application of Kenneth Burke's Pentad." *Quarterly Journal of Speech* 73 (1987): 267-279.

Brockriede, Wayne. "John Foster Dulles: A New Rhetoric Justifies an Old Policy." In *Rhetoric and Communication: Studies in the University of Illinois Tradition*. Urbana, Ill.: University of Illinois Press, 1976.

Brockriede, Wayne and Scott, Robert L. "The Rhetoric of Containment: America Develops a Policy and an Ideology." In *Moments in the Rhetoric of the Cold War*. New York: Random House, 1970.

Bruner, Michael S. "Symbolic Uses of the Berlin Wall, 1961-1989," *Communication Quarterly* 37 (1989): 319-328.

Campbell, Karlyn Kohrs. "An Exercise in the Rhetoric of Mythical America." In *Critiques of Contemporary Rhetoric*. Belmont, Ca.: Wadsworth Publishing, 1972.

Carlson, A. Cheree and Hocking, John E. "Strategies of Redemption at the Vietnam Veterans' Memorial." *Western Journal of Speech Communication* 52 (1988): 203-215.

Cherwitz, Richard A. "Lyndon Johnson and the 'Crisis' of Tonkin Gulf: A President's Justification of War." *Western Journal of Speech Communication* 42 (1978): 93-104.

Cherwitz, Richard A. "Masking Inconsistency: The Tonkin Gulf Crisis." *Communication Quarterly* 28 (1980): 27-37.

Corcoran, Farrel. "The Bear in the Back Yard: Myth, Ideology, and Victimage Ritual in Soviet Funerals." *Communication Monographs* 50 (1983): 305-320.

Corcoran, Farrel. "KAL 007 and the Evil Empire: Mediated Disaster and Forms of Rationalization." *Critical Studies in Mass Communication* 3 (1986): 297-316.

Cragan, John F. "The Origins and Nature of the Cold War Rhetorical Vision 1946-1972: A Partial History." In *Applied Communication Research: A Dramatistic Approach*, ed. John F. Cragan and Donald C Shields. Prospect Heights, Ill.: Waveland Press, 1981.

Cragan, John F. and Shields, Donald C. "Foreign Policy Communication Dramas: How Mediated Rhetoric Played in Peoria in Campaign '76." *Quarterly Journal of Speech* 63 (1977): 274-289.

Depoe, Stephen P. "Arthur Schlesinger, Jr.'s 'Middle Way Out of Vietnam': The Limits of Technocratic Realism as the Basis for Foreign Policy Dissent." *Western Journal of Speech Communication* 52 (1988): 147-166.

Dow, Bonnie J. "The Function of Epideictic and Deliberative Strategies in Presidential Crisis Rhetoric." *Western Journal of Speech Communication* 53 (1989): 294-310.

Ehrlich, Larry G. "Ambassador in the Yard." *Southern Speech Communication Journal* 38 (1972): 1-12.

Fisher, Walter R. "Romantic Democracy, Ronald Reagan, and Presidential Heroes." *Western Journal of Speech Communication* 46 (1982): 299-310.

Foss, Karen A. and Littlejohn, Stephen W. "*The Day After*: Rhetorical Vision in an Ironic Frame." *Critical Studies in Mass Communication* 3 (1986): 317-336.

Foss, Sonja K. "Ambiguity as Persuasion: The Vietnam Veterans Memorial." *Communication Quarterly* 34 (Summer 1986): 326-340.

Goldzwig, Steve and Cheney, George. "The U.S. Catholic Bishops on Nuclear Arms: Corporate Advocacy, Role Redefinition, and Rhetorical Adaptation." *Central States Speech Journal* 35 (1984) 8-23.

Goodnight, G. Thomas. "Ronald Reagan's Re-formulation of the Rhetoric of War: Analysis of the 'Zero Option,' 'Evil Empire,' and 'Star Wars' Addresses." *Quarterly Journal of Speech* 72 (1986): 390-414.

Gregg, Richard B. "The 1966 Senate Foreign Relations Committee Hearings on Vietnam Policy: A Phenomenological Analysis." In *Explorations in Rhetorical Criticism*, ed. G. P. Mohrmann, Charles J. Stewart, and Donovan J. Ochs. University Park, Pa.: Pennsylvania State University Press, 1973.

Gregg, Richard B. "Richard Nixon's April 30, 1970 Address on Cambodia: The 'Ceremony' of Confrontation." *Communication Monographs* 40 (1973): 167-181.

Gregg, Richard B. "A Rhetorical Re-Examination of Arthur Vandenberg's 'Dramatic Conversion,' January 10, 1945." *Quarterly Journal of Speech* 61 (1975): 154-168.

Hahn, Dan. "Corrupt Rhetoric: President Ford and the Mayaguez Affair." *Communication Quarterly* 28 (1980): 38-43.

Hahn, Dan. "The Rhetoric of Jimmy Carter, 1976-1980." *Presidential Studies Quarterly* 14 (1984): 265-288.

Hahn, Dan and Ivie, Robert L. "'Sex' as a Rhetorical Invitation to War." *Etcetera: A Review of General Semantics* 45 (1988): 15-21.

Haines, Harry W. "'What Kind of War?' An Analysis of the Vietnam Veterans Memorial." *Critical Studies in Mass Communication* 3 (1986): 1-20.

Heisey, D. Ray. "Reagan and Mitterand Respond to International Crisis: Creating Versus Transcending Appearances." *Western Journal of Speech Communication* 50 (1986): 325-335.

Hensley, Carl Wayne. "Harry S. Truman: Fundamental Americanism in Foreign Policy Speechmaking, 1945-1946." *Southern Speech Communication Journal* 40 (1974): 180-190.

Hikins, James W. "The Rhetoric of 'Unconditional Surrender' and the Decision to Drop the Atomic Bomb." *Quarterly Journal of Speech* 69 (1983): 379-400.

Hill, Forbes I. "Conventional Wisdom—Traditional Form: The President's Message of November 3, 1969." *Quarterly Journal of Speech* 58 (1972): 373-386.

Hoban, James L., Jr. "Solzhenitsyn on Detente: A Study of Perspective by Incongruity." *Southern Speech Communication Journal* 42 (1977): 163-177.

Hogan, J. Michael. "Public Opinion and American Foreign Policy: The Case of Illusory Support for the Panama Canal Treaties." *Quarterly Journal of Speech* 71 (1985): 302-317.

Hogan, J. Michael. "The Rhetoric of Historiography: New Left Revisionism in the Vietnam Era." In *Argument and Social Practice*, ed. J. Robert Cox, Malcolm O. Sillars, and Gregg B. Walker. Annandale, Va.: Speech Communication Association, 1985.

Hogan, J. Michael. *The Panama Canal in American Politics: Domestic Advocacy and the Evolution of Policy.* Carbondale, Ill.: Southern Illinois University Press, 1986.

Hogan, J. Michael. "Apocalyptic Pornography and the Nuclear Freeze: A Defense of the Public." In *Argument and Critical Practices*, ed. Joseph W. Wenzel. Annandale, Va.: Speech Communication Association, 1987.

Hollihan, Thomas A. "The Public Controversy Over the Panama Canal Treaties: An Analysis of American Foreign Policy Rhetoric." *Western Journal of Speech Communication* 50 (1986): 368-387.

Hunt, Everett. "The Rhetorical Mood of World War II." *Quarterly Journal of Speech* 29 (1943): 1-5.

Ivie, Robert L. "Images of Savagery in American Justifications for War." *Communication Monographs* 47 (1980): 279-294.

Ivie, Robert L. "Speaking 'Common Sense' About the Soviet Threat: Reagan's Rhetorical Stance." *Western Journal of Speech Communication* 48 (1984): 39-50.

Ivie, Robert L. "Literalizing the Metaphor of Soviet Savagery: President Truman's Plain Style." *Southern Speech Communication Journal* 51 (1986): 91-105.

Ivie, Robert L. "The Ideology of Freedom's 'Fragility' in American Foreign Policy Argument." *Journal of the American Forensic Association* 24 (1987): 27-36.

Ivie, Robert L. "Metaphor and the Rhetorical Invention of Cold War 'Idealists.'" *Communication Monographs* 54 (1987): 165-182.

Ivie, Robert L. "Metaphor and Motive in the Johnson Administration's Vietnam War Rhetoric." In *Texts in Context: Critical Dialogues on Significant Episodes in American Political Rhetoric*, ed. Michael C. Leff and Fred J. Kauffeld. Davis, CA: Hermagoras Press, 1989.

Ivie, Robert L. "A New Cold War Parable in the Post-Cold War Press." *Deadline: Bulletin From the Center for War, Peace, and the News Media* 5:1 (1990): 1-2, 8-9.

Ivie, Robert L. "AIM's Vietnam and the Rhetoric of Cold War Orthodoxy." In *The Cultural Legacy of Vietnam: Uses of the Past in the Present*, ed. Richard Morris and Peter Ehrenhaus. Norwood, NJ: Ablex Publishing Corporation, forthcoming.

Ivie, Robert L. and Ritter, Kurt. "Whither the 'Evil Empire'? Reagan and the Presidential Candidates Debating Foreign Policy in the 1988 Campaign." *American Behavioral Scientist*, 32 (1989): 436-450.

Kauffman, Charles. "Names and Weapons." *Communication Monographs* 56 (1989): 273-285.

Kelley, Colleen E. "The Public Rhetoric of Mikhail Gorbachev and the Promise of Peace." *Western Journal of Speech Communication* 52 (1988): 321-334.

King, Andrew and Petress, Kenneth. "Universal Public Argument and the Failure of Nuclear Freeze." *Southern Communication Journal* 55 (1990): 162-174.

Klope, David C. "Defusing a Foreign Policy Crisis: Myth and Victimage in Reagan's 1983 Lebanon/Grenada Address." *Western Journal of Speech Communication* 50 (1986): 336-349.

Kneupper, Charles, W. "Rhetoric, Public Knowledge and Ideological Argumentation." *Journal of American Forensic Association* 21 (1985): 183-195.

Lewis, Willam F. "Telling America's Story: Narrative Form and the Reagan Presidency." *Quarterly Journal of Speech* 73 (1987): 280-302.

Litfin, A. Duane. "Eisenhower on the Military-Industrial Complex: Critique of a Rhetorical Strategy." *Central States Speech Journal* 25 (1974): 198-209.

Logue, Cal M. and Patton, John H. "From Ambiguity to Dogma: The Rhetorical Symbols of Lyndon B. Johnson on Vietnam." *Southern Speech Communication Journal* 47 (1982): 310-329.

McBath, James H. "The War or Peace Alternative." In *Great Speeches for Criticism and Analysis*, ed. Lloyd Rohler and Roger Cook. Greenwood, Ind.: The Educational Video Group, 1988.

McKerrow, Ray E. "Truman and Korea: Rhetoric in the Pursuit of Victory." *Central States Speech Journal* 28 (1977): 1-12.

Martin, Martha Anna. "Ideologues, Ideographs, and 'The Best Men': From Carter to Reagan." *Southern Speech Communication Journal* 49 (1983): 12-25.

Mechling, Elizabeth Walker and Auletta, Gale. "Beyond War: A Socio-Rhetorical Analysis of a New Class Revitalization Movement." *Western Journal of Speech Communication* 50 (1986): 388-404.

Medhurst, Martin J. "Eisenhower's 'Atoms for Peace' Speech: A Case Study in the Strategic Use of Language." *Communication Monographs* 54 (1987): 204-220.

Medhurst Martin J. "Truman's Rhetorical Reticence, 1945-1947: An Interpretive Essay." *Quarterly Journal of Speech* 74 (1988): 52-70.

Mumby, Dennis K. and Spitzack, Carole. "Ideology and Television News: A Metaphoric Analysis of Political Stories." *Central States Speech Journal* 34 (1983): 162-171.

Murray, Michael S. "Persuasive Dimensions of *See It Now's* 'Report on Senator Joseph R. McCarthy.'" *Today's Speech* 23 (Fall 1975): 13-20.

Newman, Robert P. "The Spectacular Irrelevance of Mr. Bundy." *Today's Speech* 13 (September 1965): 30-34.

Newman, Robert P. "Under the Veneer: Nixon's Vietnam Speech of November 3, 1969." *Quarterly Journal of Speech* 56 (1970): 168-178.

Newman, Robert P. "Lethal Rhetoric: The Selling of the China Myths." *Quarterly Journal of Speech* 61 (1975): 113-128.

Newman, Robert P. "Foreign Policy: Decision and Argument." In *Advances in Argumentation Theory and Research*, ed. J. Robert Cox and Charles Arthur Willard. Carbondale, Ill.: Southern Illinois University Press, 1982.

Oliver, Robert T. "The Varied Rhetoric of International Relations." *Western Speech* 25 (1961): 213-221.

Palmerton, Patricia R. "The Rhetoric of Terrorism and Media Response to the 'Crisis in Iran.'" *Western Journal of Speech Communication* 52 (1988): 105-121.

Patterson, J. W. "Arthur Vandenberg's Rhetorical Strategy in Advancing Bipartisan Foreign Policy." *Quarterly Journal of Speech* 45 (1970): 284-295.

Procter, David E. "The Rescue Mission: Assigning Guilt to a Chaotic Scene." *Western Journal of Speech Communication* 51 (1987):245-255.

Reid, Ronald F. "Apocalyptism and Typology: Rhetorical Dimensions of a Symbolic Reality." *Quarterly Journal of Speech* 69 (1983): 229-248.

Renz, Mary Ann. "Argumentative Form and Negotiating Strategy in Three United Nations Security Council Debates." *Central States Speech Journal* 38 (1987): 166-180.

Ritter, Kurt. "Drama and Legal Rhetoric: The Perjury Trials of Alger Hiss." *Western Journal of Speech Communication* 49 (1985): 83-102.

Rosenwasser, Marie J. "Six Senate War Critics and Their Appeals for Gaining Audience Response." *Today's Speech* 17 (September 1969): 43-50.

Rosteck, Thomas. "Irony, Argument, and Reportage in Television Documentary: *See It Now* versus Senator McCarthy." *Quarterly Journal of Speech* 75 (1989): 277-298.

Rushing, Janice Hocker. "Mythic Evolution of 'The New Frontier' in Mass Mediated Rhetoric." *Critical Studies in Mass Communication* 3 (1986): 265-296.

Rushing, Janice Hocker. "Ronald Reagan's 'Star Wars' Address: Mythic Containment of Technical Reasoning." *Quarterly Journal of Speech* 72 (1986): 415-433.

Rushing, Janice Hocker and Frentz, Thomas S. "'The Deer Hunter': Rhetoric of the Warrior." *Quarterly Journal of Speech* 66 (1980): 392-406.

Ryan, Halford Ross. "Harry S. Truman: A Misdirected Defense for MacArthur's Dismissal." *Presidential Studies Quarterly* 11 (1981): 576-582.

Schiappa, Edward. "The Rhetoric of Nukespeak." *Communication Monographs* 56 (1989): 251-272.

Schuetz, Janice. "Argumentative Competence and the Negotiation of Henry Kissinger." *Journal of American Forensic Association* 15 (1978): 1-16.

Schuetz, Janice. "The Evolution of Argument and the Pursuit of Free Expression by Alexander Solzhenitsyn." *Journal of American Forensic Association* 19 (1983): 133-149.

Smith, Craig Allen. "An Organic Systems Analysis of Persuasion and Social Movement: The John Birch Society, 1958-1966." *Southern Speech Communication Journal* 49 (1984): 155-176.

Smith, Craig Allen. "Leadership, Orientation, and Rhetorical Vision: Jimmy Carter, the 'New Right,' and the Panama Canal." *Presidential Studies Quarterly* 16 (1986): 317-328.

Smith, Craig Allen. "Mistereagan's Neighborhood: Rhetoric and National Unity." *Southern Speech Communication Journal* 52 (1987): 219-239.

Smith, F. Michael. "Rhetorical Implications of the 'Aggression' Thesis in the Johnson Administration's Vietnam Argumentation." *Central States Speech Journal* 22 (1972): 217-224.

Stelzner, Hermann G. "The Quest Story and Nixon's November 3, 1969 Address." *Quarterly Journal of Speech* 57 (1971): 163-172.

Sudol, Ronald A. "The Rhetoric of Strategic Retreat: Carter and the Panama Canal Debate." *Quarterly Journal of Speech* 65 (1979): 379-391.

Theoharis, Athan. "The Rhetoric of Politics: Foreign Policy, Internal Security, and Domestic Politics in the Truman Era, 1945-1950." In *Politics and Policies of the Truman Administration*, ed. Barton J. Bernstein. Chicago: Quadrangle Books, 1970.

Turner, Kathleen J. *Lyndon Johnson's Dual War: Vietnam and the Press*. Chicago: University of Chicago Press, 1985.

Underhill, Robert. *The Truman Persuasions*. Ames, Ia.: Iowa State University Press, 1981.

Underhill, William R. "Harry S. Truman: Spokesman for Containment." *Quarterly Journal of Speech* 47 (1961): 268-274.

Vartabedian, Robert A. "Nixon's Vietnam Rhetoric: A Case Study of Apologia as Generic Paradox." *Southern Speech Communication Journal* 50 (1985): 366-381.

Wander, Philip. "The Rhetoric of American Foreign Policy." *Quarterly Journal of Speech* 70 (1984): 339-361.

Wander, Philip C. "The Place of Morality in the Modern World." In *Argument and Social Practice*, ed. J. Robert Cox, Malcolm O. Sillars, and Gregg B. Walker. Annandale, Va.: Speech Communication Association, 1985.

Wilson, John F. "Rhetorical Echoes of a Wilsonian Idea." *Quarterly Journal of Speech* 43 (1957): 271-277.

Windt, Theodore Otto, Jr. "The Rhetoric of Peaceful Coexistence: Khrushchev in America, 1959." *Quarterly Journal of Speech* 56 (1971): 11-22.

Windt, Theodore. "The Presidency and Speeches on International Crises: Repeating the Rhetorical Past." In *Essays in Presidential Rhetoric*, ed. Theodore Windt with Beth Ingold. Dubuque, Ia.: Kendall/Hunt Publishers, 1983.

Windt, Theodore. "Seeking Detente with Superpowers: John F. Kennedy at American University." In *Essays in Presidential Rhetoric*, ed. Theodore Windt with Beth Ingold. Dubuque, Ia.: Kendall/Hunt Publishers, 1983.

Young, Marilyn J. and Launer, Michael K. "KAL 007 and the Superpowers: An International Argument." *Quarterly Journal of Speech* 74 (1988): 271-295.

Zagacki, Kenneth S. and King, Andrew.   "Reagan, Romance and Technology: A Critique of 'Star Wars.'" *Communication Studies* 40 (1989): 1-12.

Index

About the Authors

ROBERT L. IVIE is Professor of Speech Communication at Texas A&M University. He is a frequent contributor to scholarly journals and is coauthor of *Congress Declares War: Rhetoric, Leadership, and Partisanship in the Early Republic* (1983). A former editor of the *Western Journal of Speech Communication,* Ivie currently serves as book review editor for *The Quarterly Journal of Speech.*

MARTIN J. MEDHURST is Associate Professor of Speech Communication at Texas A&M University. He is the author of over thirty articles and chapters, and coeditor of *Rhetorical Dimensions in Media* (1984, 1986) and *Communication and the Culture of Technology* (1990). In 1982, Medhurst received the Golden Anniversary Monograph Award for Outstanding Scholarship from the Speech Communication Association.

ROBERT L. SCOTT is Professor of Speech Communication at the University of Minnesota. He is coauthor or editor of six books, including *Moments in the Rhetoric of the Cold War* (1970) and *Methods of Rhetorical Criticism* (1972, 1980, 1990). Scott received the Winans/Wichelns Award for Distinguished Scholarship in Rhetoric and Public Address (1969) and the Charles H. Woolbert Research Award (1981) for scholarly contributions that have stood the test of time.

PHILIP WANDER is Professor of Communication Studies at San Jose State University. He is a frequent contributor to such journals as *Communication, Communication Studies, The Quarterly Journal of Speech,* and the *Journal of Communication.* Wander has also authored chapters in several standard reference works, including the *Handbook of Political Communication* (1981).